UNDERSTANDING
SECOND & FOREIGN
LANGUAGE LEARNING

Issues & Approaches

Educational Linguistics/TESOL/ICC
Graduate School of Education
University of Pennsylvania
3700 Walnut Street/C1
Philadelphia, PA 19104

UNDERSTANDING SECOND & FOREIGN LANGUAGE LEARNING
ISSUES & APPROACHES

===== **Jack C. Richards** =====
editor

NEWBURY HOUSE PUBLISHERS, INC. / ROWLEY / MASS.

Library of Congress Cataloging in Publication Data
Main entry under title:

Understanding Second and Foreign Language Learning.

Includes bibliographical references.
1. Language and languages--Study and teaching--
Addresses, essays, lectures. I. Richards, Jack C.
P51.U54   407   78-24457
ISBN 0-88377-124-1

NEWBURY HOUSE PUBLISHERS, INC.

Language Science
Language Teaching
Language Learning

ROWLEY, MASSACHUSETTS 01969

Cover design by Caroline Dickinson.

First printing: November 1978
5   4   3

CONTENTS

Alison d'Anglejan (Ph.D., Department of Psychology, McGill University, 1975), is assistant professor in the faculty of Education at the Université de Montréal. Her publications include research articles on second language acquisition and sociolinguistic aspects of speech style in Quebec. At the present time she is directing a research project on behalf of the Ministry of Immigration of Quebec, examining learning difficulties among immigrants enrolled in intensive French language courses.

S. Pit Corder holds a degree in Modern Languages from Oxford University and a graduate qualification in Applied Linguistics from the University of Edinburgh, where he now occupies the Chair of Applied Linguistics. He spent seventeen years in the service of the British Council, teaching English as a Second Language in various European countries and in Latin America, before entering University teaching in Britain, first in Leeds and then since 1964 in Edinburgh. He is the author of a textbook, *Intermediate English Practice Book*; a book on Language Teaching, *The Visual Element in Language Teaching*; a textbook, *Introducing Applied Linguistics*, published by Penguin; and co-edits *The Edinburgh Course in Applied Linguistics*.

Dr. Evelyn Hatch is an Associate Professor of English in the TESL section at UCLA, Los Angeles. Her major research area is psycholinguistics, especially second language acquisition and reading, and she has also published articles on sociolinguistic topics such as language mixing and code switching, conversational analysis, and discourse analysis. She is the editor of *Second Language Acquisition* (Newbury House, 1978). Dr. Hatch is currently in Cairo working on a project at the Centre for English Language Teaching in Egypt.

Janet Holmes is currently a senior lecturer in linguistics at Victoria University of Wellington, New Zealand. She obtained her M. Phil. from Leeds University in 1970. Her main areas of interest are sociolinguistics and the language education of minority groups. Among her publications are *Sociolinguistics*, edited with J. B. Pride for Penguin books, and articles on the acquisition of sociolinguistic competence in a second language.

Graeme D. Kennedy is currently a senior lecturer in the Department of English at Victoria University, Wellington, where he has been Dean of Languages and Literature since 1975. From 1961-1966 he taught English as a Second Language at the English Language Institute, Victoria University. In 1970 he obtained his Ph.D. from UCLA before returning to Victoria University. His main areas of interest are in language acquisition, the language education of minority groups, semantic functions of language, and language testing. Among his publications are a chapter in *Focus on the Learner* (Oller and Richards, eds.) and a chapter on the language of tests for young children in *The Language Education of Minority Children* (Spolsky, ed.). His monograph, *The Testing of Listening Comprehension*, was published by the Regional Language Center, Singapore, in 1978.

Jack. C. Richards (Ph.D. Université Laval, Quebec, 1972) is currently attached to the Regional Language Center, Singapore, as a specialist in applied linguistics, on secondment from the New Zealand Ministry of Foreign Affairs. He has taught EFL in Quebec, Indonesia, and New Zealand, and has served on the faculties of Victoria University of Wellington, Université Laval, and Satya Wacana University, Indonesia. His areas of interest are methodology in TEFL, interlanguage, and vocabulary. He has contributed numerous articles to professional journals, is the editor of *Error Analysis* (Longman); *Focus on the Learner* (Newbury House), with John Oller, Jr.; and has written several EFL texts for Oxford University Press, including *Conversation in Action, Breakthrough: A Course in English Communication Practice* (with M. Long), and *Words in Action: A Basic Illustrated English Vocabulary.*

Theodore S. Rogers is Professor of Psycholinguistics within the College of Education, University of Hawaii, and Associate Director of the Hawaii English Project—Secondary development team. He received his doctorate in Linguistics from Stanford University. His publications are in the field of applied linguistics, methodology, and individualized instruction. At the University of Hawaii he has served on the Graduate Faculties of English as a Second Language, Information Sciences, Linguistics, and Psychology. He recently spent two years in Malaysia as a Ford-Foundation-sponsored Advisor to the Malaysian government on language planning and language education.

John Schumann is an Assistant Professor of English as a Second Language at UCLA. He received his doctorate from Harvard University in 1975, and has taught ESL at junior and senior high school levels in both the United States and Iran. He is co-editor of *New Frontiers in Second Language Learning* and author of *The Pidginization Process—A Model for Second Language Learning*, both published by Newbury House. He has also published articles in *TESOL Quarterly* and *Language Learning.*

Peter Strevens has worked in the fields of phonetics, speech communication research, language teaching methodology, contemporary English language, TEFL, and applied linguistics; and he has held professorial chairs at the Universities of Leeds (1961-1964) and Essex (1964-1973). He is currently a Fellow of Wolfson College, Cambridge University, and is Director of the Bell Educational Trust. His many publications include articles, course books, and educational books; among the latter are *British and American English* (Collier-Macmillan, 1972) and *New Orientations in the Teaching of English* (Oxford University Press, 1977).

Merrill Swain is an Associate Professor at the Ontario Institute for Studies in Education (Dept. of Educational Theory, University of Toronto). She has directed the Bilingual Education Project—a large-scale research project which has evaluated bilingual education programs in Ontario—since 1972. Dr. Swain's interests in second language learning and bilingual education are represented in numerous publications in such journals as *TESOL Quarterly, Language Learning, Modern Language Journal, Language Sciences,* and others. Her doctorate is from the University of California at Irvine.

Dr. Elaine Tarone is currently the coordinator of the English as a Second Language Program at the University of Washington, Seattle. She obtained her Ph.D. in Speech in 1972 at the University of Washington, after previously obtaining a Diploma in Applied Linguistics at Edinburgh University in Scotland. She is a member of the Research Committee of TESOL and a charter member of the American Applied Linguistics Society. She has been very active in the field of second-language acquisition research, focusing primarily on the acquisition of phonology and on communication strategies in interlanguage.

G. Richard Tucker obtained his Ph.D. in Psychology from McGill University and, until his recent appointment as director of the Center for Applied Linguistics, was Professor of Psychology at McGill University. His published research includes a great number of studies of language acquisition and related issues in both monolingual and bilingual settings, as well as several monographs and books, among which are *English— Language Policy Survey of Jordan* (Center for Applied Linguistics), with C. Prator and W. Harrison; *Tu, Vous, Usted* (Newbury House), with W. Lambert; *Bilingual Education of Children* (Newbury House), with W. Lambert. Dr. Tucker has been a Project Specialist with the Ford Foundation at English Language Centers in Southeast Asia and in the Middle East. He has also been a Language Teaching Consultant with the South Shore Protestant Regional School Board, Montreal.

UNDERSTANDING SECOND & FOREIGN LANGUAGE LEARNING

Issues & Approaches

1

INTRODUCTION:
UNDERSTANDING SECOND AND
FOREIGN LANGUAGE LEARNING

Jack C. Richards

This book arose from discussions with a number of teachers and researchers at the 1977 TESOL convention in Miami, Florida. The consensus reached was that the influx of new ideas and approaches in the field of second and foreign language learning warranted a survey volume reviewing current issues in this expanding domain of research. While there is a long tradition of research into second and foreign language learning by linguists, psychologists, teachers, and others, a new impetus to such research has come from developments in the fields of psycholinguistics and sociolinguistics—itself a reflection of changing views of language associated especially with the writings of Brown, Ervin-Tripp, Clark, Slobin, Hymes, Labov, Fishman, and others. The outcome is seen in a number of new directions within second and foreign language learning. It is not necessarily the case that new answers have been found, or that today's questions are better, more informed, or more relevant. Only time will tell. The least that can be said however is that many of the questions being asked today are different questions, and that a greater amount of empirical research has been carried out. For this reason a book devoted to some of the recent directions in research in second and foreign language learning seemed timely.

The papers in this book are hence a reflection on the key theoretical and practical issues which are of concern to all who are interested in second and foreign language learning: researchers, teachers, students of foreign languages, and those involved in the planning or administration of language teaching programs. The contributors to this book seek to define some of the major issues in current theory and research, in order to provide a succinct and convenient summary for teachers, students, and researchers. I am grateful that such a distinguished group of contributors from Britain, Canada, the United States, and New Zealand agreed on the usefulness of such a review and were willing to write original survey articles summarizing their own positions and interests.

The introductory papers by Tarone and Hatch deal respectively with *The Phonology of Interlanguage* and *Acquisition of Syntax in a Second Language*. The term *interlanguage* is now frequently used to refer to the language of second and foreign language users. In talking of interlanguage, the learner's language is viewed as a corpus of sentences uniquely defined by the nature of second and foreign language learning and communication, just as *child language* similarly identifies a recognizable variety of English uniquely defined by the nature of young children's language learning and communication. The learner's interlanguage is variously considered in this volume as a dynamic linguistic system resulting from regular and systematic application of rules, strategies, and hypotheses. The growing interest in interlanguage phenomena is seen in the vast range of studies of aspects of interlanguage referred to by Tarone and Hatch, and by the appearance of journals within the field of applied linguistics devoted entirely to such phenomena. The term interlanguage is not new; it was used in Reinecke's 1935[1] study of Hawaiian pidgin. In its present meaning, however, it owes much to a paper by Selinker in 1972.[2]

Interlanguage phonology has not received the same degree of attention as the syntactic features of interlanguage, partly because the current theoretical reorientation within linguistics and developmental psycholinguistics has focused largely on syntax and the acquisition of syntax in the first language. There has not been the same degree of theoretical and philosophical reorientation within phonology and consequently we have seen much less active an interest in the acquisition of phonology in the first language, with even less spin-off into second and foreign language phonological research. Tarone's paper is therefore a valuable assessment of the state of research and knowledge about interlanguage phonology, and she demonstrates how research in interlanguage phonology has gained new insights through applying methodology from such fields as sociolinguistics, in accounting for interlanguage phonology as a variable system. She outlines different processes that interact to shape interlanguage phonology, and reviews the explanations that have been cited for the fossilization of interlanguage phonology.

Hatch's paper considers the syntax of second language learners, and provides a detailed review of some of the major questions that have motivated the study of the syntax of second and foreign language learners. Much of this research has attempted to validate the concept of a system with reference to interlanguage, in view of the evidence both for an invariant order in the acquisition of selected morphemes and structures across learners with different language backgrounds, and also in the face of evidence of variability with respect to acquisition sequences. Hatch reviews the major observational and experimental studies that have been carried out, critically assesses both assumptions and research methodology, and finally, reflecting on her own long-term interest in the development of linguistic competence in second and foreign language learners, suggests that the questions we have been asking may not necessarily have been the right ones. Much of the research on second and foreign language syntax appears to have been based on the assumption that "linguistic competence," or "language learning," is the sum total of the acquisition of individual items—morphemes, structures, etc. Hatch suggests that the reverse hypothesis is equally possible: namely, that learners *first* learn how to communicate, how to converse, and how to interpret the rules of conversation, and that morphemes, syntax, etc. arise out of this activity. The field of discourse analysis takes this assumption as its starting point in investigating second and foreign language learning, and we can expect to see a greater range of studies of this issue in the future.

Corder's paper, *Language-Learner Language,* also falls within the domain of interlanguage research and theory, and provides a global summary of current knowledge and assumptions about the linguistic systems of second and foreign language learners. Corder locates this area of research and theory firmly within the mainstream of language study, rather than treating it as a peripheral secondary issue, and suggests how the theoretical issue of the status of interlanguage can be resolved. He makes a distinction between two different types of continua involved in language change. The first is a continuum in which items from one system are gradually replaced by items from another. He describes this as a *restructuring continuum.* An example would be the learning of a standard dialect by someone who speaks a nonstandard dialect, or vice versa. Corder observes that in such cases, movement along this continuum "implies that the *overall* complexity of the language remains the same at any point along the continuum." He contrasts this type of learning situation with one where learning involves the increasing complexification of one linguistic system as it moves toward another. This, Corder refers to as a *recreation* or *developmental continuum.*

Foreign language learning can be viewed as a continuum of this sort, or as a mixture of both, as Corder points out. He then discusses the applicability of this distinction to particular problems in interlanguage research.

In his discussion of communicative strategies adopted by second and foreign language users, Corder discusses the relationship of communication strategies to learning. He sees two options open to the nonfluent language user when confronted with a situation where authentic communication is required—*message adjustment* and *resource expansion*. Message adjustment involves adapting what we want to communicate according to the resources of our interlanguage. Resource expansion involves increasing the communicative power of the interlanguage through paraphrase, circumlocution, word-coinage, borrowing, and paralinguistic behavior. Corder concludes with the alluring suggestion that perhaps the starting point in learning a new language is a simplified universal linguistic system, and that language learning is the progressive complexification of this linguistic system.

In my paper, *Models of Language Use and Language Learning*, I suggest that proficiency in a second or foreign language must be seen as more than merely the acquisition of the phonological and grammatical rules of the target language. The concept of proficiency is thus discussed in relation to grammatical well formedness, speech act rules, functional elaboration, and code diversity, and examples are given of how development along these four dimensions constitutes the acquisition of communicative competence. Then, in relation to the particular functions attributed to English as a second or foreign language in diverse settings around the world, four basic models of language are discussed: *instrumental* (language as a tool for communication and for the transmission of referential denotative information); *intergroup* (language to communicate with someone who is not a member of our group); *integrative* (language to mark affirmation and solidarity with another group); *interactional* (language to define and consolidate a group). In this way, situations where English has intergroup functions as either a foreign language or a lingua franca are distinguished from contexts where English has interactional functions. The *indigenization* English undergoes when it is used as a nonnative language for interactional functions in many parts of the world is illustrated in relation to changing roles, values, and functions for English. Models appropriate to different types of learning/ usage contexts are proposed, complementing Corder's discussion of a restructuring versus a recreational/developmental continuum.

Some justification is perhaps called for as to why this distinction is dealt with at some length in both Corder's and my own paper, in addition to what might appear as a digression into the characteristics of English in countries where it has indigenized and become a "second language." It should be emphasized that more people speak and use English in their daily lives as a "second language" in countries like Jamaica, Nigeria, India, Malaysia, Singapore, the Philippines, and Fiji, to name but a few instances, than speak English as a mother tongue or "native language" in countries like England, Canada, the United States, Australia, or New Zealand. It has been assumed for so long that English is the property of the English-speaking countries, that little serious attention has been given to the statistically more frequent situations where it functions as a second language, complementing other languages in the lives of several hundred million people. This apparent neglect of the role, status, and indigenization of English in many third world countries is being slowly rectified through the work of scholars such as Kachru for English in India, and Platt for English in Singapore and Malaysia. Anyone seriously interested in the use and acquisition of English cannot afford to be uninformed of these developments.

It would be appropriate to comment at this point on the terminology which is used throughout this book, and elsewhere, namely, the distinction between second and foreign language learning, and to clarify the ways in which these terms can be understood. First, as the usage of many of the contributors to this volume illustrates, the term *second language* is becoming increasingly used in the United States and elsewhere within applied linguistics to mean the learning of any language *after* the first language, irrespective of the status of that language vis-à-vis the learner or the country in which the language is being learned. In the rapidly developing field of "second language acquisition," second language is thus used as a cover term to include the study of the interlanguages of second and foreign language learners. Hence it includes the study of the learning of English by immigrants and non-English-speaking minority groups, as well as the learning of English by students in, say, Germany. This usage is regrettable.

Consider the term *foreign language.* This is usefully applied to a language which is studied primarily to enable one to communicate with native speakers of that language. One studies Thai, Polish, Japanese, etc. to ultimately enable communication with Thais, Poles, or Japanese, and not for use as a common language or lingua franca to permit communication between, say, Russians and Americans. Languages like Thai, Polish, and Japanese do not normally function as lingua francas. Where the orientation is primarily interaction between native and nonnative speaker and where the language has no other functions for the learner and no internal functions in the learner's country, it is useful to speak of a foreign language. Thus, if I were to study Japanese as a foreign language, it would be to communicate with Japanese people, hence a knowledge of Japanese customs and traditions would be an advantage. English can be called a foreign language when it is studied primarily to permit communication with foreigners who are native speakers of English, i.e., with Americans, Canadians, etc. In this role, cultural as well as linguistic dimensions are implied in the study of the language. For many users of English, English is primarily a foreign language, used not as a lingua franca but for communication with Britishers, Canadians, and so on. This is particularly true, of course, for people in countries bordering on English-speaking nations.

However, this is not the only function for which English is studied by millions of people around the world. English can be considered not a foreign language but an *international language,* in the sense of a language used as a lingua franca between people with no other common language and for neither of whom it is a first language. For example, a Dane speaking to a German or a Swiss is likely to use English. Here, English is not conceived of as a vehicle for interaction with British, American, or Australian people, nor for understanding the cultures of those people. Likewise a Thai speaking to another Asian uses English with a similar function, as an international, rather than as a foreign language. The differing roles of English around the world were the subject of an international conference of invited specialists sponsored by the East-West Center, Honolulu, in April, 1978, on the topic of *English as an International Auxiliary Language.* I would suggest that the cultural, that is, the foreign language component, becomes less important the further one moves away from English-speaking countries; English textbooks designed for use in Germany, France, and Scandinavia are often too British for use in Thailand or Indonesia, for example, where the international functions of English are more important than its foreign language status.

What then of the term *English as a Second Language?* In English-speaking countries, English is conveniently described as a *first language* for native speakers of English and a *second language* for speakers of other languages. The term second language implies interactional functions for English, as they are described in my paper in this book. "Second language" in this sense is widely used to apply both to English for immigrant groups and minority non-English-speaking groups within English-speaking countries, and also to describe the interactional functions of English in many third world countries where English has indigenized. It is also sometimes referred to as an auxiliary language in the latter situations (cf. Smith, 1977).[3] Hence the title of this book is intended to suggest that the terms second language and foreign language have legitimate, but distinct meanings.

Kennedy's paper, *Conceptual Aspects of Language Learning,* complements those of Tarone and Hatch by outlining some of the semantic dimensions of the learner's task, and suggesting that a consideration of the semantic dimensions of language is necessary both in order to understand the dimensions involved in second or foreign language learning, and the problems which require consideration in organizing materials for formal language instruction. Like Hatch's plea for the importance of considering acquisition as the product of interaction through language, Kennedy focuses on the function or content of utterances, particularly at the level of conceptual categories, and reviews at the same time the importance of *functional* and *notional* approaches to language learning and teaching. Though not always referred to in the same terms, this is a recurring theme in this book. Kennedy discusses a distinction made in recent years, particularly in Britain, between a *notional syllabus* for the organization of teaching materials, and a *grammatical* or *structural* syllabus. The former is an organization of teaching points in terms of content; the latter, in terms of grammatical/ linguistic form. The application of functional approaches to the analysis of language learning is seen in the work of Halliday,[4] and a statement of the basis for a notional organization of language teaching materials in the work of Wilkins.[5] In this volume such distinctions are also referred to in the contributions by Richards and Strevens.

Kennedy then goes on to discuss the conceptual categories that appear to be the basis around which language and, hence, language learning, is organized. He illustrates the complexity of the linguistic realizations of three conceptual categories—that of temporal relations, causality, and motion. His paper thus raises important questions concerning the degree to which language courses should primarily emphasize *content* and *function,* or the *code* by which content achieves linguistic expression. Similar questions are raised later in this book by d'Anglejan within the context of formal versus informal language learning.

In her paper, *Sociolinguistic Competence in the Classroom,* Holmes considers second and foreign language learning within a framework of what can be called "the ethnography of communication." By this, one refers to the total spectrum of individual, contextual, situational, functional, interactional, social, and cultural variables that influence the use and learning of a second or foreign language. In Hymes's words it includes the study of "what a foreigner must learn about a group's verbal behavior in order to participate appropriately and effectively in its activities." This is a distinct but complementary perspective from that often assumed by "second language acquisition." The latter has often been concerned primarily with the acquisition of the linguistic code of the second or foreign language, and can be approached from the interlanguage perspective, as reviewed by Hatch and Tarone. The interlanguage hypothesis is an attempt to establish "the linguistic aspects of the psychology of second language learning" (Selinker). The ethnography perspective is concerned with how a second language is actually used for the realization of meaning, for social control, for interaction, etc., and how its use reflects the goals of the users, the functions for which the second language is being used, the relationship between the participants in the speech event, and the context or setting in which the communication takes place. The isolation of relevant variables and the analysis of their contribution to second language communication constitutes the ethnography of second language communication. It includes the dynamics of the communicative act when one or both of the participants is using a nonnative language.

The importance of such an approach is underlined in Holmes's discussion of the dimensions of the acquisition of communicative competence. She examines the influence of such nonlinguistic factors as the setting, the participants, the topic, the medium, and the function of the interaction. Holmes discusses how the interaction of these factors in a speech event determines the form and appropriateness of the language that is used, and she demonstrates that the acquisition of linguistic competence in a second or foreign language involves internalizing rules by which language is used in appropriate codes, for interaction in specific settings, and shows how the role and the status of the participants as well as the nature of the transactions they are performing impose major constraints on language use, the rules for which constitute a major part of the learning task in second or foreign language learning. She focuses in particular on the classroom as a setting for language use and looks at the ways roles, functions, and interaction within a classroom situation may leave many learners, particularly minority group children, at a disadvantage. Holmes analyzes classroom language behavior in terms of amount of talk, turn-taking, types of questions used, and functions, and suggests that learning within a classroom context involves learning what the role of a pupil is, what role is reserved for the teacher, and what the norms for interaction are in such a setting. She shows that where the learner has different norms and expectations, the classroom may not be conducive to learning. Many of the practical suggestions she raises for second and foreign language teaching methods which attempt to take account of the factors she discusses are further amplified and substantiated by Rodgers in his contribution to this volume.

Schumann's paper, *Social and Psychological Factors in Second Language Acquisition,* provides a concise overview of social and psychological dimensions of second language learning. His comprehensive taxonomy of factors that are currently being investigated as influencing learning includes social, affective, personality, cognitive, biological, aptitude, personal, input, and instruction factors. Such a listing represents, in fact, the range of topics discussed by the authors of this book, who discuss particular topics from the perspective of their own particular research interests and experience. The influence of social and psychological factors is an area, like that of interlanguage studies, which has received detailed but by no means conclusive study by psychologists, linguists, and others in recent years, the most significant findings of which are discussed by Schumann. As Schumann demonstrates, an understanding of second and foreign language learning depends on what we can discover about the social forces operating between groups in contact, and the success or degree of learning achieved is viewed as the outcome of differing patterns of social dominance and social distance, as well as differing strategies of integration. Moving then from considering language as the vehicle for the realization of social roles, to language as the expression of the individual. Schumann considers the psychological variables affecting individual learning patterns, and discusses affective, personality, cognitive style, and personal factors. His paper demonstrates the social and psychological validity of the distinction between second and foreign language learning proposed above. In the case of foreign language learning, the major variables would appear to be psychological variables affecting the individual as a language learner and language user. With second language learning the focus is on social factors and the role of the individual in relation to groups in contact.

The remaining chapters in this book deal in the broadest sense with aspects of language teaching, treating both the nature of formal language teaching, how it differs from informal language learning, and with how the application of insights into the processes of second and foreign language learning such as those discussed by the contributors to this book can be applied to the problem of optimizing the efficiency of language learning within an educational system. Thus the five remaining chapters deal with formal language teaching, the implementation of language teaching programs, informal language learning, bilingual education, and individualized language learning.

We begin with Strevens's invaluable discussion of the nature of institutionalized language teaching. The teaching of a foreign language, Strevens demonstrates, is a multidimensional activity. He identifies four principal elements as relevant to an understanding of language teaching: the learner, the teacher, the community, and the language teaching profession. Strevens suggests that the description of language learning and the teaching of foreign languages are separate though related activities. Whereas the linguist and the psycholinguist are concerned chiefly with *the learner*, with *learning*, and with *the learned*, the language teacher is concerned with the relationship between herself/himself, the community, the subject matter, and the learner. Strevens emphasizes that the current interest in second language acquisition should not lead us to undermine the status or value of good foreign language teaching. Language teaching is more than applied linguistics or applied psycholinguistics. It derives its principles and procedures from observation and experience of language teaching and classroom language learning. Linguistics, psycholinguistics and sociolinguistics may enable us to interpret the results we get, but teaching strategies and procedures are determined independently and are not dependent for their validity on the current state of knowledge in any of these disciplines. Second and foreign language learning is, among other things, attitudinal, intellectual, social, cultural, personal, and interactive. Strevens isolates relevant variables in the total teaching/learning process including social and community factors, teacher variables, method and instructional factors, and learner variables, and shows how the interaction among these variables accounts for the success or failure of language teaching in particular circumstances.

In his paper on the implementation of language-teaching programs, Tucker likewise shows how language teaching cannot be considered apart from the broader social, cultural, and ultimately political factors which determine language teaching policies and which create the conditions for their implementation. He emphasizes that language-teaching programs must be in harmony with government policy and with the goals of educational planning in society, reflecting what Strevens refers to as "the public will." Tucker's discussion of the relationship between language-teaching policy and its effects upon classroom practice in the Sudan and Quebec demonstrates the need for more serious consideration, not merely of the minutiae of the acquisition processes in second and foreign language learning, but of the interrelationship between learner achievement, educational planning, structures for the implementation of language policy, the school language-teaching curriculum, tests, employment language requirements, and those of higher education, for example. Tucker suggests that such factors define the parameters within which language-teaching programs operate and can be planned. Many language-teaching programs fail because they take insufficient account of these factors. Tucker refers to research on individual and instructional factors in second language learning to see in what ways language teaching can accommodate the variety of individual factors that have been associated with successful second and foreign language learning. Tucker suggests that language-teaching goals should be established with the help of sociolinguistic information on the role of the second or foreign language within the context where it is being taught, on teachers' and learners' perceptions of goals, as well as on information on resources available, attitudes and motivation.

In the next paper, *Language Learning In and Out of Classrooms*, d'Anglejan compares the classroom as a context for language learning, with informal nonclassroom language acquisition. She distinguishes between formal and informal learning by demonstrating how informal language learning takes place within the context of social interaction, without the articulation of formal rules. By comparison, formal language teaching often emphasizes the code, rather than the content of communication, and hence may be relatively untransferable to unstructured situations outside the classroom. D'Anglejan suggests that foreign and second languages are best learned as the product of communicative interaction between a learner and a native speaker, and that such interaction need not necessarily take place in a classroom. At the same time one must remember that for millions of students around the world, such contexts are not available, and as Strevens emphasizes, when good foreign language teaching is matched by favorable learner, community, and method factors, many people do succeed in learning foreign languages through formal language teaching. D'Anglejan, however, is concerned with the equally frequent situation where learners fail to learn foreign languages within formal teaching programs, and she reviews approaches to foreign and second language teaching which try to make formal language teaching more like informal language learning. These may involve the teaching of specific content through the second or foreign language rather than teaching the language mainly to illustrate grammatical or other teaching points; they may involve the learning of the language via the integration of it into a job-skills program, or through changing the focus of classroom activities so that there is a need for real communication in the target language, for problem solving and information seeking.

The acquisition of content through a second or foreign language, or the existence of a home-school language switch is, of course, the model followed in many multilingual countries around the world, and indeed the norm for sections of the population even in English-speaking countries. Merrill Swain's paper, *Home-School Language Switching*, i.e., bilingual education, reviews approaches and implications of this model of language teaching/learning. She discusses three different types of program: *second language immersion*, where the learner encounters a language in school which is not the language of the home or of the immediate community environment; *second language submersion*, where some children must make a home-school language switch but for others in the school no such switch is involved since the school language is their home and community language. In comparing academic and language achievement for students in these different types of programs, Swain refers to the social status in the community of the child's home language, the socio-economic background of the learner, and other factors which might make an apparently similar language situation a positive one for one group of learners, but a negative one for others. The third model Swain discusses is the *transitional and maintenance bilingual education program* which involves utilizing the home language initially in the education program, shifting later to a partial or total use of the school language. Such programs are designed to lead to acquisition of second language skills without a decrease in academic achievement or mother tongue development. Swain then discusses the level of second language achievement reached by students in immersion programs compared with mother tongue speakers of the school language. She refers both to the limited functions of the second language in the school setting and the lack of peer group reinforcement for the second language as possible explanations for the syntactic simplifications found in the immersion student's speech.

Finally, Rodgers's paper, *Strategies for Individualized Language Learning and Teaching*, explores in greater detail how the focus of classroom activity in second and foreign language classes can be organized so that language learning becomes the outcome of doing things, performing tasks, solving problems, communicating about real content, and interacting with both teacher and peers. He discusses a variety of instructional techniques and activities which have been used in different language learning situations. Common to the various techniques he discusses—programmed learning, sequential learning kits, factlets, contracts, flow-charting, group work, peer teaching, games, and simulations—is an attempt to match instructional activities and systems to individual differences in learning and teaching. We see a move away from materials based on memorization and repetition which highlight the formal code of the language and toward the organization of the classroom in terms of creating opportunities for learners to participate in the teaching process through using language creatively as an instrument of learning. The additional motivation and level of personal involvement generated by such procedures as Rodgers outlines is said to make second and foreign language learning more effective.

What then are the common themes and directions which emerge from the diverse yet convergent viewpoints on second and foreign language learning presented in this book? First, the contributors demonstrate that the study of second and foreign language learning, viewed either from a *learning* or a *teaching* perspective, constitutes an independent domain of activity and is not merely a secondary aspect of linguistics, psycholinguistics, sociolinguistics, or the language arts. What characterizes recent research in this area is a growing body of empirical investigation of individual, social, cognitive, cultural, and pedagogic variables that influence the acquisition and use of second and foreign languages. The papers in this book show how our understanding of second and foreign language learning draws on insight from linguistics, sociolinguistics, psycholinguistics, psychology, sociology, and pedagogy, while developing its own theoretical foundations as models of the teaching/learning process emerge.

Second, the papers collected in this volume identify a number of key issues which have emerged from recent research. Some of these may be stated as follows:

(1) Successful second and foreign language learning results from a convergence of positive teacher, instructional, social, learner, and method factors, though none of these factors in isolation can guarantee successful language learning.

(2) The acquisition of communicative competence in a second or foreign language involves learning how the target language reflects the influence of functional, setting, topic, participant, medium, and other sociolinguistic factors in speech events.

(3) Second and foreign languages are learned and used not as formal codes but as vehicles for social interaction and for the expression and comprehension of complex semantic, social, and psychological content.

(4) Relevant input factors to the learning process need further study and should lead to a better understanding of the relative importance of linguistic, cognitive, social, psychological, and pedagogic factors.

(5) Although individual variables such as age, aptitude, and attitude make for differences in learning styles and may account for differences in levels of attainment, regular systematic strategies, modes, and processes appear to characterize many of the formal aspects of second and foreign language learning.

(6) Language teaching research and language learning research complement each other, but are not identical. Language teaching is concerned with procedures intended to produce desired ends. Second and foreign language research is not limited to settings where teaching is necessarily a part of the input. It is concerned with explaining how and why particular ends result from language learning.

The student or instructor may care to extend or revise this list after reading the papers in this book and discussing or reflecting on the questions at the end of each chapter.

While there may be disagreement as to what the most crucial issues are in the field of second and foreign language learning, there will surely be agreement that to try to understand second and foreign language is to acknowledge both the complexity of what is known and the degree to which many crucial factors are still little understood. Hence, there is little room for dogmatism or fervent conviction, either by researchers or language teachers, but rather a recognition that our attempt to understand the nature of second and foreign language learning is an ongoing process, requiring revision and rejection of hypotheses as research proceeds and as further factors come to light. At the same time it should be stressed that the problems involved are not merely academic. They often have important implications for educational policy, and may even have political overtones. It is hoped that this volume therefore will play some small part in contributing to the better understanding of what is involved in second and foreign language learning, as well as highlighting questions for which answers are still to be found.

NOTES

1. John E. Reinecke, *Language and Dialect in Hawaii*. Honolulu: University of Hawaii Press, 1969 (reprint).

2. Larry Selinker, *Interlanguage*. *IRAL*, Vol. X/3, 1972, 219-231.

3. Larry E. Smith. *English as an International Auxiliary Language*. *RELC Journal*, 7/2, 1976, 38-49.

4. M. A. K. Halliday. *Learning How to Mean—Explorations in the Development of Language*. London: Arnold, 1975.

5. D. A. Wilkins. *Notional Syllabuses*. London: Oxford University Press, 1976.

2

THE PHONOLOGY OF INTERLANGUAGE

Elaine E. Tarone

The phonology of interlanguage is an area which was largely neglected by second language acquisition research until very recently. There seemed to be very little interest in the pronunciation patterns of the speech of second language learners. When Schumann summarized existing second language acquisition research in 1976, he found absolutely no studies on the phonology of interlanguage. Even now, we have only a small amount of phonological data collected from second language learners in reasonably natural speech situations. The reason for the dearth of studies is hard to pin down. Perhaps one reason is the commonly held belief (commonly held even among researchers) that the learner's pronunciation of the sounds of a second language is influenced more strongly by negative transfer from the first language than is the learner's interlanguage grammar. Thus, studies of interlanguage phonology would be likely to produce the least amount of interesting data in support of a creative construction or interlanguage theory of second language acquisition. However, as we shall see, the research which *has* been done in this area quite clearly shows that transfer is only a part—and often a small part—of the influence on interlanguage phonology. Another, perhaps more decisive, reason may be a general conviction on the part of second language acquisition researchers, second language teachers, and students, that pronunciation of a second language is simply not very important. This conviction is more difficult to fight, but I think the evidence will show that it too is incorrect. It is essential not only that second language learners should acquire the grammar system and vocabulary, but also that

15

they should be *intelligible* to other speakers of that language; it is clearly possible for a learner to master the syntax of a language but not the phonology. Further, it is my belief that research in this area will shed much light on our understanding of the process of speech perception in general.

Whatever the reasons, however, the studies on interlanguage phonology have been sparse. This chapter will examine the nature of the data and the major issues involved in current research on interlanguage phonology. The two central issues seem to be:

(1) the nature of the processes which shape interlanguage phonology;

(2) the phenomenon of fossilization of interlanguage phonology.

THE PROCESSES SHAPING INTERLANGUAGE PHONOLOGY

In the 1960s, there were quite a few papers written which claimed to be able to predict errors in the pronunciation of second language learners on the basis of a contrastive analysis of the phonologies of the native language (NL) and target language (TL). All learner errors in pronunciation were felt to originate from negative transfer—that is, the learner's attempt to use inappropriate sound patterns of the NL in place of the sound patterns of the TL. A very simplistic contrastive analysis of the NL and the TL might reveal the following patterns:

	Native Language	Target Language
(1)	/t/	/t/
(2)	/f/ ⎱ /v/ ⎰	/f/ ———
(3)	/l/ ———	⎱ /l/ ⎰ /r/

In example (1) we have a case of *positive transfer*: both the native language and the target language have the phoneme /t/, so we would expect that the learner will have no difficulty with this sound in the target language. In example (2) we have an example of *negative transfer* which we might call *convergence*: where there are two phonemes /f/ and /v/ in the native language, these two sounds are considered variants in the target language of a single phoneme /f/. We would predict few if any problems for the learner in this case, either, since the learner does not have to learn to make or hear any new distinctions in the TL. It is example (3), a case of *divergent negative transfer,* which would predict the most difficulty for the learner; where his native language has only one phoneme /l/, the target language has two, /l/ and /r/. These two are likely to be perceived and uttered by the learner as minor variants of the NL phoneme /l/, and the learner would be predicted to have much difficulty in discriminating between them.

It is important to note that few of the early papers on contrastive analysis made any attempt to go beyond anecdotal examples in support of their claim that *all* learner errors in pronunciation could be predicted in this way. The concept seemed to make sense intuitively, and so it was never rigorously tested experimentally.

Those experiments which *were* run to measure empirically the degree of negative NL transfer effects in the learners' pronunciation of TL sounds were all run in more or less artificial experimental situations, presenting TL words and sounds in isolation and examining the learners' ability to perceive or produce the sounds being studied. I will not attempt to summarize all of the early experimental studies here; for a complete summary of these studies see Johansson (1973).

Brière (1966) reports on one of the most thorough of these early experiments. Words containing 14 non-English sounds (from Arabic, French, and Vietnamese languages) were presented on tape as targets for 20 American students. The students repeated the words as they heard them, and their responses were recorded and transcribed. Based on the mean number of correct responses by the subjects, a hierarchy of difficult sounds was established. It is interesting to note that while most of the results of Brière's investigation were predicted by his contrastive analysis, some were not. For example, when /ɡ/ (a voiced uvular fricative), was the target, subjects substituted several American English sounds as predicted—but they also substituted /ʀ/ (a uvular trill), a sound which does not occur in American English. Generally, Brière found that NL and TL sounds which were similar were easy for learners to pronounce; the major exception to this finding was /x/, which, while very different from any American-English (AE) sound, was still easy for the subjects to learn. Also the non-AE sound /t/ (a voiceless nonaspirated fortis dental stop) was significantly easier to learn than the dentalized /tˡ/, very close to AE. Finally, in his contrastive analysis, Brière found it necessary to use the syllable as the prime unit of analysis, showing that the American-English rules for distribution of /ž/ within the syllable affected the students' ability to learn the sound in other syllable positions. Hence, any contrastive analysis had to take the syllable structures of the two languages into account. Thus, Brière's results showed in 1966 that contrastive analysis, as it was commonly being used to predict pronunciation problems for second language learners, was not completely successful in its predictions of learner performance on an experimental task.

Other experimental studies using isolated words and syllables examined the perception of speech sounds by speakers of several languages. Carroll and Sapon (1957-1958), Lotz (1960), and Scholes (1968) had results indicating that negative transfer from the NL was influencing subjects' performance on experimental perception tasks, while Stevens (1969) and Singh and Black (1966) concluded that the subjects' perception of some TL features operated independently of their first language background.

So, even though contrastive analysis was claimed to be able to predict all learner errors in pronunciation, experimental evidence from the 1960s showed that processes other than negative transfer were also at work.

It is important to reiterate that these studies did not look at spontaneous interlanguage (IL) performance—that is, they did not examine the IL speech of second language learners engaged in communication. Indeed, Brière's was the only study which looked primarily at pronunciation rather than perception. All these studies artificially isolated TL words and sounds, and examined the perception and repetition skills of subjects in a fairly limited environment.

The limitations inherent in such a reductionist experimental approach are highlighted in a paper by Nemser (1971). Nemser ran an experiment using Hungarian subjects learning English, and showed that the nature and number of the sound substitutions made by subjects in his study depended on the experimental task used (e.g., transcription of sounds in nonsense syllables, translation from NL to TL, etc.). That is, the method used to gather data on interlanguage phonology influenced the nature of the data gathered. Nemser's results have serious implications for second language acquisition researchers interested in studying phonology. As we shall see later, interlanguage phonology happens to be variable, that is, highly sensitive to shifts in communication situation, speaker mood, etc. Researchers in this area should be aware of this fact. It is this writer's opinion that if researchers' results are to be at all applicable to L2 learner speech and speech perception in the classroom and in the real world, an attempt should be made to gather spontaneous speech data. Certainly researchers should avoid the testing of isolated speech segments in artificial settings.

The earliest study of which I am aware which gathers data at the sentence level is that of Johansson (1973). Johansson reports on a very extensive study which analyzes the segmental interlanguage phonologies of 180 native speakers of nine different languages, who were asked to repeat Swedish (TL) words and sentences which they heard on tape.

Johansson's subjects were not engaged in spontaneous communication when her data were collected, and hence, as she herself notes, "it is possible that our results would be different in a different testing situation." She justifies her method of data collection, however, by noting that the repetition of sentences involves the skills of both speech perception and production, and by pointing to first language acquisition studies indicating that sentence repetition tasks elicit better performance in pronunciation than spontaneous speech elicited by the description of pictures (p. 48). A similar position has been taken by researchers using elicited imitation tasks in second language acquisition research. Certainly, the fact that the TL materials were presented at the sentence level is a vast improvement over all the previous experimental studies, and Johansson's careful detailed analysis of the results of her multiple contact study produce a significant contribution to our understanding of second language learner phonology.

Johansson's subjects were 20 native speakers each of nine different languages: American English (AE), Czech, Danish, Finnish, Greek, Hungarian, Polish, Portuguese, and Serbo-Croatian. The subjects' repetitions of Swedish words and sentences were recorded and transcribed; deviations from the Swedish model were recorded in narrow phonetic transcription. The quality and quantity of each of these segmental deviations from the Swedish model were recorded and the results are presented in great detail by language group. After an extensive review of the literature on contrastive analysis and error analysis, with particular reference to phonology, Johansson analyzes her data to determine the extent to which errors seemed to be caused by negative NL transfer and hence were predictable by contrastive analysis. She concludes that "a large number of the substitutions made could have been predicted by contrastive analysis"; however, she also concludes that there were some general common directions for substitution followed by all language groups. There was a general "tendency [in substituting for TL sounds] to move from the extreme higher and lower positions in the articulation area toward the middle height, the tongue's rest position." Further, there were some very real limitations to the power of contrastive analysis to predict the shape of interlanguage phonology:

> There is definite evidence for the claim that learners confronted with a new language use not only sounds which occur in L1 and L2 but also other sounds which could not be directly predicted by contrastive analysis.

For example, she found that her subjects seemed to be trying to modify certain sounds away from L1 and toward L2, as when her American-English and German subjects produced [ʉ] for the Swedish [ɯ:]. She found examples of overgeneralization, with learners who used "one Swedish sound for another where neither has a counterpart in the speaker's L1"; an example of this type of overgeneralization occurred when native speakers of Czech and Polish used [y] for the Swedish [ɯ:]. Finally, Johansson notes that

> contrastive analysis provides for no way of determining where differences between languages will not lead to difficulty or where seemingly similar differences lead to various degrees of difficulty.

For example, contrastive analysis could not predict that higher vowels and some long and back vowels would be more difficult for all groups.

Johansson's study is a valuable contribution to our understanding of the relative effect of transfer on segmental interlanguage phonologies. Her data seem to indicate that language transfer does operate to shape certain aspects of the IL phonology, but that other processes, such as overgeneralization and approximation, also operate. In addition, her study repeats Brière's finding that it is not enough to predict that differences between two phonological systems will automatically create learning problems in exact proportion to the degree of difference between them. In some cases, NL and TL sounds which seemed to be very similar were very hard to learn, and in others, NL and TL sounds which seemed to be very different presented no learning problem. Johansson's data suggest that one of the constraints involved in shaping the relative difficulty of the learning of new L2 sounds may have to do with the *intrinsic* difficulty of those L2 sounds, an effect operating independent of the process of negative transfer, but interacting with it. That is, given that higher vowels in Swedish were usually more difficult for all groups, was there an interaction effect such that those learners whose L1s had similar vowels found the Swedish vowels somewhat less difficult than those learners whose NLs had no such similar sounds? It seems to me that a theory of interlanguage phonology would have to take into account any such interaction effects of the several processes which seem to be identified as operating to shape IL phonology.

Wode and Felix have reported recently on the findings of an extensive first and second language acquisition project in Kiel, Germany, which is investigating German L1 children learning English L2 and English L1 children learning German L2. This is a longitudinal study collecting data in real communication situations and analyzing its syntactic, morphological, and phonological characteristics. The Kiel findings on the IL phonologies of children seem to be quite consistent with those of Johansson for adults. Wode (1976) finds evidence that some phonological elements are strongly affected by negative transfer from the NL, while other elements seem to be acquired with no influence from the NL, but rather in the same way that a child would acquire them in a L1 phonology. For German children learning English as a L2, those elements which did evidence negative transfer were

the stressed and unstressed vowels/vocoids, the syllabic and non-syllabic consonants/contoids except /r/ possibly /w/. The acquisition of the latter two, especially /r/, was parallel to the development sequence when English is acquired as L1.

Lonna Dickerson (1974) sheds considerable light on some of the reasons why contrastive analysis may be so limited in predicting the shape of segmental IL phonology. Dickerson studied the IL phonologies of Japanese university students learning English as a second language. Her analysis is different from any of the preceding ones in that it takes into account the effect of phonological variation in both the NL and IL on the process of acquisition of the TL. Her central claim is that the acquisition of a L2 phonology proceeds by the movement of variations within the environments of variable word classes. In this study she makes no claim as to the directionality of the variable IL phonological system, the rate of its change, or the influence of any community of IL speakers on its development; her focus is on the mechanism whereby acquisition of the L2 proceeds. Dickerson concludes:

The learner's performance is essentially the output of a *variable system*. As such, predictions about this output which deny its source, as the CA [contrastive analysis] hypothesis does, will always be rejected.

One reason that the CA hypothesis will always be rejected is that positive and negative transfer do not work invariably but variably.

Note here that Dickerson is not absolutely rejecting the notions of positive and negative transfer in shaping an IL phonology. In fact, she clearly finds evidence for the existence of transfer in her data.

In many cases the learner's output does contain phones which are those used in the NL. Furthermore, they appear in environments which are often similar to NL environments. There is every reason to believe that these variants originate in the NL. . . .

She is simply stating that these processes operate variably *as they interact with other processes and constraints*. Wayne Dickerson suggests (personal communication) the following variable rule as a representation of Lonna's findings as to the linguistic constraints on the production of [s] and [z] by Japanese students learning English as a second language:

$$\left(\begin{bmatrix} +ant \\ +cor \\ +cont \\ +str \end{bmatrix}\right) \blacktriangleright \left\langle \begin{bmatrix} +ant \\ +cor \\ +cont \\ +str \end{bmatrix} \right\rangle / \left\langle [-seg] \right\rangle \left\langle \begin{bmatrix} +syl \\ -bk \end{bmatrix} \right\rangle \left\langle \begin{bmatrix} +syl \\ -bk \end{bmatrix} \right\rangle \underline{\quad} \begin{bmatrix} +syl \\ +high \\ -back \end{bmatrix}$$

To break this rule down, we can say that in this Japanese learner's interlanguage, certain phonological environments are more favorable to the production of [s] and [z] than others. One of the most difficult environments is when this segment occurs initially in front of a high front vowel:

$$\emptyset \quad \underline{\hspace{2cm}} \quad \begin{bmatrix} +syl \\ +high \\ -back \end{bmatrix} \qquad \text{(e.g., see, zip)}$$

Even harder for a Japanese speaker is the [s] or [z] sound in a medial position, between an initial front vowel, and a following high front vowel.:

$$\begin{bmatrix} +syl \\ -back \end{bmatrix} \quad \underline{\hspace{2cm}} \quad \begin{bmatrix} +syl \\ +high \\ -back \end{bmatrix} \qquad \text{(e.g., easy, Lassie)}$$

Most difficult is the medial position between an initial central back vowel and a following high front vowel:

$$\begin{bmatrix} +syl \\ +back \end{bmatrix} \quad \underline{\hspace{2cm}} \quad \begin{bmatrix} +syl \\ +high \\ -back \end{bmatrix} \qquad \text{(e.g., music, position)}$$

W. Dickerson (1977) develops this notion of sociolinguistic variation ·in IL phonology further, showing, in his longitudinal analysis of the IL phonology of a single Japanese learner of English as a second language, not only that the usage of phonological variants was correlated with linguistic environment for this learner, but also that progress was attained over time by the increasing approximation of the TL variants in each relevant linguistic environment. Further, he shows that nonlinguistic constraints such as the nature of the task (whether free speaking, dialogue reading, or word list reading) produce systematic style shifting in the interlingual phonology. He expresses such nonlinguistic constraints in this manner:

$$\emptyset = f(\text{Proficiency Level})(\text{Style: WL} > \text{DR} > \text{FS})$$

The similar variation observed by Nemser (1971) in learner perform-ance on various experimental tasks could be systematically described by variable rules. Other researchers, such as Schmidt (1977), have also begun to explore the influence of sociolinguistic variation on IL phonology. For further details on the variable analysis of IL phonology, see W. Dickerson (1976), and Dickerson and Dickerson (1977).

It is this writer's opinion that some sort of variable system of phonological description will go far toward accounting for the relative importance of all the processes we have considered thus far in shaping an IL phonological system: negative transfer from the NL, L1 acquisition processes, overgeneralization, approximation, as well as certain external constraints such as inherent difficulty of the TL system, or, as we shall see next, even psychological constraints.

The phonological environments described by Dickerson as "favorable" to the production of a TL sound might be favorable due to transfer effects—i.e., the existence or nonexistence of those environments in the NL—or to more universal effects. As Johansson points out, some aspects of the TL (Swedish higher vowels and some long and back vowels) seemed to be inherently more difficult, and certain processes seemed to operate equally for all learners, such as the tendency of the articulators toward a neutral rest position. Tarone's research (1972, 1976) explores another area of hypothesized universal physiological constraint, which relates to the constraints on the syllable structure of IL. A language transfer hypothesis would maintain that the syllable structure of the NL would be transferred in the learner's attempt to produce the TL. So, if the NL contains only syllables of a vowel-consonant (VC) type, such as [ab], [ik], and so on, the CA hypothesis would predict a tendency for the L2 learner to transform the TL syllables into VC types. Another hypothesis as to the processes shaping IL syllable structure would be that L1 learning processes are reactivated. So, different syllables of the TL would be simplified by the L2 learner in the same way that they are by the L1 learner. In order to understand this position, it may be helpful to consider a theoretical paper by D. K. Oller (1974) in which he compares the process of consonant cluster simplification used in L1 acquisition and L2 acquisition. His conclusions are limited in that his data on L2 acquisition are gleaned from anecdotal comments in the literature of the 1960s. However, they are interesting. According to Oller, epenthesis (vowel insertion) is a characteristic strategy of L2 learners. However, in L1 acquisition of phonology, learners under three years of age usually simplify by reducing or deleting difficult sounds, e.g.:

(a) cluster reduction: blue → bue
(b) final consonant deletion: big → bi
(c) weak syllable deletion: banana → nana

But Oller's understanding of the L2 literature is that L2 learners operate quite differently:

(a) epenthesis is used rather than cluster reduction: tree → təree
(b) epenthesis is used rather than final consonant deletion: big → bigu
(c) weak syllable deletion was reportedly uncommon

Thus epenthesis seems to have been a favored strategy for L2 learners, while consonant deletion was favored for L1 learners. This epenthesis could be a result of transfer from the NL. Tarone supports another hypothesis, however, arguing that the simple open CV syllable may be a universal articulatory and perceptual unit such that the articulators tend to operate in basic CV programs in all languages. Different languages elaborate on this basic program in various ways, adding different combinations of permissible initial and/or final consonants. However, researchers such as Kozhevnikov and Chistovich (1965) have shown that in stressful situations of various kinds, speakers tend to revert to the simple CV pattern of pronunciation in their NL—i.e., they stutter. Tarone's (1976) research shows in L2 learners a similar tendency to revert to a CV syllable pattern in IL. She analyzed the spontaneous speech of six students learning English as a second language—two native speakers each of Cantonese, Korean, and Portuguese. These adult subjects were asked to describe a series of pictures. While the dominant process influencing the IL syllable structure seemed to be transfer from the NL, the preference for the CV syllable clearly operated as a process independent of the transfer process. Subjects would simplify TL consonant clusters which occurred also in their NL, reducing them to simpler CV patterns. Second language learners used *both* epenthesis *and* consonant deletion to accomplish this CV patterning.

Thus, one of the universal constraints which may shape phonological environments favorable or unfavorable to the production of TL-like sounds may be the physiological constraint of the articulators' tendency to operate in CV-like, close-open patterns.

Celce-Murcia's (1977) observations of a child learning English and French simultaneously have revealed another process which is clearly operating to shape IL phonologies—a process not clearly predictable by either contrastive analysis or error analysis—the process of avoidance. Celce-Murcia analyzed the spontaneous speech of the learner and observed that her daughter consistently attempted to avoid what were for her physiologically difficult forms. Living in a bilingual home, the child tended to prefer those lexical items which were easiest to pronounce, and thus mixed languages. For instance, she had a great deal of difficulty with fricatives, and therefore consistently used the lexical item "couteau" and avoided "knife." And, rather than say "football," she created a new word, "piedball," and insisted on using it for a long time. Here again, there are clearly some physiological constraints—in this case, developmental ones—which activate a process—in this case, a process of avoidance—to shape a learner's IL phonology.

The only other study on IL phonology I know of which relates to the issue of the processes shaping IL phonology is Backman's (1977) study on intonation in interlanguage. It describes the interlanguages of eight Spanish-speaking university students learning English. The data were collected by asking the subjects to listen to English dialogues on tape (the dialogues were not made up by the experimenter, but were dramatizations of earlier conversations which had really occurred) and then to repeat them on tape. Backman found that 78% of the learners' utterances had inappropriate intonation. The learners generally used a smaller overall range of pitch: smaller pitch rise, especially on yes-no questions and prefinal rises to stressed syllables; a higher pitch for unstressed syllables; and a movement of pitch prominence to the left in declarative statements and wh-questions. Not all of these characteristics could be accounted for in terms of transfer. Backman concludes:

> The Spanish [NL] data then had explanatory power in certain respects; it did not however provide all the answers for the subjects' intonation errors.

Thus, even in the area of prosodic features, it would appear that the process of transfer from the NL is by no means the only process operative, and that an adequate theory of acquisition of L2 phonology must take other processes and constraints into account. To summarize, then, the following processes are claimed at this time to be operative in shaping IL phonology:

(1) negative transfer from NL (all studies)
(2) first language acquisition processes (Wode, Tarone)
(3) overgeneralization (Johansson)
(4) approximation (Johansson, Nemser)
(5) avoidance (Celce-Murcia)

And, the following constraints appear to be operative:

(1) the inherent difficulty of certain TL sounds and phonological contexts (Johansson)
(2) the tendency of the articulators to rest position (Johansson)
(3) the tendency of the articulators to a CV pattern (Tarone)
(4) the tendency to avoid extremes of pitch variation (Backman)
(5) emotional and social constraints (Dickerson, Schmidt)

The Dickerson studies suggest that all these processes and constraints may interact with one another in such a way that the rules of a learner's IL phonology must be considered variable. The degree of influence which these processes and constraints have on an IL phonology must be experimentally determined and incorporated into a variable rule system which can accurately describe IL phonology.

THE FOSSILIZATION OF INTERLANGUAGE PHONOLOGY

One of the central issues in the study of interlanguage phonology is that of the fossilization of IL phonologies in adult L2 learners. There are two related questions here: the first has to do with whether this fossilization is inevitable when adults learn a L2, and the second has to do with the causes of such fossilization. Researchers are divided in their answers to both questions.

First, is phonological fossilization inevitable for adult L2 learners? Scovel (1969) says yes; he maintains that no adult ever achieves perfect native pronunciation in a L2. He has labeled this the "Joseph Conrad phenomenon," in honor of the famous British author who achieved unquestioned native-like fluency in the syntax of English, his second language—yet retained a Polish accent all his life. Scovel has gone so far, in these days of inflation, as to offer a free dinner to anyone who can show him an individual who learned a L2 after puberty and who now speaks that L2 with perfect native pronunciation. As of April 1977 no one has been able to produce such an individual.

Other researchers disagree with Scovel. Hill (1970) maintains that this kind of fossilization is by no means inevitable, being the result of social and cultural factors in Western culture. She points to native peoples like the Vaupés Indians of the Amazon, and the Siane of New Guinea, who reportedly learn several L2s as adults and achieve native-like fluency. However, evidently Scovel remains unconvinced; presumably, he has not yet met one of these individuals and been able to determine the degree of acceptability of their accents. More recently, Neufeld (1977) has experimented with methods of teaching L2 pronunciation which, he maintains, are successful in helping adults to acquire native or near-native proficiency in pronunciation of new languages. (More will be said about Neufeld's technique later.) It is not known at this writing whether Scovel has had a chance to deliberate upon the nativeness of the pronunciation of Neufeld's subjects. Hence, at present, it would appear that the question of the inevitability of phonological fossilization in adults is still undecided.

The second question is related: what causes phonological fossilization to occur? There are several possible explanations. Some of them fall into a general category of physiological explanations. For example, a popular explanation among L2 learners themselves seems to be that when learners get older "their tongues get stiff"—that is, the muscles and nerves of the tongue and mouth have been practicing the same set of pronunciation habits for years. This theory might maintain that the nerves and muscles necessary for the pronunciation of new L2 pronunciation patterns have atrophied so that native-like pronunciation is impossible. I am aware of no research evidence that this sort of atrophy takes place. Another physiological explanation, originally supported by Scovel (1969), is based on Lenneberg's (1967) suggestion that "lateralization"—the completion of cerebral dominance—affects the learning of language. Somehow, with lateralization the brain loses its capacity for language learning, and this loss affects the pronunciation of the L2 more than the syntax or vocabulary of the L2. However, recently some questions have been raised about the lateralization hypothesis. Krashen (1973) reanalyzed data used by Lenneberg and also dichotic listening data, and showed that lateralization actually seems to take place much earlier—before the age of five, in fact—than the critical period for language learning, which is commonly supposed to occur at around puberty.

Another group of explanations can be grouped as pointing to psychological causes of phonological fossilization. In fact, Krashen has his own theory about the causes of fossilization. Krashen (1977) maintains, as does Rosansky (1975), that the close of the critical period is related to the onset of Piaget's stage of formal operations. In this stage of cognitive development, adolescents begin to conciously construct abstract theories about the world. Hence, they tend to *learn* L2s, that is, to abstract rules of grammar and pronunciation and consciously apply them, rather than to *acquire* L2s, that is, to activate the same unconscious processes that children do in acquiring a L1. The formal operations type of psychological explanation for phonological fossilization is being strongly pushed at present. However, to my knowledge, it does not explain the Joseph Conrad Phenomenon—that is, the learner who acquires the syntax and vocabulary of the L2 but not the pronunciation. Why should formal operations affect only the pronunciation, and not the syntax or morphology in cases such as these?

Another psychological explanation of phonological fossilization in adults is based on *psychological habit formation* and is related to the language transfer question. That is, theoreticians have claimed that language transfer has its strongest effect on the pronunciation of a second language. Though we have seen that this claim has been considerably weakened by recent research results, there has been no comparative study to determine the *relative* influence of language transfer on pronunciation as opposed to syntax or morphology of a IL. If this claim proves to be validated by such a comparative study, then we might say that it is psychological habit formation and negative transfer that for some reason selectively operate to make IL phonology singularly resistant to change.[1] An interesting experiment was done recently which was essentially based on a psychological habit formation hypothesis.

Neufeld (1977) reports on a study in which he experimentally tested a new technique for teaching L2 pronunciation to adults. Essentially, he maintains, the problem is that we expose adults to inappropriate learning situations where they form inaccurate acoustic images of the target language sound patterns. Once formed, those acoustic images are set, and so are the learners' pronunciation patterns. (It is not clear from Neufeld's discussion why adults are negatively affected by malformed acoustic images and children are not.) In his experiment, Neufeld instructed 20 young adults in three non-Indo-European languages—Chinese, Japanese, and Eskimo. The students watched videotaped lessons consisting of 100 stock phrases in these languages. They were given no explicit instruction in the meaning or pronunciation of the utterances or the grammatical rules of the languages, since the purpose of the study was to force the subjects to focus on the sound patterns of the languages. For the first part of the study the subjects merely watched and listened and were prevented from speaking. Later they traced intonational contours of the utterances they heard and saw correct contours traced for them on the videotape. Later they were allowed to whisper repetitions of what they heard. Only in the last three lessons of the 18 were the subjects allowed to repeat the utterances in a normal voice; by this time it was assumed that they had received enough accurate input to have formed a correct acoustic image of the languages and were unlikely to destroy that image by their own pronunciation. Neufeld's subjects (Ss) then recorded the phrases on tape, and native speakers of the three languages judged the nativeness of the subjects' pronunciation. Almost half the Ss were judged to have native or near-native pronunciation. Clearly, this experiment needs to be expanded so that we can judge whether their pronunciation ability persists when they are using the TLs for real communication. But Neufeld's results are most interesting and indicate some future directions for research. Research on the processes underlying IL phonology indicates that language transfer is only one of several processes; hence one would surmise that this kind of psychological habit formation theory of IL phonological fossilization would be similarly limited in its explanatory power. But to the degree that transfer is an effect, the psychological habit formation theories must be accorded validity.

A third type of explanation very different from psychological habit formation uses the affective argument and focuses on the adult learners' essential lack of empathy with the native speakers and culture of the L2. Guiora et al. (1972) attempted to artificially increase the empathy levels of L2 learners by administering gradually increasing amounts of alcohol. They found that the learners' pronunciation of the TL improved up to a certain point and then, as subjects drank greater amounts of alcohol, rapidly deteriorated. Guiroa et al. feel that IL pronunciation is a much more sensitive indicator of empathy than either syntax or morphology (and Dickerson's comments on the influence of speakers' mood on pronunciation might support this feeling). Since children have more fluid language ego boundaries, they are much more likely to identify with speakers of a TL than are adults, who have more rigid language ego boundaries. Essentially, adults have decided on their cultural identity and use their *accent* to identify themselves appropriately. They essentially have no motivation to change their accent when it communicates perfectly well who they are. Hill (1970) implicitly supports a similar position when she points to native tribes whose cultures highly value multilingualism and encourage this capacity in adults. Where the culture encourages adults to achieve multilingualism, they achieve it, according to Hill. However, Hill's tribespeople have not been studied by L2 acquisition researchers to determine the exact extent of their native-like proficiency. Another plausible explanation for Guiora's results is simply that muscle-relaxation induced by the alcohol allowed the subjects to achieve better articulation of the TL sounds (H. D. Brown, personal communication).

However, intuitively, the socio-emotional factors would seem to be especially powerful in determining degree of proficiency in pronunciation. These factors are hard to measure unambiguously in an experimental setting, but there are many anecdotes suggesting their power. For one, there have been many observations that children are particularly susceptible to an at-times cruel form of pressure to conform to (empathize with?) their peer group in all matters, including pronunciation. In her work on children at play in L2 learning situations, Peck (1977) has quite clearly shown that mockery of aberrant learner accents is a very common and particularly effective form of peer teaching. It is clearly the case that children mock the accents of child L2 learners directly and frequently, but that adults do *not* directly mock the accents of adult L2 learners. Could this be one of the reasons why children acquire native-like accents and adults do not;? The possible implications for teaching are appalling; negative reinforcement has been most unpopular for years. Guiora's approach may have more pleasant implications for the use of socio-emotional factors in facilitating the learning process.

But here again, the causes of phonological fossilization are not clear. There seems to be persuasive evidence supporting several different forces active in causing this phenomenon. There seems to be less and less evidence for physiological sources of the problem. The formal operations argument and the psychological habit formation argument both seem to have some potential explanatory power, but are limited in important ways. The affective factors arguments, dealing with empathy and cultural identity, seem to provide some very strong directions for future research.

SUMMARY

We have seen that much productive research has taken place recently on different aspects of interlanguage phonology. Most of this research has focused on the collection of data and the analysis of this data in an attempt to determine the nature of the processes shaping interlanguage phonology, and the causes of fossilization of interlanguage phonology. While much progress has been made, there are many questions which remain to be answered:

— What are the relative influences of such processes as transfer, overgeneralization, avoidance, and first language acquisition processes on the shape of IL phonology?

— In viewing interlanguage as a variable system, can we account for those relative influences?

— What are the physiological and social constraints on IL phonology?

— Is it possible for adults to acquire a L2 without an accent? If not, why not?

In our attempts to answer questions such as these, undoubtedly we will learn much about the complex interrelationships of language, mind, body, and society in the process of second language acquisition.

NOTE

1. Adjemian (1976) suggests that the mental processes commanding muscle control may be slower to change than cognitive processes governing syntax; thus "habit formation" is not the only possible explanation here.

REFERENCES

Adjemian, Christian. "On the Nature of Interlanguage Systems," *Language Learning* No. 1, 1976.

Backman, Nancy. "Intonation problems of eight Spanish-speaking adults learning English," Ph.D. dissertation, Boston University, 1977.

Brière, Eugene. "An investigation of phonological interference," *Language* 42, 4, 1966, 768-796.

Carroll, J., and S. Sapon. "Discriminative perception of speech sounds as a function of native language," *General Linguistics, 3,* 1957-58, 62-71; cited in Johansson, *Immigrant Swedish Phonology,* Lund, Sweden: Gleerup, 1973.

Celce-Murcia, M. "Phonological factors in vocabulary acquisition: a case study of a two-year-old English-French bilingual," *Working Papers in Bilingualism, 13,* May, 1977, 27-41.

Dickerson, Lonna. "Internal and external patterning of phonological variability in the speech of Japanese learners of English," Ph.D. dissertation, University of Illinois, 1974.

Dickerson, Lonna, and Wayne Dickerson. "Interlanguage Phonology: Current Research and Future Directions," *The Notions of Simplification, Interlanguages and Pidgins.* Ed. Corder and Roulet. Faculté des Lettres, Neuchatel, 1977.

Dickerson, Wayne. "Language Variation in Applied Linguistics," *ITL Review of Applied Linguistics 35,* 1977, 43-66.

———. "The Psycholinguistic Unity of Language Learning and Language Change," *Language Learning 26,* 2, 1976, 215-231.

Felix, S. "Some Differences Between First and Second Language Acquisition." Paper presented at the 3rd International Symposium on Child Language, London, 1975.

Guiora, Alexander, et al. "The effects of experimentally induced changes in ego states on pronunciation ability in a second language: an exploratory study," *Comprehensive Psychiatry 13,* 1972, 421-428.

Hill, Jane. "Foreign accents, language acquisition and cerebral dominance revisited," *Language Learning 20,* 1970, 237-248.

Johansson, Faith Ann. *Immigrant Swedish Phonology: A Study in Multiple Contact Analysis.* Lund, Sweden: CWK Gleerup, 1973.

Kozhevnikov and Chistovich. *Speech: Articulation and Perception.* Moscow: Nauka, 1965.

Krashen, Stephen. "Lateralization, language learning and the critical period: some new evidence," *Language Learning 23,* 1973, 63-74.

———. "Some issues relating to the monitor model," paper presented at the TESOL Convention, Miami Beach, Fla., 1977.

Lenneberg, E. *Biological Foundations of Language.* New York: J. Wiley & Sons, Inc., 1967.

Lotz, J. et al. "The perception of English stops by speakers of English, Spanish, Hungarian, and Thai: a tape-cutting experiment," *Language and Speech 3,* 1960, 71-77; cited in Johansson, *Immigrant Swedish Phonology.* Lund, Sweden: CWK Gleerup, 1973.

Nemser, W. *An Experimental Study of Phonological Interference in the English of Hungarians.* Bloomington, Ind.: Indiana University Press, 1971.

Neufeld, Gerald. "Language learning ability in adults: a study on the acquisition of prosodic and articulatory features," *Working Papers in Bilingualism 12,* Jan. 1977, 45-60.

Oller, D. K. "Toward a general theory of phonological processes in first and second language learning," paper presented at the Western Conference on Linguistics, Seattle, Wash., 1974.

Peck, Sabrina. "Language play in child second language acquisition," paper presented at the First Annual Second Language Acquisition Research Forum, UCLA, 1977.

Prator, C., and B. Robinett. *Manual of American English Pronunciation.* New York: Holt, Rinehart & Winston, 1972.

Rosansky, Ellen. "The critical period for the acquisition of language: some cognitive developmental considerations," Ph.D. dissertation, Harvard University, 1975.

Schmidt, Richard. "Sociolinguistic variation and language transfer in phonology," *Working Papers in Bilingualism* 12, Jan. 1977, 79-95.

Scholes, R. "Phonemic interference as a perceptual problem," *Language and Speech* 11, 1968, 86-103; cited in Johansson, 1973.

Schumann, John. "Second language acquisition research: getting a more global look at the learner," *Papers in Second Language Acquisition,* ed. H. D. Brown. Ann Arbor, Mich.: Language Learning, 1976.

Scovel, Tom. "Foreign accents, language acquisition and cerebral dominance," *Language Learning* 19, 1969, 245-254.

———. "The ontogeny of the ability to recognize foreign accents," First Annual Second Language Acquisition Research Forum, UCLA, 1977.

Singh, S., and J. Black. "Study of 26 intervocalic consonants as spoken and recognized by four language groups," *The Journal of the Acoustical Society of America* 39, 1966, 372-387; cited in Johansson, 1973.

Stevens, K. L. "Crosslanguage study of vowel perception," *Language and Speech* 12, 1, 1969, 1-23; cited in Johansson, 1973.

Tarone, Elaine. "Some influences on interlanguage phonology," *IRAL* (forthcoming), and *Working Papers in Bilingualism* 8, Feb. 1976, 87-111.

———. "A suggested unit for interlingual identification in pronunciation," *TESOL Quarterly* 6, 4, Dec. 1972, 325-333.

Wode, Henning. "Developmental sequences in naturalistic second language acquisition," *Working Papers in Bilingualism* 11, Aug. 1976, 1-31.

STUDY AND DISCUSSION QUESTIONS

(1) Research has revealed several limitations to the use of contrastive analysis in predicting errors in the speech of second language learners. What are those limitations? Is it possible for researchers who still believe in the value of contrastive analysis to get around those limitations?

(2) The author referred to several processes and constraints which seem to affect interlanguage phonology. What other processes or constraints might be operative? How could they be studied?

(3) What is the best way to describe the variable nature of interlanguage? Are Labov-type variable rules the best, or is there some other way in which to describe this variability?

(4) Do you know anyone who first came into contact with their second language after the age of 12, and now speaks that second language with no accent? If so, what could account for this ability?

(5) What do you feel are the most likely causes of the Joseph Conrad effect? Defend your position. Outline a research project which could test your thesis.

(6) What reasons can you offer for the observation that interlanguage phonology is highly sensitive to shifts in communication situation and speaker mood? Can you give examples of this phenomenon?

(7) Which processes affecting interlanguage phonology and which constraints as mentioned on page 25 appear to be the most crucial in your experience? Are some learners more likely to make use of certain processes than others?

3

ACQUISITION OF SYNTAX
IN A SECOND LANGUAGE

Evelyn Hatch

Zoila: I never ... I never listen, you know, the ... the words
           little uhh small words for continue conversation.
Rina: What, like what?
Zoila: "Ah," "and," and "that," [əm] [ipidit] (= examples of
           "little" words as observed by Zoila). You know? "If";
           [bin], [it] sometimes ... (unintelligible) ... well, maybe
           because I no study ... never, and only hear the people
           and ... and talking.
Rina: Yeah, but people talk with these words.
Zoila: Yeah, pero [əs, əh], I'm ... hear and put more attention
           the big words. You know and ... something "house." I
           know "house" is the casa for me. And [əs əs] and little
           words is no too important for me.

                                                    —Shapira, 1976

If many learners of ESL feel as Zoila does—that the acquisition of the
"little words" that mark many of the syntactic relationships for English
is unimportant—why do we as teachers and researchers believe that the
little words are important? What can we learn from the study of the
learner's acquisition of syntax that might be valuable to the learner, or to
us as teachers and researchers?

    For many learners, teachers, and researchers, language learning means
learning syntax, a bias we will discuss in this chapter. If syntax is central
and crucial to language learning, it is well worth investigating how it is

34

acquired. There are at least ten questions that have been asked and many others are possible.

(1) Is interlanguage real (systematic) or is it just a cover term for random fluctuation between accuracy/error or learning/backsliding as the learner strives to acquire the target language?

(2) If interlanguage is systematic, what is the system? Can a sequence for acquisition of syntactic structures be shown? How similar and definable are the stages in interlanguage for all learners (e.g., how much variability is there)?

(3) If there is a sequence in the acquisition of structures, is it the same regardless of the native language of the learner?

(4) Is the sequence the same for child and adult learners?

(5) Is the sequence the same if the learner does/does not receive instruction?

(6) Is the sequence the same if the learner is immersed, submersed, or not mersed at all in the language community?

(7) If there is a sequence in second language acquisition, is it the same as that described for first language acquisition?

(8) If there is a sequence, can norms be set on where a learner might be expected to be after X amount of exposure to the language?

(9) If there is a sequence, is it the same as the pedagogical sequence given in language textbooks? If not, should a pedagogical sequence follow a learning sequence?

(10) If there is a sequence, and if that sequence appears to be similar across learners, how can we explain it?

In order to find the beginnings of answers to these questions, researchers and teachers have searched the literature on first language acquisition looking for procedures which might be useful in second language research as well. Two major research techniques—observational and experimental—were adopted from first language research.

Observational studies usually take the form of weekly observations where conversations with the learner(s) are taped, transcribed, and analyzed for evidence of syntactic development over time. (Some researchers record data on a daily schedule; others have used a bimonthly or monthly schedule for recording.) Since most observational studies are continued for nine months a year, most investigators have worked with only a few learners. In order to shorten the data collection period and still have data that cover many months of development, some researchers have used a pseudolongitudinal format where several subjects from the same first language background but at various stages of exposure to the language are observed, as shown in Table 3-1. The data collected at Time 1 from four learners gives us a picture of what we might expect to occur

Table 3-1   Learners' Exposure to English at 4 Data Collection Times

Learner	Time 1	Time 2	Time 3	Time 4
A	1 month	2 months	3 months	4 months
B	2 months	3 months	4 months	5 months
C	3 months	4 months	5 months	6 months
D	4 months	5 months	6 months	7 months

in four months of language acquisition. It is, of course, possible that the composite picture shown at Time 1 for the four subjects may not reflect with complete accuracy the actual development of any one subject. By looking at the data from Learner A, horizontally, we obtain longitudinal data which can show us how valid we are in making generalizations from the composite picture of learners at the Time 1 period. The Time 2 composite can be checked against Learner B's acquisition over the total data collection period, and so on.

There are two major problems with observational studies, whether longitudinal or pseudolongitudinal. We never know whether the language produced by the learner actually reflects the syntactic sophistication he possesses. There may never be an instance where, for example, he is called upon to produce a negative question. Yet he may, in fact, be able to use negative questions. In any case, the data are bound to be incomplete but, at the same time, so voluminous that only parts of it can be analyzed, given normal life expectancies of the researchers. The second problem is one of generalizability. Since observational studies are extremely time-consuming (primarily because of transcription time requirements), most researchers study only one learner. It is difficult to know how many case studies with similar findings must be obtained before we are able to generalize from them.

The time factor has led many researchers to turn to experimental measures. In the earliest studies, these were traditionally composed of variations on the Berko test ("This is a wug, now there are two of them, there are two_____") to study the acquisition of English morphology: asking learners to change affirmative sentences to negatives and statements to questions in order to study Aux development; or repetition and translation tasks to study a wider variety of syntactic forms.

Experimental measures allow us to test large numbers of learners on whatever syntactic structure we wish to investigate. These tests, frequently called cross-sectional studies, look at the learner at *one* point in his development. If several syntactic structures are tested, an accuracy order for those structures can be obtained. Hopefully, that accuracy order is similar to an acquisition order.

Such studies allow for stronger claims regarding generalizability of findings. However, unless repeated at time intervals, the tests only reflect accuracy at one point, not acquisition over time. We are not certain that accuracy data are always a true reflection of acquisition.

Using these two research techniques—observational studies and experimental measures—along with a healthy dose of error-analysis work, research was begun on the acquisition of syntax in second language learning. The research falls into a number of natural groups. The methods, findings, and claims made for each will be presented in detail in the following sections.

MORPHEME STUDIES

Brown, Cazden, and others studying children learning English as a first language found that certain grammatical morphemes do not appear until fairly late in language development. For example, a child may not mark plurals or show possessives by addding an "s" morpheme. In order to trace the acquisition of such morphemes, Brown and Cazden worked out a methodology which required counting the number of such morphemes used correctly in obligatory instances, setting a 90% criterion level (where the child produces correct forms at this level in two consecutive data collection sessions) for the acquisition of each morpheme. Since the early studies were based on observations of only a few children, deVilliers and deVilliers (1973) elicited spontaneous speech data from 21 children in a cross-sectional study, comparing the accuracy order they obtained with the acquisition order found by Brown for his three subjects. They found that the accuracy order data correlated highly with those found in the observational data.

Researchers in second language acquisition wondered, then, if the same order of acquisition of these morphemes might be revealed if we looked at second language learner data. Using observational data on a Japanese child learning English, Hakuta scored the following morphemes:

Present Progressive	-ing	My father is read*ing* a book.
Copula	be, am, is, are	Kenji *is* bald.
Aux. (Prog.)	be, am, is, are	She*'s* eating a money.
Past Aux.	didn't, did	Margie *did*n't play.
Prep. *in*	in	Policeman is hiding *in* Kenji's shoes.
Prep. *on*	on	Don't sit *on* bed.
Prep. *to*	to	He come back *to* school.
Poss.	's	My father*'s* teacher.
Plural	-s	My hand*s* is dirty.
Art.	a, the	She's in *a* house. Gimme *the* playdough

Past Regular	-ed	The policeman disappear*ed*.
Past Irregular	go-went	She *came* back.
3rd Pers. Reg.	-s	This froggie want*s* more milk.
3rd Pers. Irreg.	has, does	She *has* mother, right?
Gonna Aux.	am, is, are	I'*m* gonna died today.

These were scored and then ranked in the order that they were acquired by his second language learner. A comparison of the ranks obtained in the studies by Brown, de Villiers and de Villiers, and Hakuta is presented in Table 3-2.

Table 3-2   Morpheme Rank Orders in Several Studies

Brown's Longit. Order		de Villiers and de Villiers		Hakuta	
$n = 3$		$n = 21$		$n = 1$	
1	Pres. Prog.	2	Pres. Prog.	2	Pres. Prog
2.5	*on*	2	Plural	2	Copula
2.5	*in*	2	*on*	2	Aux
4	Plural	4	*in*	4.5	*in*
5	Past Irreg.	5	Past Irreg.	4.5	*to*
6	Poss.	6	Arts	6	Aux Past
7	Uncontract Cop.	7	Poss.	7	*on*
8	Arts	8.5	3d Person Irregular	8	Poss.
9	Past Reg.	8.5	Contr. Cop	9	Past Irreg.
10	3d Person Regular	10.5	Past Regular	10	Plural
11	3d Person Irregular	10.5	3d Person Regular	11	Arts
12	Uncontr. Aux.	12	Uncontr. Cop.	12	3d Person Reg.
13	Contr. Cop.	13	Contr. Cop.	13	Past Reg.
14	Contr. Aux.	14	Uncontr. Aux.	14	*Gonna* Aux

Dulay and Burt (74)		Bailey et al.*		Larsen-Freeman		Rosansky*	
$n = 60$		$n = 73$		$n = 24$		$n = 6$	
1	Art	1	Pres. Prog.	1	Pres. Prog.	1	Pres Prog. *ing*
2	Cop	2	Plural	2	Cop	2	Short Plural
3	Prog	3	Cont. Cop	3	Art	3	Pro Case
4	Plural	4	Art	4	Aux	4	Art
5	Aux	5	Past Irreg.	5	Short Plural	5	Cop
6	Reg Past	6	Poss	6	Reg. Past	6	Aux
7	Irreg Past	7	Contr Aux	7	Sing.	7	Poss
8	Long Plural	8	3d Pers. Pres.	8	Past Irreg.	8	Past Irreg.
9	Poss			9	Long Plural	9	Long Plural
10	3d Pers. Sing.			10	Possessive	10	Past Reg.
						11	3d Pers. Reg.

*The rank numbers do not represent true ranks but rather a listing which reflects the Group Means for each morpheme. In addition, the Rosansky data should *not* be interpreted as anything more than a list since her contention is that the Group Means and the rank order obscure the variability present in the data.

Following the deVilliers and deVilliers model, Dulay and Burt began a series of studies using accuracy rather than acquisition data. Using a set of seven cartoon pictures and a series of questions to elicit spontaneous data, they first looked for the accuracy order of morphemes of children whose native language was Spanish (the Sacramento study, 1973). They found that while there were similarities in the data of their second language learners with first language data, the correlation of the rank orders for the morphemes was not statistically significant. They attributed the lack of a significant correlation to the greater cognitive development of second language learners. One should, they argued, expect differences since the child is already mature and has acquired one language. They next looked at the accuracy order of morphemes for two language groups—learners whose native languages were Spanish and Chinese (the 1974 study)—and found the order of morpheme accuracy was the same for the two groups, as shown in Fig. 3-1. This led them to suggest that, at least for child second language learners, first language transfer/interference was unimportant in the acquisition of syntax.

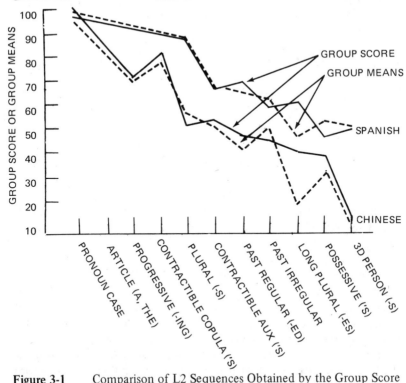

Figure 3-1   Comparison of L2 Sequences Obtained by the Group Score and the Group Means Methods

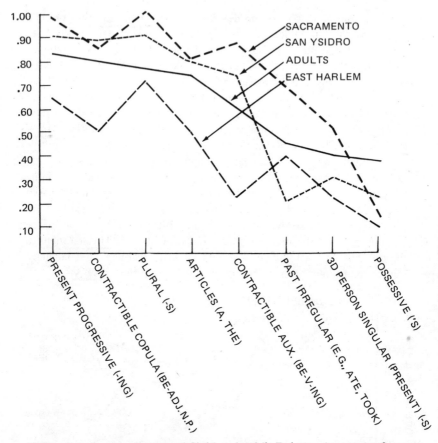

Figure 3-2   Comparison of Child and Adult Relative Accuracies for 8 Functors

Bailey, Madden and Krashen (1974) replicated these studies using adult second language learners who were receiving language instruction. Using Dulay and Burt's picture cards, the Bilingual Syntax Measure, they found an accuracy order which correlated highly with that of the child second language learners, as shown in Fig. 3-2. Larsen-Freeman, also testing adult second language learners, found a healthy correlation on accuracy for her learners with child second language learners when the data were obtained on the Bilingual Syntax Measure. However, the accuracy orders she obtained on other tasks, using other instruments, did not all reach the same level of significance but rather varied with the task. This led her to suggest that we should be cautious in interpreting our results and in claiming an invariant order for morpheme acquisition.

Claims

On the basis of the similarity of findings in these studies of morpheme acquisition, an *invariant order* of acquisition was proposed for second language learners. The order did not appear to be amenable to the effects of instruction or to the pressures of first language transfer/interference. Claims were made that, at least for children, language instruction was not necessary and that, since the first language of the learner made no difference in the acquisition order, materials based on a contrastive analysis approach were ill-conceived.

On a more theoretical level, the data were said to support a model of language learning which in some of the literature has been called a *creative construction hypothesis*. The model assumes that the learning process is automatic, that each learner creates his language anew via innate language learning ability. The learner's *language acquisition device* reacts to unrestricted input data to create the system for the learner. The invariant order of morphemes was thought to be a reflection of that internal rule-making device.

The claims, stated rather baldly here, were extreme and have, of course, received a great deal of attention and criticism. A first problem was the simple matter of scoring. How did one define an obligatory instance? For example, looking at a picture book, the investigator might ask the child learner, "What does the little boy do?" And the child might respond, "Jumping, jumping, jump!" Is the response an obligatory instance for present tense -s since the investigator has set up that context in his question? Or is it an obligatory use of present continuous since the picture shows ongoing action? Are there two correct and one incorrect uses of present continuous or three incorrect uses of present tense "-s"? Many arbitrary decisions had to be made or else a good deal of the data must be discarded as ambiguous.

Second, the criterion of 90% correct in obligatory instances also loses much information. For example, if we count all instances of *be* as copula, we may find the learner has produced the copula correctly in 90% of the obligatory cases. A closer look at the data, however, may reveal that only copula form *is* appears in the data in *this is/that's/(it)'s.* There may be no examples of *am, are, was,* or *were.* Yet the learner is credited with acquisition of the copula.

It is also possible to score morphemes as acquired when, in fact, the function of the morpheme has not been learned. For example, many learners produce large numbers of -*ing* verb forms in the beginning stages of learning. In counts, the morpheme may appear in 90% of the obligatory instances. On the other hand, the learner may also use -*ing* verb forms everywhere else as well. Gough found this to be true for the

Table 3-3   Percent of Ss Using 8 Verb-related Morphemes at 90%, 80% and 70% Criterion

Criterion	Cop n = 83	Aux n = 83	-ing n = 83	Past Irreg. n = 72
90-100%	94	53	48	31
80-100%	98	66	61	45
70-100%	99	70	66	53

Iranian child she studied, who even used "ings" for imperatives! Another example is found in Plann's study. She found that children learning Spanish as a second language appeared to have acquired the masculine agreement rules for articles and adjectives. Using a confusion matrix, however, she was able to show that they had acquired number agreement rules but simply used masculine agreement rules for all nouns, thereby scoring as having acquired them correctly for masculine nouns. Mikeš and others have long suggested that we not claim acquisition of various forms until those forms appear in contrast to others in their class. We would, then, not count *-ing* as acquired until it was used appropriately in contrast to present, past, etc., and we would not score learners as producing masculine article and adjective agreement rules until they contrasted masculine and feminine endings appropriately.

Not only does the scoring method cover up the use of a form when it should not be used and prevent us from finding out whether all variants of a form or only one are produced, it also prevents us from seeing what acquisition looks like below the 90% criterion level. That is, the criterion treats all performance above that level as + acquired and everything below it as − acquired. That leaves out everything in the 0-90% range.

To solve this problem, Andersen (1977) suggested using a Group Range Method for scoring, a method which helps reveal the variability within the data. It shows us much more about individual performance on each morpheme. It can show us the percentage of subjects who used any particular morpheme correctly 90-100% of the time, 80-100% of the time, 70-100% of the time, and so on. See Table 3-3. It can also show us the percentage of learners who never make an error in using the morpheme, the percentage of learners who never use the morpheme correctly, and percentages of learners at any point in between. See Table 3-4. While Andersen still found a significant correlation on the data he collected from 89 Spanish speakers with the studies reported earlier (in Table 3-3 the rank order is from left to right, each morpheme produced correctly more frequently than those in the columns to its right), the

Table 3-3 (continued)

	Past Reg.	*Perf.* have	*3d Pers.*	*Perf.* -en
Criterion	n = 40	n = 70	n = 73	n = 70
90-100%	20	11	6	6
80-100%	25	14	13	7
70-100%	32.5	17	16	8

Source: Andersen, 1977.

method gives us much more information for it allows us to see important individual patterning within the data.

Andersen also questions the choice of morphemes we have decided to study. The morphemes were chosen for specific reasons by first language researchers. They were adopted by second language researchers who were interested in comparing second language data with that of first language learners. In taking over this list of morphemes, we have lumped together morphemes which should not be grouped, and separated morphemes which should be grouped if we are to address the questions of second language learning. For example, Andersen has shown that lumping articles together has covered up variability of performance on definite/indefinite/∅ article accuracy. He found that his learners did much better on definite articles than indefinite and much better on *the* than on ∅, as shown in Figs. 3-3 and 3-4. These differences show native language transfer/interference as an important factor—a sharp contrast to findings

Table 3-4   The 1-99% Range of Morpheme Use Expanded into Intervals

Percent	*Cop.*	*Aux.*	-ing	*Past Ir.*	*Past Reg.*	*Perf.* have	*3d Pers.*	*Perf.* -en
100%	90	51	41	24	15	11	3	6
90-99%	4	2	7	7	5	0	3	0
80-89%	4	13	13	14	5	3	7	1
70-79	1	4	5	8	7.5	3	3	1
60-69	1	5	8	10	15	3	7	3
50-59	0	7	1	1	7.5	4	7	4
40-49	0	2	4	6	7.5	1	1	1
30-39	0	1	2	4	5	3	7	3
20-29	0	2	6	11	12.5	7	5	6
10-19	0	5	5	4	5	11	10	9
1-9	0	0	1	1	0	0	5	1
0	0	7	6	10	15	53	42	64

Source: Andersen, 1977

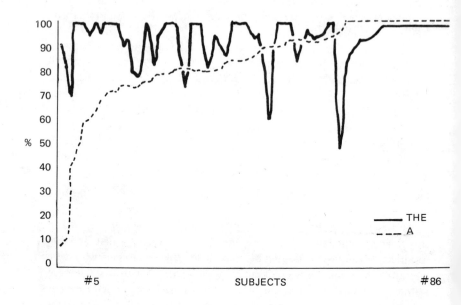

Figure 3-3

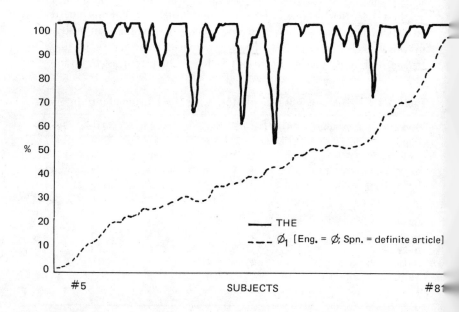

Figure 3-4

of no first language interference when the articles are grouped together as one morpheme.

While there are problems in scoring morphemes and in the criterion level being insensitive to variation, there are even more objections to the analysis of rank orders. Once rank ordered, the differences between the morphemes are assumed to be equidistant, that is, the difference between 1 and 2 is assumed to be the same as the difference between rank 5 and 6. If you look at mean scores, this is not always the case. In some studies, morphemes acquired early cluster together and those acquired last cluster together. Imagine a hypothetical case where Japanese students had mean scores far apart on copula and articles and yet they still ranked as 2 and 3 in accuracy, while Persian students had mean scores close together for the same morphemes which also ranked as 2 and 3. The differences are completely wiped out in the analysis.

Rosansky (1976) has shown that the correlation figures for cross-sectional studies do not make much sense when subjected to fine-grained analysis. She first notes that the 1973 Sacramento sample obtained an order which correlated with the 1974 Spanish-speaking sample but not with the 1974 Chinese sample in the Dulay and Burt studies. This makes little sense since the Spanish and Chinese samples in the 1974 study were highly correlated and cited as evidence that native language of the learner was unimportant in the acquisition of syntax. Rosansky next found that the order of morpheme acquisition of the six Spanish speakers in the Cazden, Cancino, Rosansky, and Schumann report (1975), collected in observational studies rather than cross-sectionally, correlated with the Dulay and Burt, Bailey, Madden, and Krashen, and Larsen-Freeman Bilingual Syntax orders. However, it also correlated with the deVilliers' first language order. Since none of the other studies correlated with the first language order, again the correlations were suspect. Her conclusion is that the individual variability gets washed out little by little through each part of the scoring and analysis. Once ranks are assigned, the variability is lost to the analysis and the correlations are meaningless.

Despite all the problems with morpheme methodology, the studies have given us a good deal of information about the second language learner's problems with English morphology. They have given us some first answers to many of the questions posed at the beginning of this paper. The answers, however, require careful interpretation given the methodological problems apparent in the research.

AUX STUDIES

A second area of investigation has been the acquisition of the Aux system, which includes the acquisition of negation, yes/no and wh-questions, and of *do* as a tense carrier in negatives and questions. The data have been presented in three ways: formal rule descriptions comparing first and second language learners, descriptions of stages of acquisition, and implication scales and variable rules.

Rule descriptions

Following the work in first language acquisition, Huang (1970) described the acquisition of questions and negation for his Taiwanese child learning English. Brown had established the average length of a child's utterance in morphemes, the Mean Length of Utterance (MLU) as a measure of language development. Using the MLU, he divided acquisition into a series of stages. In a series of studies, the first language learners' acquisition of questions and negatives was described by writing formal phrase structure and transformational rules at each of these periods. Huang hoped to follow this method but immediately found that the MLU could not be used to set periods of development for the second language learner. His learner was able to produce very long utterances (e.g., "It's time to eat and drink") almost immediately. Huang's solution was to divide the data into months of exposure to English and to write formal rules to describe negatives and questions within these time periods.

Ravem, studying his two Norwegian children as they learned English, also was interested in using formal rules to show the development of negation and questions, since different sets of rules would have to be generated for the two languages. Comparing his rules for negation in English and Norwegian:

English

$$\text{NEG-X-Tns-} \left\{ \begin{array}{l} \text{M} \\ \text{have} \\ \text{be} \\ \text{cop} \end{array} \right\} \text{- X} \quad \Rightarrow \quad \text{X-Tns} \left\{ \begin{array}{l} \text{M} \\ \text{have} \\ \text{be} \\ \text{cop} \end{array} \right\} \text{NEG-X}$$

Norwegian

$$\text{NEG-X-Tns} \left\{ \begin{array}{l} \text{M} \\ \text{ha} \\ \text{cop} \\ \text{MV} \end{array} \right\} \text{-X} \quad \Rightarrow \quad \text{X-Tns} \left\{ \begin{array}{l} \text{M} \\ \text{ha} \\ \text{cop} \\ \text{MV} \end{array} \right\} \text{-NEG-X}$$

Ravem predicted that the children would produce correct negatives except in the case of main verb negation. Based on the Norwegian rules, they should produce forms like "He like not the house" or "He like it not." However, he found that his learners instead used negatives similar to those of first language learners of English (e.g., "He not like the house" and "He don't like it").

Nor was the development of question structures traceable to Norwegian. Rules predicted from Norwegian would generate wh--questions like "Where live Tom?" Again, the children produced instead sentences similar to first language learners' "Where Tom live?"

In copula yes/no questions, Ravem's children Reidun and Rune typically used inversion at an early stage. Only occasionally (and optionally) did Reidun make use of intonation alone as a question signal. Ravem attributes this to transfer from Norwegian which also requires inversion. Yes/no questions which require *do*-support have two possible favored patterns for the learner: either use of intonation as the question signal (e.g., "You like ice cream?") or transfer of the Norwegian rule (e.g., "Like you ice cream?"). Reidun typically chose intonation while Rune chose the Norwegian inversion pattern.

Though similar patterns were found in his learners' development of questions and negations to that found by Brown and Bellugi, there were enough differences to lead Ravem, to state that neither the L2 = L1 learning hypothesis nor the contrastive analysis hypothesis of interference/transfer in their extreme formulations were supported in his data. Huang, on the other hand, found strong similarities between his Taiwanese learner's acquisition of negatives and questions and those of first language learners.

Stages

Adams, working with 10 Spanish-speaking children as they learned English, also charted their acquisition of the Aux system in questions and negatives. Pooling the data from her subjects (collected in observational sessions, and in translation and story-telling tasks), she developed the notion of stages. While she acknowledged a good deal of overlap between the stages, she felt that the data could be described in terms of sequential development for all her learners.

Her learners followed this sequence for negation: While there were a few examples of *no* placed either immediately before or after an utterance (e.g., "No dis one no"), these were not as numerous as those found in data of first language learners. The negative element appeared within the sentence—*no* directly before the main verb (e.g., "I no sing it") and *not* before predicates where a copula would be required in adult speech. However, the copula was frequently omitted by the children (e.g., "It not hot"). One of the ten learners, however, had a more general rule which was to place *no* immediately before main verbs, modals, and even forms of *be* (e.g., "I no wanna play," "We no can go on the bars," "He no was there"). In this early stage, *don't* appeared only in a few chunk-learned utterances such as "I don't know." The next stage showed an increase in the use of *don't* plus main verb as the *no* plus main verb pattern subsided. *Don't* was quickly overgeneralized and used as a negative filler in place of other forms (*doesn't, won't, can't,* etc.). *Not* was still used with auxiliary *be* and the copula. Next, the use of *don't* as a negative filler became more limited and the modal auxiliaries began to emerge. *Can't* and *won't* were the first to appear. Then, *do* began to emerge as a tense carrier as the distinction between *don't, doesn't,* and *didn't* began to emerge. Double marking of tense was common (e.g., *didn't found, doesn't wants*). In this period the indeterminates also began to appear, again with frequent double marking (e.g., *don't want nothing, ain't gonna never, nobody won't, doesn't have no crayons,* etc.).

At the end of two years of observation, most of Adams's learners still hadn't produced sentences with the Aux element *have + en*. Two learners were beginning to acquire the structure, making errors such as *haven't do* for *haven't done*.

The yes/no question data could be divided into three stages. In the first stage, the children used rising intonation as the only signal for a question (e.g., "Is good?" "Play blocks?" "Wanna see something?"). In the second stage, rising intonation was still the common question form for yes/no questions, but there were also a few chunk-learned questions using *do*. "Do you got X?" "Do you know?" *Can* questions with inversion ("Can I go?") also appeared at stage 2. The use of *be* in yes/no questions was variable. Sometimes the copula was omitted, sometimes it was inverted correctly. By the third stage, *be* inversion stabilized for all learners and more modals began to appear inverted in question forms (*will, could, should*).

Wh-questions also fell into three stages of development. In the first, the wh-word appeared at the beginning of the question followed by declarative word order (e.g., "What you want?"). This was the most common form in stage 2 as well; however, *be* was now frequently inverted. This inversion of *be* was then overgeneralized to embedded questions as well (e.g., "I don't know where is mines"). There were a few examples of verb inversion (e.g., "What say that?") perhaps testing out transfer of a possible Spanish rule. By the third stage, *be* was used correctly in wh-questions. Modals were also correctly inverted in wh-questions. *Do*-support appeared in yes/no questions first. Shortly thereafter, it began to emerge in wh-questions. Again, tense was often doubly marked ("Where did he found it?" "Where's this one belongs?").

The Cazden, Cancino, Rosansky, and Schumann study also discusses the developmental patterns of negatives, interrogatives, and Aux *do*. For negatives they found their six Spanish-speaking learners began with *no +*

verb ("I no can see"; "But no is mine"; "I no use television"). Simultaneously or shortly thereafter, the learners started to use *don't* + verb. Here *don't* was considered simply an allomorph of *no* (rather than *do* + *not*). The subjects produced sentences like "I don't hear," "He don't like it," "I don't can explain." In the third stage, auxiliary + neg, the subjects learned to place the negative after the auxiliary. In general, the first auxiliaries to be negated in this way were *is* (*isn't*) and *can* (*can't*). In the final stage, the learners acquired the analyzed forms of *don't* (*do not, doesn't, does not, didn't, did not*): "Because you didn't bring," "He doesn't laugh like us," etc. At this point *don't* was no longer a negative chunk but consisted of *do* + neg.

Like Adams's child learners, these learners—two children, two adolescents, and two adults—showed some variable behavior within the stages. In order not to lose the individual variation in the acquisition process, line drawings were used to display the data. Figure 3-5 shows an adult's variable used of *no + v* and *don't*.

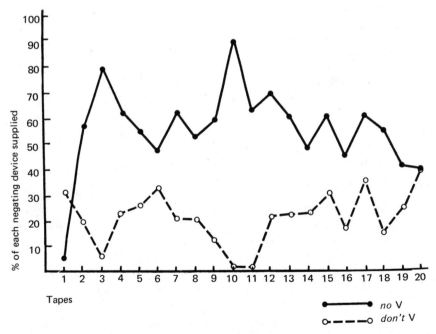

Figure 3-5 Development of Negation in Alberto Showing Proportion of Each Negating Device to Total Negatives in Each Sample

Wh-questions were described as follows:

Stage 1—Undifferentiation: learner did not distinguish between simple and embedded wh-questions
  (a) Uninverted: both simple and embedded wh-questions were uninverted
  (b) Variable Inversion: simple wh-questions were sometimes inverted, sometimes not
  (c) Generalization: Increasing inversion in wh-questions with inversion extended to embedded questions
Stage 2—Differentiation: learner distinguished between simple and embedded wh-questions

(Cazden, Cancino, Rosansky, and Schumann, 1975)

As you can see, the findings of the Cazden, Cancino, Rosansky, and Schumann study are similar in broad outline to those for Adams's Spanish speakers. Data from other observational studies of Spanish speakers (cf., Butterworth, Young, etc.) also corroborate the notion of stages of development. Nevertheless, it is difficult to make strong claims of generalizability for the notion of stages on the basis of so few studies, particularly since most of the learners are from the same first language background. Is there systematicity for all learners acquiring English negatives and question-formation or have these studies only shown that there are similarities in stages for Spanish speakers learning English as a second language?

Implicational Scales

To remedy the problem of generalizability, Hyltenstam turned to an experimental approach. Using a modified cloze procedure, he tested 160 adult students learning Swedish as a second language. The test was administered twice. Time 1 refers to the first test given three weeks after instruction began; Time 2 refers to the second test given after eight weeks of instruction.

Swedish requires that the neg particle be placed after the main verb in main clauses (e.g., Kalle *kommer inte* idag = Charlie comes not today), while it is placed before the verb in subordinate clauses (e.g., Det är skönt att Kalle *inte kommer* idag = It's fine that Charlie not comes today). When an Aux is present, the neg particle follows it in main clauses and precedes it in subordinate clauses. (Deviations in the rule are possible but all test items concurred with this rule.) In looking for overall patterns, Hyltenstam found that two ranks could be constructed for accuracy of negative placement in main clauses and in subordinate clauses. In main clauses, all Aux verbs were negated according to the rules but main verbs were not. In subordinate clauses, just the opposite was the case. There, negatives were placed appropriately for main verbs while negs used with Aux were incorrect. In other words, the two ranks were almost exactly reversed. This order remained the pattern at Time 2 though many more learners gave correct responses at Time 2 than at Time 1. What appears to be happening is that the learners put the negative in front of all verbs whether in main clauses or subordinate clauses, whether an Aux preceded the verb or not. This gave them correct responses to sentences with Aux in main clauses and incorrect responses with Aux in subordinate clauses. It gave them correct responses to sentences with main verbs in the main clauses and correct responses to negs with verbs in subordinate clauses.

Hyltenstam, realizing this overall picture might be due to certain learners who followed this pattern and variable behavior by other learners, checked for individual variable behavior in the data. To do this he used implicational scales (as described by DeCamp). Test items are listed in columns across the top of the table and subjects' responses are coded as correct (+) or incorrect (−) for each item. The pattern of +/− is then scanned for regularities of responses across all subjects and within each subject's data. Separate scales were set up for the main and subordinate clause data. Tables for those learners who were native speakers of English are illustrated in Table 3-5. Notice, first of all, that there is a pattern to the data. There are always more pluses to the left of the scales than to the right. The line drawn separates Aux verbs from main verbs. Subjects, particularly at Time 1, responded more accurately on negatives for Aux verbs in main clauses. However, individual learners show other patterns. Subject 47, for example, got all main clause negation right and all subordinate clause negation wrong at Time 1—he did not differentiate clause types. At Time 2, he had learned to make this distinction. Learner 193 usually put the Neg before verbs and after Aux verbs, though there is some variability in his responses. By Time 2, he had learned the rule correctly. None of the learners show absolutely random performance. The learners can be identified along the continuum according to the parts of the Neg rule they have acquired. Their progress on the continuum can be shown in line drawings, as seen in Fig. 3-6. Learners who have only acquired the Neg after the Aux in main clauses would appear at the lower left. If the learner had acquired both Aux + Neg and MV + Neg placement, he would be on the second step of the continuum. Learners who acquired all the rules would appear at the top right-hand corner of the continuum chart. Once the learner is placed on the continuum, we can check to see whether first language of the learner makes a difference. In this case, we find that the individuals of each language group are spread over the continuum rather than grouped together.

Table 3-5   Scales 1-4. Native Speakers of English

Time 1

Main clauses

S/C[1]	kan 1	vill 2	vill 3	får 4	ska 5	hinner 6	stannar 7	arbetar 8	kommer 9	börjar 10	bor 11	sover 12
284	+	+	+	+	+	−	−	−	−	−	−	−
28	+	+	+	−	+	+	−	−	−	−	−	−
34	+	+	+	+	+	+	−	−	−	−	−	−
193	+	+	+	−	+	+	−	+	−	−	−	−
264	+	+	+	+	+	−	−	+	−	−	−	−
50	+	+	+	+	+	−	+	−	+	+	−	−
22	+	+	+	+	+	+	+	+	+	−	+	−
215	+	+	+	+	+	+	+	+	+	+	+	−
33	+	+	+	+	+	+	+	+	+	+	+	+
37	+	+	+	+	+	+	+	+	+	+	+	+
47	+	+	+	+	+	+	+	+	+	+	+	+
56	+	+	+	+	+	+	+	+	+	+	+	+
69	+	+	+	+	+	+	+	+	+	+	+	+
86	+	+	+	+	+	+	+	+	+	+	+	+
301	+	+	+	+	+	+	+	+	+	+	+	+
79	+	+	+	+	+	+	+	+	+	+	+	+
202	+	+	+	+	+	+	+	+	+	+	+	+
247	+	+	+	+	+	+	+	+	+	+	+	+
257	+	+	+	+	+	+	+	+	+	+	+	+

Time 1 (continued)

Subordinate clauses

S/C	sover 1	kommer 2	stannar 3	arbetar 4	bor 5	börjar 6	hinner 7	ska 8	får 9	vill 10	vill 11	kan 12
257	−	−	−	−	−	−	−	−	−	−	−	−
247	−	−	−	−	−	−	−	−	−	−	−	−
79	−	−	−	−	−	−	−	−	−	−	−	−
301	−	−	−	−	−	−	−	−	−	−	−	−
86	−	−	−	−	−	−	−	−	−	−	−	−
69	−	−	−	−	−	−	−	−	−	−	−	−
56	−	−	−	−	−	−	−	−	−	−	−	−
47	−	−	−	−	−	−	−	−	−	−	−	−
37	−	−	−	−	−	−	−	−	−	−	−	−
215	−	−	−	−	−	−	−	−	−	−	−	−
33	−	−	−	−	+	−	−	−	−	−	−	−
202	+	+	−	−	−	−	−	−	−	−	−	−
22	+	−	−	+	+	−	−	−	−	−	−	−
193	+	+	+	−	−	−	−	+	−	−	−	−
264	+	+	−	−	+	+	−	−	−	−	−	−
50	+	+	−	+	+	+	−	−	−	−	−	−
28	+	+	+	+	+	+	−	−	−	−	−	−
34	+	+	+	+	+	+	−	−	−	−	−	−
284	+	+	+	+	+	+	+	−	−	−	−	−

Table 3-5 (continued)

Time 2

Main clauses

S/C	1	2	3	4	5	6	7	8	9	10	11	12
50	+	+	+	−	+	−	+	−	+	−	−	−
28	+	+	+	+	+	+	+	+	−	+	+	−
22	+	+	+	+	+	+	+	+	+	+	+	+
33	+	+	+	+	+	+	+	+	+	+	+	+
34	+	+	+	+	+	+	+	+	+	+	+	+
37	+	+	+	+	+	+	+	+	+	+	+	+
47	+	+	+	+	+	+	+	+	+	+	+	+
56	+	+	+	+	+	+	+	+	+	+	+	+
69	+	+	+	+	+	+	+	+	+	+	+	+
86	+	+	+	+	+	+	+	+	+	+	+	+
79	+	+	+	+	+	+	+	+	+	+	+	+
193	+	+	+	+	+	+	+	+	+	+	+	+
202	+	+	+	+	+	+	+	+	+	+	+	+
215	+	+	+	+	+	+	+	+	+	+	+	+
247	+	+	+	+	+	+	+	+	+	+	+	+
257	+	+	+	+	+	+	+	+	+	+	+	+
264	+	+	+	+	+	+	+	+	+	+	+	+
284	+	+	+	+	+	+	+	+	+	+	+	+
301	+	+	+	+	+	+	+	+	+	+	+	+

Time 2 (continued)

Subordinate clauses

S/C	1	2	3	4	5	6	7	8	9	10	11	12
37	−	−	−	−	−	−	−	−	−	−	−	−
56	−	−	−	−	−	−	−	−	−	−	−	−
69	−	−	−	−	−	−	−	−	−	−	−	−
28	+	+	+	−	−	−	+	−	−	−	−	−
50	−	+	+	+	+	+	+	−	−	−	−	−
33	+	+	+	+	+	+	+	−	−	−	−	−
86	+	+	+	+	+	−	+	+	−	−	−	−
202	+	+	+	+	+	+	−	+	−	−	−	−
34	+	+	+	+	+	+	+	+	+	+	+	+
47	+	+	+	+	+	+	+	+	+	+	+	+
301	+	+	+	+	+	+	+	+	+	+	+	+
79	+	+	+	+	+	+	+	+	+	+	+	+
193	+	+	+	+	+	+	+	+	+	+	+	+
215	+	+	+	+	+	+	+	+	+	+	+	+
247	+	+	+	+	+	+	+	+	+	+	+	+
257	+	+	+	+	+	+	+	+	+	+	+	+
264	+	+	+	+	+	+	+	+	+	+	+	+
284	+	+	+	+	+	+	+	+	+	+	+	+
22	+	+	+	+	+	+	+	+	+	+	+	+

[1]S = subject, C = context

Figure 3-6   The Buildup of the Interlanguage Continuum for
Syntax of Negation

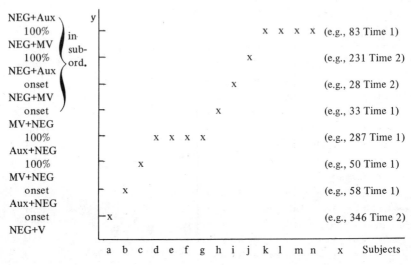

On the basis of the scales, Hyltenstam concludes that his 160 learners used a highly regular route in acquiring negatives in the second language (a route undifferentiated by background language, length of education, knowledge of foreign languages, etc.).

The final description sounds very similar to that presented by Adams and by Cazden, Cancino, Rosansky, and Schumann. First the negative marker is placed before the verb—this is the same as the *no + v* stage described by Adams and Cazden et al. Soon the learner realizes that *no + v* is not the way native speakers of either Swedish or English form negatives. So the learner of English changes his *no + v* to *don't + v*. The learner of Swedish begins by putting negatives after Aux verbs; then, slightly later, he begins to put the neg after the main verb. However, these solutions are not completely right and he discovers his negatives still aren't quite the same as the native speaker's. The learner of Swedish has to differentiate main clause negation from subordinate clause negation. He begins to sort out this distinction. For the learner of English, *don't* has to become an analyzed form of *do* (*do not, doesn't, does not, didn't, did not*) plus neg.

There is, of course, variation among the learners at various times along the road to acquisition of the negative. Some backsliding might be expected since many parts of the language are being learned simultaneously. As new forms come in, the learner's attention may be diverted from newly acquired rules and some backsliding into earlier stages might be expected.

Claims

The claims in the Aux literature are somewhat less sweeping than those made in the morphology studies. The search is for regularity in the learning process that would allow us to believe in the systematicity of interlanguage. Since they look at process rather than at the end product, the findings are not radically different from the approach used by Slobin in looking for universals in first language acquisition. They all describe a set of operation principles that the learner appears to use as he gradually differentiates the rules for the system.

One reason that the task has been difficult is the degree of variation from subject to subject and even in the performance of one subject during the process. In observational data, the learner may produce lots of "I don't know" utterances at an early stage. Or he may produce lots of "whatcha" questions. Are these to be counted as forerunners of *do* in negatives and questions? The problem of *memorized chunks* (also called *prefabs* by Hakuta and *formula utterances* by Wong-Fillmore) and how they are to be dealt with in tracing acquisition has not been solved to anyone's real satisfaction. We can look for *do* elsewhere in the data and decide to throw out chunk-learned utterances as being outside the real data. But some learners also learn "I don't want," "I don't like," and other "I don't v" along with "I don't know." How many of these do we need to find in the data before we decide that they may have an effect on the learning process?

The variability in early stages between correct and incorrect forms is complicated by the large number of chunk-learned utterances. The degree of variability from learner to learner has led to some speculation on how much variation is allowed before the claim of systematicity has to be discarded. Taylor (1974), finding that adult ESL learners showed great variability in producing correct/incorrect verb forms on a written translation task, argued that interlanguage is, indeed, a suspect concept when variation is found not only among learners but within each learner's performance as well. Nevertheless, Hyltenstam and others believe that implicational scales and variable rules can deal with variable data and can reveal the interlanguage continuum for second language structures. Others argue that the rather small amount of variation found in his data may be due to the cloze procedure task which does not allow for much variation in choice. If we agree with Hyltenstam's position, the question still to be answered is whether such a continuum can be found for other syntactic structures as well.

ADVANCED SYNTACTIC STRUCTURES

Two other favorite areas of first language research have been relative clauses and a set of four structures which are associated with the Minimal Distance Principle. Second language researchers have wondered whether tests of these structures would reveal similar patterns for first and second language learners.

In her dissertation (1969), C. Chomsky tested whether children acquiring English as a first language would simply attend to surface proximity of nouns and verbs in processing sentences or whether syntax would make a difference. She assumed that children might interpret the noun closest to the verb as the subject of the verb in such sentences as:

(1) The doll is easy/eager to see. (Child assumes doll does all the seeing)

(2) Bozo asked/promised Mickey to sing. (Mickey does the singing)

(3) Ask/tell Bozo what to eat. (Bozo does all the eating)

The fourth area of investigation involved pronoun reference. Would the child, for example, identify the correct pronoun referent in such sentences as "After *he* got the candy, Mickey left," and "Pluto thinks *he* knows everything." And, if so, would they recognize the nonidentity of the pronoun in such sentences as "*He* found that Mickey won the race."

Van Mettre (1972) tested 32 Spanish-English bilingual children on these structures and found an "orderly sequence of the structures" which paralleled that of first language learners. Cook (1973) tested 20 adult ESL learners on the *easy/eager* distinction and found similar stages to those described for first language learners. D'Anglejan and Tucker (1975) found adult ESL learners, particularly beginners, relied on surface proximity rather than syntax in processing the sentences. Syngle tested 198 adult ESL learners from various native-language backgrounds and 16 child second language learners and found "essential similarities" in adult and children's comprehension of the sentences. He also found no differences which could be attributed to the learners' native language.

The relative clause studies, on the other hand, do not turn out to so exactly mirror first language data. First, Schachter in her now-famous "Error in Error Analysis" paper, showed that ESL learners vary not only in accuracy in producing relative clauses but also in frequency of use of relative clauses according to their native language membership. Students whose first language has relative clause structures similar to English in most details (e.g., Persian or Arabic) use as many relative clauses in writing as do native speakers, but they make relatively large numbers of errors on the finer details of English relative clauses. Students from language backgrounds which have radically different relative clauses structures (e.g., Japanese or Chinese) use few relative clauses when writing English but they make few errors in those they do produce. First language does make a difference here.

Bertkau's work (1974) on comprehension and production of relative clauses by adult ESL learners further substantiates the claim for differences. She found Japanese students scored lower on comprehension of relative clauses than Spanish ESL learners, and that Japanese students had special problems in comprehension on relative clauses following subject-noun phrases. She concludes from the production data that individual learners vary greatly on relative clause production. She claims individual idiolects, rather than one discernible interlanguage continuum, exist at least in the area of relative clauses.

Other researchers are currently working on relative clause data using scaling techniques (cf., L. Anderson, forthcoming). However, at this point, the findings on whether or not patterns have been discerned for all learners regardless of first language are not available.

PROFICIENCY TESTS

If accuracy orders do mirror acquisition orders and if native language has no important effect on the interlanguage sequence (as has so often been claimed in the literature), then proficiency tests should be able to give us an overall idea of what is learned first, second, and so on for all second language learners. Many tests (cf., Ilyin Oral Interview) allow the examiner to terminate testing after the learner is unable to respond to several test items in a row. This assumes an order of acquisition for the items on the test.

Fathman, the developer of the SLOPE test, reported an accuracy order on the items of that test for 200 ESL children (6-15 years). Older children received higher scores on morphology and syntax subtests but the accuracy *order* for the structures did not differ across the age range. In a second report, she found no differences for 60 ESL learners (6-14 years) in the accuracy order on this test for language background (Spanish or Korean), age, or learning method of the learners. The subtests for the SLOPE cover most of the areas mentioned in the morphology and Aux studies discussed above.

To really discover the sequence of interlanguage we need proficiency tests with a broad range of items on syntactic structures. The problem is that such tests are usually constructed to discover what the learner does (not) know in the smallest number of items. Further, most test designers feel that global measures (such as cloze and dictation tests) can more accurately place students than can discrete point grammar tests.

Nevertheless, in order to preserve face validity, many entrance exams include a sampling of syntactic structures.

The few studies I have found which look at proficiency test data are not very encouraging if we want to discover one interlanguage continuum which is not influenced in any way by the first language of the learner. Kempf took data from entrance exams (Michigan Test of English Language Proficiency) of 423 foreign students (1976). Fifty-five error types were identified and cross-tabulated for students' native language and proficiency level. Significant differences were found among language groups on nine error types while 15 error types differed according to the students' proficiency level. In other words, both first language and the students' level in language development made a difference on the kinds of errors s/he made. Data from entrance exams which test grammatical items could be coded to replicate Kempf's findings. Meanwhile, we might look to other sources of error analysis for similar validation.

Linguists such as Goerge and Richards have discussed the similar characteristics of all second language learner errors. Neuman, in an attempt to document these similarities for the intermediate-level learner as contrasted to the shared errors of beginning learners, analyzed errors made in compositions of 158 learners. Her classification system and the errors made in each category is much too lengthy to display here, but the most frequent errors of intermediate-level students may be of interest. She found raw error scores as follows:

885 Noun modification (262 omissions of def. art, 206 omissions of indef. art, 226 arts used where not needed)

501 Verb errors (including 260 tense substitutions, largely present for past; 95 voice errors showing confusion of passive/active)

493 Preposition errors (240 substitutions, especially of locatives; 172 omissions again especially of locatives, 81 supplied where not needed)

404 Lexical errors (251 semantic errors especially in verbs; 132 morphology word class errors)

281 "Sentence structure" errors (146 fragments; 100 word order errors)

234 "Complex syntax" errors (114 for gerund/infinitive forms; 73 relative clause)

172 Number agreement (114 in determiner-noun agreement)

145 Noun errors (113 singular/plural errors, especially generic nouns)

65 Logical clause relationships (39 in conjunction choice error)

30 Adverbs of time or place not requiring prepositions

18 Negation

Error figures were converted to means and adjusted for length of composition to check for reliability of the findings for different intermediate classes and for differences among beginning, intermediate, and advanced learner classes. The part of the study that concerns us here is whether errors on structures would differ according to the native language of the learner and whether the scores would vary according to the proficiency level of the student. In order to check this, eight error-type groups were identified and compared across beginning, intermediate, and advanced levels. Surprisingly, the mean number of errors in each of the categories failed to show significant change across levels with one exception—word order errors. And, in this, beginning and advanced learners made more errors than the intermediate group (perhaps showing that beginners and advanced learners are more adventurous in experimenting with word order). It is surprising to see little evidence of progress (and therefore no discernible continuum) across levels. Unfortunately, standard deviations are not given, so we do not know the extent of variability. Either the students show a great deal of variability in errors (and therefore no continuum) or else there is a plateau where little progress is being made on these structures.

Neuman also found that the native language of the learner did make a difference on two error types. Japanese and Korean students made more article omission errors than other learners; students from Germanic/ Slavic and from Japanese and Korean differed from other language groups on preposition omissions. While mean scores seemed to show that students from certain language backgrounds made more errors overall than students of other language groups, when scores were adjusted for length of composition the differences were not significant.

Neuman's study, like most error-analysis work, used written data. In contrast, Linde worked with oral data, tabulating errors made by Japanese speakers during conversations. He found that each of his Japanese learners made the same error many times in his speech sample. This might be evidence (contrary to Taylor's findings) that each learner's interlanguage is consistent. However, error ranks across his subjects did not agree. That is, not all subjects made the same errors despite their common first language—evidence for variability and the lack of influence from the native language. Linde also claims that frequency counts in error analysis are misleading. As teachers, we all are aware that Japanese students have problems with English articles. We would expect the accuracy sequence to change, then, for Japanese students with articles acquired late. At least, articles would be out of line in the learning sequence compared to other language groups. Linde found extremely high error counts on articles for his learners. However, articles are high frequency words in English; they occur everywhere. If scores are adjusted for frequency of appearance in English, then the errors on articles for Japanese speakers are no more common than verb tense errors.

While Linde urges that scores be converted for frequency (which might help to reveal the interlanguage continuum), one could argue that corrected scores are also misleading. Yet that is precisely what we do on proficiency exams. We control for frequency of error. There may be two multiple choice questions on articles in a complete test and one of these may do double duty in testing for mass-count noun distinctions. It isn't surprising, then, that native language of the learner does not turn out to be a large factor in accuracy orders from proficiency exams. Again, variation among learner groups as well as individuals is being lost because of our instruments and data analysis procedures.

Obviously, proficiency exams alone cannot answer the question of systematicity in the learning sequence. Error-analysis studies can help remedy this, but they too must be carefully thought out in order to answer the questions we pose. The main purpose of both proficiency exams and error-analysis studies has been a very practical one of getting information to teachers about the common errors and the specific errors of second-language learners.

> While approximative systems of language learners may be studied as entities worthy of attention in and of themselves, the results of such study should also provide feedback to language teaching practice and to general linguistic theory.
>
> Richards and Sampson, 1974

Even with all the problems discussed above, proficiency tests may be one way of getting the kind of information about the order of acquisition of syntactic structures that teachers need.

The beginning research in each of the areas has given us the following answers to the questions posed at the beginning of this chapter:

(1) While there is a good deal of argument about the degree of systematicity in interlanguage, many researchers and teachers believe that the move from the beginning stages of language learning to later fluency follows a sequence which is not random.

(2) While each learner's interlanguage may show systematic changes, that system is not an invariant one for all learners. There is a good deal of overlap within even one learner's data as he moves from one stage to the next. He may, for example, begin by using *me* as first person pronoun, then use *me* and *I* interchangeably for some period of time, and finally arrive at *I* as the correct form. While all this can be systematically described, the correct/incorrect forms may shift back and forth several

times as the learner sorts out the rules for any part of the language. In addition, there is variation among learners. Part of this may be due to the native language of the learner (unpopular though that notion may still be). In other words, the "invariant sequence" is not all that invariant. Despite the variance found within data of one subject and the data between subjects, most researchers still feel there is enough similarity to allow us to talk about interlanguage as systematic changes in the learners' learning of syntax. With these qualifications, the studies do show us which morphemes are learned early and which late.

(3) There is a good deal of difference of opinion as to whether transfer/interference from the first language makes any difference in the order of acquisition of syntactic structures or the speed of acquisition.

(4) The sequence is thought to show the same systematicity and the same variability in data from adults and child learners.

(5) The literature which discusses the effect of instruction is weak. One reason is that ESL instruction, bilingual instruction, and monolingual instruction are seldom, if ever, operationally defined. We do not know what methods are involved or whether they are or are not mutually exclusive. Fairly strong claims have been made in favor of various programs on the basis of slight differences found only in certain structures for certain children. Fairly strong claims have been made that instruction has no effect on learning though it may have some effect on speed of learning. Hopefully, much more careful research can be done in the future.

(6) With the exception of Canadian studies, subjects and their schooling have seldom been appropriately described. "Children who speak one language at home and another at school" is not an adequate definition. We need to know who speaks the other language at school. Do the children use the home language in talking with each other and only use the other language when speaking with the teacher? Does the teacher use both languages or only one? Does she understand both? The general findings of these studies do show that children who receive their education in a second language do learn more of that language than learners who only receive foreign language instruction.

(7) Claims and counterclaims regarding the similarity of the second language data and first language learning data have been made. Similarities are there, but differences have also been shown. Differences have been attributed to a number of causes—the greater cognitive development of the learner, the effect of the first language on second language learning, etc.

(8) Norms have not been set. While the stages may be similar, there is considerable variation in how quickly learners move through the stages.

Some learners (cf., Schumann, 1975) appear to fossilize at points along the continuum. Generally, adolescent and adult learners appear to make the most rapid *initial* progress in second language learning.

(9) The morpheme sequence has been claimed to follow the pedagogical sequence presented in textbooks for ESL to some extent. Certainly, the present progressive is presented before the past tense, and both before the present perfect. And "What's this?" is usually one of the first questions presented in texts. But much of the material is present simultaneously or in quick sequence in language texts. Most teaching materials take into account the gradual sorting out of the language by planned cyclical review. All teachers know how difficult questions involving *do* are for students. They have to be reviewed many, many times before they are finally really acquired by the learner. Pedagogical sequence is similar in some respects to the natural order of acquisition of structures, but pedagogical sequence has to be based on many other criteria as well.

(10) The final question will be discussed in the remainder of this paper.

EXPLAINING THE SEQUENCE

In a number of earlier papers, I have argued that if we want to learn anything meaningful about the acquisition of second languages, we cannot just study production data. We have suggested that in observational studies the researchers must transcribe and examine not just the learner's production of speech but also the speech of those with whom he talks. We assume that input (some portion of which must be intake) is an extremely important factor in the order of acquisition of various syntactic forms and syntactic functions.

The first step in investigating the importance of input was simply to look at frequency of forms in the language addressed to the learner and the language produced by the learner. We were, on the basis of case study data, able to show that the frequency in the input directly influenced the child's acquisition/production of those forms. Larsen-Freeman (1976) further tested this claim by correlation frequency of forms in parent speech and in teacher speech in the ESL classroom with the morpheme accuracy orders of learners. The correlations were highly significant.

But if we look at the language of the learner and his conversational partners, we find that these interactions shape the frequency of forms, especially for the beginning learner. Just as Snow (1972) and others have shown that mother language to child learners is systematically simplified, the "foreigner talk" of native speakers to second language learners is also simplified in important ways (Hatch, Shapira, and Gough, 1975; Katz, 1977). This simplification is not so much a conscious simplification to make the syntax simple for the learner. Rather, it appears to be the native speaker's way of making it possible for the learner to carry on a conversation, to be able to take his turn to talk, and to be able to contribute something relevant to the conversation.

Our basic premise has long been that the child learning his first language learns some basic set of syntactic structures, moving from a one-word phase to a two-word phase to more complex structures, and that eventually the child is able to put these structures together in order to carry on conversations with others. This notion seems to be even stronger in second language learning. In actuality, the reverse may be closer to the truth. That is, language learning evolves out of learning how to carry on conversations, out of learning how to communicate.

Early conversations of child second language learners show the child interacting with others to produce sentences together:

Paul:	Oh-oh!	Paul:	This
Native Speaker:	What?	Native Speaker:	A pencil.
Paul:	This. (Points to ant.)	Paul:	Pencil.
Native Speaker:	It's an ant.		
Paul:	Ant.		

Out of these vertical structures using *this* and a noun supplied by the partner evolve the early *This* + noun two-word utterances. Scollon (1974) believes that "this interaction with other speakers may well be the means by which (the learner) has learned how to construct" syntactic structures.

When a child learner says "this" in opening a conversation, the native speaker must, by the rules of conversation, make a relevant reply. However, the rules of conversation also put him under two constraints: (1) what information about "this" is shared background for adult and child; and (2) what are the attributes of "this" that one can talk about? That is, there is nothing obvious about "this" when the child points to a pencil that would allow one to make a relevant remark about much of anything beyond identifying the object as a pencil, asking "what is it?", or talking about where, whose, what color, how many, or what it can be used for—"Can you write?" "Are you writing?" And the first constraint prevents the adult from saying such things as "Speaking of pencils, what do you think about the Sierra Club pressuring Congress to enlarge the Redwood National Forest?" or "How do you suppose they get the lead inside pencils?" The point is that conversational constraints, rather than conscious "making-language-easy," can account for the high frequency of simple structures in the input data to the child learner.

However, once we begin to look at conversations between adult learners and native speakers of English, we find that communication takes place in conversations with a minimum of syntactic organization. Here is a sample exchange between an adult learner and a native speaker:

Native Speaker: You don't like shorts?
Rafaela: No . . .
my sister
my sister
oh
the lady
lady no, no, no use many short.
For me is muy . . . (laughs)
Native Speaker: (laughs) Latin American men . . . yeh!
Rafaela: Si.

How important is syntax in the example; does the listener understand? Even more important, at the moment, are the claims that we might make about the learner's acquisition or nonacquisition of syntax based on such data? We might go through the data counting morphemes or looking for verb tense and, when we finish the counts, assign percentage figures on the assumption that native speakers would have used correct forms in these places.

But, once we begin looking at real conversations of native speakers of English, we find that our comparison standards are faulty. E. Keenan has been doing some interesting work on the differences in unplanned talk data, planned speech, and highly planned written language samples of native speakers. She has found that the talk data of native speakers are not as syntactically organized as one might suppose. Perhaps a sample of a native speaker engaged in story telling (a fairly planned sample of talk data) will make this clear:

ONE of them was—uh— . . . back in . . . what 66? . . . 67 . . . when I FAINTed on the subway. It was very UM . . . UH . . . FRIGHTening experience. I had DON'T even remember FAINTing before in my life let alone on the subway . . . A—nd UH— . . . it was h . . . very hot . . . August day . . . and I was going into the city . . . from Queens? . . . A—nd . . . I was standing . . . a very crowded car . . . And I remember standing . . . I was standing up . . . and I remember holding on to the . . . center pole, . . . a—nd . . . I remember (chuckle) saying to myself . . . there is a person over there that's falling to the ground . . . and that person was me.

—Tannen, 1977

Notice the number of syntactic errors, the number of repetitions of words, the use of conjunction over subordination, etc.

Tina Bennet, working with Keenan, has suggested that the talk data of native speakers share many features of pidgins, creoles, and second language learner talk. We need to know much more about the spontaneous speech of native speakers. If Bennet is right, talk data of second language learners may be much closer to talk data of native speakers than we think.

Yet, I do not think one would confuse this beginning learner of English with a native speaker:

Ricardo:	Saturday, Sunday
	me
	how do you say . . .
	Saturday, Sunday. (trying for "last weekend"?)
	Me in . . .
	in car of my father.
Native Speaker:	Where? In your father's car? Where did you drive? (note correction of poss. morpheme)
Ricardo:	Capistrano
	me
	my mother me go for my mother watch
	she watch house.
	Me (+ gesture of driving)
Native Speaker:	Oh, are you looking at a house in Capistrano?
Ricardo:	Yeah
	Mama say me
	Mama say me
	Mama no understand car
	You know?
Native Speaker:	Yes, she doesn't know how to drive. (restatement for learner)
Ricardo:	Mama say me . . .
	"Ricardo, you me go de Capistrano?"
	Me.
	"Fred.
	Fred, please, keys for car."
	Me a this for police (+ gesture) . . . .

Butterworth data, 1972

Instead of highly organized syntax, the story follows the conventions of highly organized narratives. First, time must be presented (*"Once upon a time"*); then place ("Once upon a time *in a kingdom by the sea"*). Note that Ricardo specifies the car in the place slot and the native speaker says "Where?" Next comes who ("Once upon a time in a kingdom by the sea there lived *an old woman"*). Ricardo manages to identify the "goers" as himself and his mother. The story then proceeds, with a recounting of events in the order of occurrence (getting the keys, showing his license, etc.). The learner is attending to the requirements of conversation in constructing the narrative; however, his syntactic organization leaves much to be desired.

It seems unlikely that this particular learner attends to the corrections included in the replies of the native speaker. More likely, he "hears" them only as signals that his listener understands what he is trying to tell him. Perhaps at some later stage he will hear them and match them to his own performance. At the moment, however, he is not unlike Zoila, the learner who told us that the little words which mark syntactic relationships are unimportant.

It may be that the talk data of language learners bears as much resemblance to the dialogues of an ESL textbook as the speech of native speakers does to the lines a playwright might create. Yet, some native speakers do approach the articulateness of the playwright's imagination and some ESL learners become more fluent than some native speakers. If input were the only explanation, this would never happen. The order of acquisition of syntactic structures may be based on input, on frequency, on numbers of forms to be sorted out, grammatical complexity, semantic weight, perceptual saliency, or even pronunciation problems with consonant clusters. How far and how fast the learner progresses may be much more related to instruction, learner interest in the finer points of syntax, and innumerable personal variables.

In our search for system in the learner's acquisition of second language syntax, the beginning research has shown us overall general patterns of development. We have looked for similarities among our learners in that development and we have found them. We have also found considerable variation among learners and variability in the language produced by each learner. Considering how little we know about the specifics of anything beyond a few morphemes, question formation, negation, and relative clauses, it may be premature to offer explanations. As we refine our research techniques and begin to look at language learning in real-life context (whether that is a foreign language classroom, conversations with native speakers, or conversations with other learners), the continuum and the reasons for variation may become much clearer to us.

REFERENCES

Adams, M. A. "The Acquisition of Academic Skills and a Second Language Through a Program of Total Immersion," MA-TESL thesis, UCLA, 1974.

Andersen, R. W. "The Impoverished State of Cross-Sectional Morpheme Acquisition/Accuracy Methodology," in Henning, C. A., ed., *Proceedings of the Los Angeles Second Language Acquisition Forum*, UCLA, 1977.

Anderson, L. "Discovering Intermediate Stages in Language Learning Through Scaling Analysis," paper presented at NWAVE-V, Georgetown University, 1976.

d'Anglejan, A., and R. G. Tucker. "The Acquisition of Complex English Structures by Adult Learners," *Language Learning*, 1974, 25, 2, 281-296.

Bailey, N., C. Madden, and S. Krashen, "Is There a 'Natural Sequence' in Adult Second Language Learning?" *Language Learning*, 1974, 24, 235-243.

Bertkau, J. "Comprehension and Production of English Relative Clauses in Adult Second Language and Child First Language Acquisition," *Language Learning*, 1974, 24, 2, 279-286.

Brown, R. *A First Language*. Cambridge, Mass.: Harvard University Press, 1973.

Brown, R., C. Cazden, and U. Bellugi. "The Child's Grammar from I to III," in Hill, J. P., ed., *Minneapolis Symposium on Child Psychology*. Minneapolis, 1968.

Butterworth, G. A. "A Spanish-Speaking Adolescent's Acquisition of English Syntax," MA-TESL thesis, UCLA, 1972.

Cazden, C. B., H. Cancino, E. J. Rosansky, and J. H. Schumann. "Second Language Acquisition Sequences in Children, Adolescents and Adults," final report, NIE Grant No. NE 6-00-3-0014, Harvard, 1975.

Chomsky, C. *The Acquisition of Syntax in Children From 5 to 10*. Cambridge, Mass.: MIT Press, 1969.

Cook, V. J. "The Comparison of Language Development in Native Children and Foreign Adults," *IRAL*, 1973, 11, 1, 13-28.

deVilliers, J., and P. deVilliers. "A Cross-Sectional Study of the Acquisition of Grammatical Morphemes in Child Speech," *Journal of Psycholinguistic Research*, 1973, 2, 3, 267-278.

Dulay, H., and M. Burt. "Should We Teach Children Syntax?" *Language Learning*, 1973, 23, 235-252.

Dulay, H., and M. Burt. "Natural Sequences in Child Second Language Acquisition," *Language Learning*, 1974, 24, 1, 37-53.

Fathman, Ann. "The Relationship Between Age and Second Language Productive Ability," *Language Learning*, 1975, 25, 245-253.

George, H. V. *Common Errors in Language Learning*. Rowley, Mass.: Newbury House, 1972.

Gough, J. W. "Comparative Studies in Second Language Learning." Unpublished M.A. thesis. Los Angeles: UCLA, 1975.

Hakuta, K. "Development of Grammatical Morphemes in a Japanese Girl Learning English as a Second Language," in Hatch, E., ed., *Second Language Acquisition*, Rowley, Mass.: Newbury House, 1978.

Hatch, E. "Discourse Analysis and Second Language Acquisition," in Hatch, E., ed., *Second Language Acquisition*. Rowley, Mass.: Newbury House, 1978.

Hatch, E. "Discourse Analysis, What's That?", in Celce-Murcia, M., *Teaching English As a Second Language*. Rowley, Mass.: Newbury House, in press.

Hatch, E., R. Shapira, and J. Gough. "Foreigner Talk," paper presented at the Second Language Acquisition Forum, UCLA, 1975.

Hatch, E., and J. Wagner-Gough. "Explaining Sequence and Variation in Second Language Acquisition," in Brown, H. D., ed., *Papers in Second Language Acquisition*, Proceedings of the 6th Annual Conference on Applied Linguistics, Ann Arbor, Mich., 1975, 39-58.

Huang, J. "A Chinese Child's Acquisition of English Syntax," MA-TESL thesis, UCLA, 1970.

Hyltenstam, K. "Implicational Patterns in Interlanguage Syntax Variation," unpublished paper, Dept. of Linguistics, University of Lund, Sweden, 1977.

Katz, J. T. "Foreigner Talk Input in Child Second Language Acquisition: Its Form and Function Over Time," in Henning, C. A., ed., *Proceedings of the Los Angeles Second Language Research Forum*, 1977.

Kempf, M. A. "A Study of English Proficiency Levels of the Composition Errors of Incoming Foreign Students at the University of Cincinnati During 1969-1974," Ph.D. dissertation, Ohio State University, 1975.

Larsen-Freeman, D. "The Acquisition of Grammatical Morphemes by Adult ESL Learners," *TESOL Quarterly*, 1975, *9*, 4, 409-419.

Larsen-Freeman, D. "An Explanation for the Morpheme Accuracy Order of Learners of English as a Second Language," *Language Learning*, 1976, *26*, 1, 125-135.

Linde, R. "A Diagnosis of Grammar Errors Made by Japanese Persons Speaking English as a Second Language," Ph.D. dissertation, American University, 1971.

Mikeš, M. "Acquisition des Catégories Grammaticales dans le Langage de l'enfant," *Enfance*, 1967, *20*, 289-298.

Neuman, R. A. "An Attempt to Define Through Error Analysis the Intermediate ESL Level at UCLA," MA-TESL thesis, UCLA, 1977.

Plann, S. "The Spanish Immersion Program: Towards Native-like Proficiency or a Classroom Dialect?" MA-TESL thesis, UCLA, 1976.

Ravem, Roar. "Language Acquisition in a Second Language Environment," in Richards, Jack C., ed., *Error Analysis*. Longman, 1974, 124-133.

Richards, J. C. (ed.). *Error Analysis, Perspectives on Second Language Acquisition.* London: Longman, 1974.

Richards, Jack C., and Gloria P. Sampson. "The Study of Learner English," in Richards, 1974.

Rosansky, E. J. "Methods and Morphemes in Second Language Acquisition Research," paper presented at the 8th Annual Stanford Child Language Research Forum, Stanford, Cal., April, 1976.

Schachter, J. "An Error in Error Analysis," *Language Learning*, 1974, *24*, 2, 205-214.

Schumann, John H. *The Pidginization Process: A Model for Second Language Acquisition.* Rowley, Mass.: Newbury House, 1978.

Scollon, R. "One Child's Language From One to Two: The Origins of Construction," Ph.D. dissertation, University of Hawaii, Honolulu, 1974.

Shapira, R. "A Study of the Acquisition of Ten Syntactic Structures and Grammatical Morphemes by an Adult Second Language Learner," MA-TESL thesis, UCLA, 1976.

Slobin, D. I. "Cognitive Prerequisites for the Development of Grammar," in Ferguson, C. and D. I. Slobin, eds., *Studies in Child Language Development.* New York: Holt, Rinehart, and Winston, 1973.

Snow, C. E. "Mothers' Speech to Children Learning Language," *Child Development,* 1972, *43,* 549-565.

Syngle, B. "Second Language (English) Acquisition Strategies of Children and Adults: A Cross-Sectional Study," Ph.D. dissertation, Louisiana State University, 1973.

Tannen, D. "Well What Did You Expect?" In *Proceedings of the 3rd Annual Meeting of the Berkeley Linguistics Society,* Berkeley, Cal., 1977.

Taylor, B. T. "Overgeneralization and Transfer as Learning Strategies in Second Language Learning," Ph.D. dissertation, University of Michigan, 1974.

Van Mettre, P. D. "Syntactic Characteristics of Selected Bilingual Children," Ph.D. dissertation, University of Arizona, 1972.

Wagner-Gough, J., and E. Hatch. "The Importance of Input Data in Second Language Acquisition Studies," *Language Learning,* 1975, *25,* 2, 297-308.

Wagner-Gough, J. "Comparative Studies in Second Language Learning," CAL ERIC/CLL Series on Language and Linguistics, *26,* 1975.

Wong-Fillmore, L. "The Second Time Around: Cognitive and Social Strategies in Second Language Acquisition," Ph.D. dissertation, Stanford University, 1976.

STUDY AND DISCUSSION QUESTIONS

(1) How can we reconcile the findings of cross-sectional studies which show adolescents and adults as good second language learners with case studies which show them to be very poor learners?

(2) Translations tasks frequently have been used to elicit data. Imagine a research report that showed that contrastive analysis could predict errors. The data in the experiment were elicited via translation. Would you accept the findings?

(3) Assume you wanted to study the acquisition of time connectives (*first, and then, before, after, when,* etc.). You have four subjects that you tape record every two weeks, but they seldom produce the connectives. How can you elicit them?

(4) It frequently has been suggested that language lessons ought to follow the "natural sequence" shown in language development of untutored learners. What arguments can you give for and against this suggestion?

(5) There are many fields which discard any model that can be shown not to cover *all* data. Other fields allow models to "leak" a lot—that is, a few counterexamples do not discredit the model. Other fields never test models but accept them if they "make sense." How would you characterize the interlanguage model: watertight, leaky, or a sieve? If it makes sense to you, can you think of more appropriate ways of testing the model? If it doesn't make sense to you, can you think of ways to modify the model so that it does make sense?

(6) Many L2 studies reflect or replicate L1 research methods. Can you think of questions which relate to the acquisition of syntax that would be designed just for work in *second* language learning?

(7) In acquiring negation, many learners use *not* before nouns, adjectives, and locatives, and *no* before verbs (e.g., She *not* smart. He *not* in Colombia./I *no* have time. I *no* go there.) How do you account for this?

(8) If a learner began verb negation with *no* + verb (I no go there) and then added *never* + verb (I never go there) would this really be counter evidence to the notion of stages?

(9) Try to replicate Schachter's study using a syntactic structure which contrastive analysis predicts will be difficult for your students. Do your findings show your students avoid using the structure? How might avoidance data effect the notion of a natural order of acquisition (e.g., a natural order unchanged for age, language background, or degree of instruction of the learner)?

(10) If your students are from many different language backgrounds, what evidence do you have that interlanguage is systematic? What evidence do you have of variability? How can you account for the variation?

4

LANGUAGE-LEARNER LANGUAGE

S. P. Corder

It is not so long ago that people ceased to think of dialect speakers as some sort of second-class citizens because the language they spoke was considered to be no more than a distorted, incorrect, or defective form of their mother tongue. It is only more recently that people have come to think of pidgins and creoles as languages in their own right and not some "inferior, haphazard, broken, bastardised version of older, longer-established languages," as Loreto Todd (1974) puts it. It is even more recently still that some people have been prepared to consider the language of the second language learner as other than a defective, distorted, or incorrect form of the language they are learning. And yet to do so is now coming to be seen as a necessary preliminary step toward investigating objectively the whole phenomenon of second language learning and second language use. Only by treating language learners' language as a phenomenon to be studied in its own right can we hope to develop an understanding of the processes of second language acquisition, just as it is only by treating child language as a phenomenon to be studied in its own right that we can hope to understand something about the processes of first language acquisition and the use that infants make of language.

When we consider that the majority of the human race has attempted to acquire some second language beside its mother tongue, usually, of course, outside the classroom, we must realize the all-pervasiveness of the phenomenon of language-learner language and recognize that no account

71

of human language itself can be complete without an understanding of this phenomenon any more than it can be without taking account of the existence of child language, pidgins, creoles, and dialects.

Although most of us have no doubt succeeded in making the conceptual readjustment required in considering dialects, pidgins, and creoles as languages in their own right, I do not underestimate the difficulty of doing the same for language-learner language. The main problem, which it shares with child language, is its dynamic nature. It would appear to be difficult to pin down because of its heterogeneity; all speakers of it speak a slightly different version, depending upon how far they have progressed toward their target language. But if we reflect for a moment, the same is true of dialects and creoles, only they change more slowly over time or as the observer moves through geographical or social space. Variability is the rule in human language and the language-learner language is no exception.

Another problem in conceptualizing the language-learner language is that it is the possession of an individual or set of individuals and not of a community which can be independently identified on nonlinguistic criteria. Again this is a property shared by child language. There is no natural social community of speakers of language-learner language or of child language, as there is of dialect, creole, or pidgin languages. We find it difficult to think of a language as existing which does not correspond to an identifiable social group. But just as it is now possible to accept the variability and dynamic nature of child language, it should also be possible to do the same for learner language. And for the same reason. The utterances made by a child, while having certain characteristics of adult language, are manifestly different and, furthermore, different in systematic and predictable ways. This is also true of learner language. As Larry Selinker pointed out in 1971, since the utterances of the learner and

> those that would have been produced by a native speaker of the target language, had he attempted to express the same meaning as the learner, are not identical, we would be justified in hypothesizing the existence of a separate linguistic system—this system we will call "interlanguage."

It is this linguistic system which I have been calling the *language-learner language* and will hereafter, following Selinker, also call *interlanguage*. It is therefore because the learner attempting to communicate one and the same set of messages produces utterances which, while *similar to those of other language learners,* are different from those of the native speaker of the target language, child or adult, dialect or standard speaker, that the concept of interlanguage is justified.

It is customary to characterize the differences I have referred to as *errors,* and in the context of language teaching discourse it may be useful to do so since it is clearly the task of the teacher to help and encourage the learner to approximate his language progressively in the direction of the target language. We might equally well wish to persuade a dialect speaker to adjust his language in the direction of the standard language. But if we are considering interlanguage as a form of language to be studied in its own right, it is as illogical to refer to differences between utterances in an interlanguage and some related target language as errors as it is to describe the utterances of a dialect speaker as erroneous by comparison with those in the standard language, or to regard the utterances of the infant as deviant forms of the adult language. The extension of this illogical procedure would eventually lead us to talk of French as erroneous English!

I have already identified one of the difficulties in conceptualizing the notion of interlanguage as being due to its heterogeneity. Language learners do not speak the same interlanguage any more than infants all speak the same version of child language. The reason for this is obvious: their interlanguage is undergoing constant change in the process of learning. It is this salient characteristic of interlanguage which leads us to talk about it as a *dynamic system.* But there are difficulties here because our ordinary experience of a language is of the apparent high degree of homogeneity that we find among adult native speakers of what we think of as the same dialect. That this degree of invariability is more apparent than real is due to the fact that we ourselves have a variable repertoire within a certain range and our own linguistic performance varies largely in the same way as that of our interlocutors. Hence we are normally unaware of it. It has, however, given difficulty to linguists when they have attempted to describe the linguistic behavior of individuals or groups. Language behavior is far from homogeneous and linguistic systems are not, and cannot adequately be, described by means of the categorical rules favored by linguists, who have been forced as a consequence to invent such fictional beings as "ideal speaker-hearers in a homogeneous society" in order to accommodate their data to their theories. As Bailey (1973) has said:

> Describing the competence of speakers in formulations represent-
> ing the internalized grammars which generate all the differences
> with which they deal competently is impossible with static models.

The linguist's *language system* then is a static system, and when linguists have been forced to deal with obviously dynamic phenomena they have, until very recently at least, done so by positing a sequence of static but overlapping systems (polylectal grammars). It is in this way that Nemser

(1974) attempted to cope with the essentially dynamic nature of interlanguage, speaking about an evolving series of approximative systems, each successively more similar to the target. Brown (1973), in accounting for the dynamic process of child language acquisition similarly describes the developmental sequence in terms of a series of stages. In the final analyses, the identification of one stage or system as separate from the next is an arbitrary decision. This form of idealization is essentially counterintuitive; neither the infant nor the language learner jumps, as it were, overnight, from one system or state of knowledge to the next in the series. Typically, as any teacher or mother could tell us, the process is smooth, though change may be slower or faster in individual cases or at different times. There is a time at which the learner does not appear to know or use some bit of language, and there may be a later time when he always uses it correctly when the context requires, but in between these times there is a longer or shorter period during which he sometimes uses it and sometimes doesn't, when his behavior is apparently inconsistent. Interlanguage, like child language, is a continuum of more or less smooth change, and we can locate learners, like infants, along the continuum of change or development. This is what we mean by a dynamic system and new ways of describing this sort of system must be found if present linguistic theory proves inadequate for the task. For, as Bickerton (1975) says:

> The language learning continuum between two distinct languages must equally constitute a system, and the "Anglo-Chinese" and "Anglo-Spanish" of native English-speaking learners of Chinese or Spanish must have as much right to the title of "system" as English, Spanish or Chinese.

In this paper, however, I am going to concern myself not with the technical problem of how theory is being, or should be, adapted to deal with dynamic systems, but only with the nature of the interlanguage continuum and how interlanguage is learned and used.

INTERLANGUAGE AS A CONTINUUM

We may revert for a moment to the quotation from Bickerton. It is clear that he conceives of the interlanguage continuum as stretching from the mother tongue to the target language and it is clear that, in adopting the term "interlanguage" Selinker had in mind that the interlanguage system was in a sense *intermediate* between the first and the second language. Nemser's term "approximative system" is noncommittal as to the nature of the continuum; he merely envisages learning as a movement through a series of stages (along some sort of continuum—nature unspecified) in the direction of the target language.

There are, in fact, two types of continua which are candidates for the continuum we are interested in, and possibly some mixture of the two. The first is the Selinker-Bickerton continuum. This envisages the learner as engaged in a process of progressively adjusting his mother tongue system to approximate it ever more closely to the target. This process can be called *progressive restructuring* and the continuum a *restructuring continuum*. Movement along this continuum means gradually replacing features of the mother tongue, one by one, with features of the target language. We will leave aside any consideration of how this process could be adequately described linguistically, and the obvious problem, from a theoretical point of view, that it cannot be a case of simple substitution of mother tongue forms, since few languages have any features or aspects in the one-to-one relationship that this implies, except perhaps at some very deep or abstract level. One may add here in parentheses that it is precisely the task of so-called contrastive linguistic studies to discover the relationship between mother tongue and target language structure. Continua of a progressively restructuring kind are, however, being intensively studied by creolists and dialectologists, as well as by historical linguists. In this context they are referred to as *lectal continua*. The changes a language undergoes through time and space are essentially a process of restructuring.

The salient characteristic of a continuum of this sort is that movement along it implies that the overall complexity of the language remains the same at any point along the continuum. This runs counter to the experience of any language teacher, who would surely claim that language-learner language is in some sense a good deal less complex than that of either his mother tongue or the target. It does, however, account for the well-attested fact that, particularly in the early stages of learning a language, the learner's interlanguage frequently shows in its grammar and phonology certain characteristics of features which can be related readily to his mother tongue. This is what one would expect if he were engaged in a task of restructuring and it is often referred to as the process of *transfer* from the mother tongue. Whether the term transfer is a happy one, if the learner is indeed engaged in progressively *removing* features of his mother tongue *from* his interlanguage, is a matter of argument.

Not all learners, however, show evidence of transfer on the same scale; indeed it has been claimed (Dulay and Burt, 1974) that some learners studied, especially children, do not show any clear evidence of it at all in their utterances. Furthermore, we have the intuitive feeling that the learner's language is simpler overall than that of the adult native speaker of the target language and that learning is more readily conceived of as a process of increasing complexification of the interlanguage. This suggests that second language acquisition resembles perhaps in some respects the acquisition of the mother tongue, which is quite evidently a process of increasing complexification of the child's language. Such a continuum of increasing complexity we can call a *recreation* or *developmental* continuum. Child language and interlanguage are perhaps not the only language phenomenon which can be described as developmental in this sense. The post-pidgin continuum, that is, the developmental sequence followed by a pidgin language in the course of acquiring native speakers (Sankoff and Laberge, 1973), during its development into a creole, also follows a continuum of increasing complexity. There is, however, some doubt as to the existence of post-pidgin continua (Bickerton, 1974).

The question that immediately jumps to mind is this: if interlanguage does indeed follow a continuum of increasing complexity, what is its starting point? The infant's starting point in his language acquisition career is presumably, linguistically speaking, zero. (I shall not here get involved in the nativist versus interactionist controversy.) The post-pidgin continuum, if it exists, presumably starts from an existing pidgin. (What about the pre-pidgin continuum?) It is somehow counterintuitive to suggest that the second language learner starts from scratch, that he is in effect learning language all over again. Does the fact that he already possesses language and is a language user count for nothing? Somehow we must reconcile the notion of increasing complexity with the notion of restructuring. We must propose some starting point for the learner in his career along the interlanguage continuum which does not offend our intuitions and which can be reconciled with the actual and, at present, conflicting data from interlanguage research.

We have not, I am sure, finished with questions which jump to mind. Granted, you may say, that the learner moves along some continuum or other in his learning of a second language, this says no more than that his knowledge of the target language is increasing all the time. Why all this talk about interlanguage? May not every learner follow his own idiosyncratic course in his discovery of the target language? If this were so then there would be nothing worth investigating; if in the course of his development each learner was peculiar to himself, then no generalization would be possible, no significant principles of learning could be discovered, and the concept of interlanguage would be vacuous. But the same could be said about the study of child language acquisition and the concept of child language. The concept of interlanguage presupposes that interesting and important generalizations can be made about the process of second language learning, specifically that all language learners do show similarities in their acquisition of a second language and consequently in their interlanguage grammars at various points along the continuum of change or development. This is the hypothesis of the *built-in syllabus*, first proposed by the author in 1967 (Corder, 1967) and later taken up by others (cf. Bailey et al., 1974). There is now a considerable body of evidence which supports this view. The relevance of such studies to language teaching is obvious. We may remind ourselves at this point that the so-called structural element in language-teaching syllabuses is not based upon any understanding of the developmental processes of natural language learning, and although it represents what we attempt to teach, it does not follow that it is what is learned.

The hypothesis of the built-in syllabus takes two forms, the strong and the weak, each corresponding to one of the two types of continua discussed above. The strong hypothesis proposes that there is a degree of uniformity about second language learning such that all learners of a particular second language follow roughly the same sequence of development, *whatever their mother tongue.* This implies that the starting point for all learners is the same whatever their mother tongue and that the continuum along which they move must be purely developmental. Such a hypothesis could be disproved by evidence that the learners, particularly in the early stages, showed clear traces in their utterances of influence from their mother tongue. I want to point out at this stage the difficulties, which will be dealt with later, in identifying the processes by which features of the mother tongue (or indeed any other language known to the learner) may find their way into his utterances. The mere presence of such features does not automatically invalidate the strong hypothesis.

The weak form of the built-in syllabus hypothesis claims no more than that all learners *having a particular mother tongue* will follow the same sequence in the acquisition of some second language. This form of the hypothesis relates to the notion of a restructuring continuum. It could be disproved by evidence which supports the strong hypothesis, namely, that at least some learners show no evidence in their interlanguage utterances of the influence of the mother tongue.

The strong and weak forms of the built-in syllabus hypothesis represent two extremes, but are not necessarily mutually exclusive. It is entirely possible that certain aspects of the mother tongue do play a part in second language acquisition and others do not. For instance, it is perfectly possible to accept the weak hypothesis (restructuring continuum) in relation to the acquisition of the phonological system of the target language, while maintaining the strong hypothesis in regard to the syntax (recreation continuum). It is also plausible to suggest that, for example, children, or indeed some adults, learning in a free learning situation follow a recreation continuum, while adults under formal tuition follow a restructuring continuum. It is further possible that there is some hypothesis intermediate between the two extremes which better fits all cases, namely, that second language learning is a process of both restructuring and complexification and that there is indeed a starting point other than zero but one that is not specifically that of the mother tongue but some more basic, simpler, or more universal system: that there is some process of *reculer pour mieux sauter*! And that the influence of the mother tongue may be less in controlling the sequence of development than in the facilitation of the acquisition of certain features: the mother tongue may affect the *speed* of development at certain points rather than the *sequence* of development.

THE LANGUAGE LEARNING PROCESS

Some readers may react adversely to the expression "built-in syllabus" with its implication of a learner being programmed, genetically perhaps, to develop in a fixed and immutable way, such that neither he nor the teacher can do much about it—in other words, that learners are automata. No such extreme implication is intended. What is implicit in the notion is that all human beings, endowed as they are with the same cognitive learning capacities, when faced with a similar learning task will tend to find roughly similar solutions to that problem in a roughly similar way; that language learning, as indeed all learning, is constrained within certain limits by the inherent properties of the human mind. But that does not mean there is no scope for variability. There is a multiplicity of environmental and personal factors in the learning situation that can affect to some degree both the course and the speed of learning. We can surely envisage a state of affairs in which there is an overall similarity in the course of learning but at the same time a degree of individual difference. The program may interact differently with various factors in the learning situation to produce a somewhat different sequence of events. After all, the current view of language is that while there are obvious superficial differences between one language and another there are at the same time certain deeper and more abstract ways in which all languages resemble each other. This is precisely what one would expect if language learning were both a product of nature and of nurture.

What I have just said indicates that the view of language learning which I am adopting is that it is a cognitive process whereby the learner, through interacting with his environment, creates for himself an internal representation, or hypothesis, about the nature of that environment. In the case of language learning it is, of course, his linguistic environment with which he is interacting. This means no more than that learning results from interaction with speakers of the language, native or otherwise. "Speakers" here is understood to include "writers" since some part of the learner's linguistic environment is written communication and, more specifically, written discourse whose function is to help him develop this internal representation. One may, of course, learn a language inside or outside the classroom. Anyone with whom a learner interacts linguistically in writing or speech is in a sense his teacher and provides the data upon which his learning capacities operate.

The learner, then, is engaged in developing an internal representation of the nature of the language data and how it is used; but, unlike the infant acquiring his mother tongue, the second language learner not only has a more or less developed adult view of the nonlinguistic environment but also possesses a mature internal representation at least of his mother tongue linguistic environment. He has available, then, whether he uses it or not, a rather rich and specific set of hypotheses about human language which he can use to process the data of the second language. If he makes heuristic use of these hypotheses, he will be likely to follow a restructuring continuum in his development, progressively accommodating his mother tongue representation to the data of the second language. If he does not use the mother tongue hypothesis, he will resemble a child acquiring language for the first time, the difference being that his knowledge of the world and his cognitive learning capacities are mature; and these may significantly affect the speed, and perhaps the course, of his progressive development of an internal representation of the second language environment. We can now, for the sake of brevity, translate the terms "internal representation of a language" or "hypothesis about a language" into the more usual term "grammar of a language" and hence the term "hypothesis about the second language" into his "interlanguage grammar." In short, the learner, as a result of his interaction with speakers of the target language, is engaged in the task of creating for himself an ever more adequate internal grammar of the language. He does this by the two basic processes of *accommodation*—adapting his interlanguage grammar to fit the perceived facts of the language, and *assimilation*—attempting to fit newly perceived facts into the present state of his interlanguage grammar.

Any internal representation of the nature of the environment can be regarded as an hypothesis about that environment. To test the adequacy or "good fit" of his hypothesis about the target language, the learner makes utterances which derive from that hypothesis or, in technical terms, are generated by his internal interlanguage grammar, to see whether they work, i.e., achieve their communicative intent. If they do, he has no reason to doubt the validity of his hypothesis; if they don't (if his interlocutor reacts in such a way as to indicate that he does not understand or accept the utterance) then the learner will attempt to improve his hypothesis. This is what we mean by "interaction with his linguistic environment." We should note here that this account is not to be understood to mean that these processes are above the level of consciousness, or that the intentions of the learner in attempting to communicate are to test his interlanguage grammar. His intentions are presumably to communicate as best he can. Fundamentally it is by attempting to communicate with speakers of the target language that the learner learns. Outside the classroom, interaction in the interlanguage covers some part of the whole range of functions and types of discourse which is served by the mother tongue. This is sometimes called "authentic communicative activity," as if what went on inside the classroom is not authentic. This is a misconception. Discourse inside the classroom is authentic but has the severely limited function of instruction, merely one among many functions of discourse in the world at large. Inasmuch as our study of language learning has been based upon classroom interaction alone, our picture has been distorted. Hence the profound importance of recent emphasis in language teaching on a much wider range of communicative activity in the language classroom.

The feedback a learner receives from his environment, i.e., his interlócutors, may be more or less directly useful to him in upgrading his interlanguage grammar. It may take the form of correction, either reformulation, expansion of his utterance in the target language form, or statements by the teacher about the inadequacy of his utterance, i.e., reference grammatical statements; or it may be no more than a momentary hesitation in the response of a native-speaker interlocutor. Whether feedback—confirmation or disconfirmation of his hypothesis—is an essential feature of language learning is still open to question. There are anecdotal accounts of learners making considerable progress in the development of their interlanguage without ever opening their mouths.

INPUT AND OUTPUT

In discussion of learning processes it is now fashionable to use the functioning of a computer as an analogy, particularly in terms of the relation between *input, program,* and *output.* While the analogy is helpful, it has its limitations, as all analogies do when we use them as explanations, quite apart from the neomechanistic view of cognitive human behavior it may encourage, namely that a learner behaves in an entirely predictable fashion when placed in a particular environment. The analogy is, however, highly misleading if we consider that the interaction, if we may call it that, between the computer-user and the computer is similar to, let alone identical with, the interaction between a learner and his interlocutors. However, it is useful if we are interested in the relation between the linguistic data made available to the learner—sometimes called the input—and the interlanguage grammar—the output—that results from his programmed processing of that data. We are interested in this relationship because we should be able to infer from it something about the nature of data processing, or learning. It will also tell us something about how variability in the data is reflected in the interlanguage grammar which results from the processing. In the teaching situation this means no more than the relationship between what we attempt to teach a learner and what he actually learns. As I have suggested, it is part of the folklore of teaching that the learner learns what we set out to teach him. This is a belief which tends to be reinforced by the results of our tests and exercises, which are designed upon that assumption. Tests and exercises are not communicative activities in the ordinary sense and we cannot safely assume that we can infer from them the nature of the learner's interlanguage grammar at any particular time. Their object is to measure or quantify the learner's knowledge of the target language, not to elicit the sort of data which will give us a picture of the current state of his interlanguage grammar. For that we need some elicitation procedure which yields qualitative analysis. A truer picture can be obtained of the state of his interlanguage from a study of his spontaneous utterances made when attempting to use his language for communicative purposes, in interaction with other speakers. To base one's account of a learner's interlanguage on the data from tests and exercises is like inferring something about a learner's mathematical knowledge from his manipulation of a pocket calculator.

While there may be some similarity between the output of a computer and the result of a learner's learning activity in the form of an interlanguage grammar (although the one is overt and susceptible of direct inspection, while the other is only indirectly investigable), the analogy between the computer input and the data available to the learner is misleading. I have suggested that there is no necessary connection between what we teach and what is learned. The teaching syllabus is certainly not input. Neither, however, is the language data to which the learner is exposed. Properly speaking, input is what goes in. What elements are, in fact, processed from the data that is available is determined by what the current state of the learner's interlanguage grammar permits him to *take in* at that moment. If the basic learning processes are accommodation and assimilation, then what can be assimilated from the data is constrained by the state of the internal representation; and the way that that representation can be modified to accommodate new information is also determined by its current state, not by the data available, except in the limiting case that the data lack the information processable at that moment. This is no more than to restate a general principle of learning, that we can only teach someone something if he already possesses the necessary conceptual framework to accommodate the new information.

Part of the study of interlanguage development is an investigation of the nature of the data to which the learner is exposed. In the classroom the data have characteristics which normally sharply distinguish them from the data available outside the classroom. First, as we have seen, classroom discourse is essentially pedagogic in function. It is therefore constrained in a particular way that relates to its function. The data a learner is exposed to are typically constrained by the so-called linguistic or structural syllabus. Only the data which are believed to be relevant for the learning of the "next item on the menu" are available to the learner. There is, however, no good reason to suppose that whatever logic such a grading has is related to the internal logic of a learner's program, or built-in syllabus. No syllabus yet proposed has been constructed upon a sustained investigation of the sequential development of interlanguage grammars as manifested by learners acquiring a language in a free learning situation. It is therefore entirely plausible to suppose that if the language data are tightly controlled by a linguistic syllabus and the learner is never allowed access to any form not prescribed by that syllabus, he may well be deprived of precisely the information which the current state of his interlanguage grammar requires in order to develop. Luckily recent teaching methodology has considerably relaxed the tight control over the linguistic data which was fashionable some years ago. Since we do not yet know very much about the sequence a learner's interlanguage development takes, the wise course would be to relax even further our control over the linguistic forms he is exposed to, indeed perhaps to abandon all control of a structural sort.

This proposal may sound like an abdication of all accepted pedagogical principles. Our task is to make the processing of the data as easy as possible and this implies a different sort of control. For want of a better term I shall call this *rhetorical control*. It is now well established that mothers or other adults, when interacting with infants and young children acquiring their mother tongue, simplify their language in various ways which correspond to the age or linguistic development of the child

(Snow and Ferguson, 1977). This simplification is not so much in terms of the range of structures employed but rather in terms of the range of speech functions and topics, the length of utterances, the tempo, pitch, and other prosodic features as well as the amount of partial or total repetition, rephrasing, and redundancy in their speech. This means that, in general, *mother talk* is an adaptation of the adult's normal language behavior which has the effect of facilitating the child's perceptual processes and interpretation of utterances. Mother talk is perceptually simpler and more explicitly related to situational context.

When we turn to the way native speakers modify their speech when interacting with interlanguage speakers, we frequently find similar, though not quite identical, adaptations. There is rarely any simplification of the structure employed. Normally the utterances are fully grammatical, but the rhetoric is adapted to assist the learner in processing the signal and the range of speech functions is limited and closely related to context (Hatch, 1978). If we observe a sensitive teacher interacting with his pupils or other interlanguage speakers in authentic communicative activity we can observe the same thing happening. The data available to the learner can be, and normally are, controlled, but not in the way specified in a linguistic syllabus. The data available to the language learner we can refer to as *teacher talk*. This, if we really must use the term, is input.

COMMUNICATIVE STRATEGIES

If those who interact with interlanguage speakers adopt a strategy of rhetorical simplification to maximize the probability of successful communication, what strategies does the learner adopt to achieve the same end? Let us start by adopting the common sensical assumption that in a free learning situation it is through attempting to communicate that a learner acquires his grammar, that necessity is the mother of invention in a very true sense. He develops his interlanguage system in response to his experienced communicative needs (Schumann, 1974). The logical implications of this are twofold: if he experiences no needs he won't learn at all; if he finds that he can manage with whatever knowledge he has, he won't go on learning. His interlanguage grammar will *fossilize* at the point in its development where his needs are satisfied. As Valdman (1978) has pointed out, learning in a classroom situation is the exact converse. There are fewer, if any, communicative demands of an authentic sort on the learner in most classrooms; he experiences no needs and, therefore, what we can regard as the immediate motivations for interlanguage development do not exist and have to be replaced artificially either by long-term motivations or basically irrelevant incentives. At the present time we do not know very much about the relationship between different kinds of communicative needs or types of discourse and the levels of complexity in the interlanguage grammar that are required to meet them. But that there is such a relationship is certain and is felt by anyone who cares to observe his own reactions when confronted by the need to engage in different types of discourse in his interlanguage.

The question is: what strategies do we employ when we find ourselves in such a situation? Again common sense supplies at least a framework for discussion. We can adopt the basically conservative risk-avoiding strategy of *message adjustment,* either refusing further interaction or trying to sidestep certain topics, saying less than we would wish to, or otherwise opting out in various degrees. Or we can adopt a risk-taking strategy, the risk being that we shall fail to some degree in achieving our communicative ends. Basically this strategy is aimed at increasing by one means or another our linguistic resources, either by skillful manipulation of what we already know: paraphrase, circumlocution or principled guessing, word-coinage, borrowing from whatever resources we have available, notably our mother tongue, but often from other languages we know, greater recourse to paralinguistic behavior (gesture, etc.), and only in extreme cases switching to another language or seeking our interlocutor's help by asking for a translation, or picking up clues from his language. These I shall call *resource-expansion* strategies.

The study of communicative strategies of learners was initiated by Varadí (1973), who was interested in explaining the origin of certain types of errors produced by interlanguage speakers. It is fairly clear that it is the risk-taking strategies which are most likely to result in unacceptable utterances. But this merely highlights the principle that it is by taking risks that we develop our interlanguage, that we learn. The pedagogical moral of this is obvious: the encouragement of the learner to take risks even at the expense of committing errors and, by implication, a willingness on the part of the teacher, beyond what is usually found in most classrooms, to accept error as a sign of a motivation for learning, or indeed a strategy of learning, and not something to be deprecated, let alone penalized. As Holley and King (1975) say:

> A case can be made for permitting and even encouraging foreign language students to produce sentences that are ungrammatical in terms of full native competence. This would allow the learner to progress like a child by forming a series of increasingly complete hypotheses about the language.

One might note here that it is well established that the feedback the infant receives from his adult interlocutors is almost always related to the *content* of his utterances and not to their *form*, that is, their adequacy or otherwise as attempts at communication.

The theoretical interest, then, in studying the interlanguage speaker's communicative strategies lies in their relation to learning. I have already enunciated the principle that learning derives, in a free learning situation, from the attempt to communicate. How do these strategies lead to learning, that is, development of the interlanguage grammar? The risk-avoiding strategies (too often encouraged in the classroom because they do not produce errors), can scarcely lead to learning. If we are never prepared to operate beyond our self-assessed capacities then we never enlarge our knowledge. The risk-taking strategies, on the other hand, may all yield in principle, learning outcomes. If a guess is accepted by our interlocutor, then the form is incorporated into our repertoire as part of the target language. A translation or borrowing that succeeds is similarly incorporated. Those that fail provide information about the limits of the target language. Analogizing errors (overgeneralization of a learned rule) may be evidence of guessing which proved unsuccessful. But we learn something about the scope of a rule by doing such guessing. Principled guessing and hypothesis testing are one and the same thing.

There is one type of guessing strategy which is of particular theoretical interest: that of borrowing from the mother tongue. I have already noted that the utterances of language learners may frequently show features which resemble those of the mother tongue. Where there is a similarity between the mother tongue and the target language in respect to these features they will, of course, pass unnoticed by the native speaker, since they do not produce errors and are communicatively successful. We are, therefore, in some difficulties in deciding on any particular occasion whether these features are the result of a restructuring process or the result of creative learning (Tarone, 1976). Where there is a difference, of course, the result is error. We cannot immediately distinguish those erroneous mother tongue features which are a result of restructuring from those which are borrowings resulting from a guessing strategy of communication, but which do not derive from (are not generated by) the current state of the speaker's interlanguage grammar. We must, therefore, make an important distinction between transfer features in utterances, which may be the result of either a restructuring process or a creative learning process, and borrowed features, which are the result of a communicative strategy. I have already pointed out that successful borrowing may lead to learning—incorporation into the learner's interlanguage system. In the end the only way we can distinguish between the two is the systematic nature of transfer features and the nonce occurrence of borrowings.

The theoretical import of this distinction between transfer as a learning process (restructuring) and borrowing as a strategy of communication is that the mere presence of mother tongue-like features in learners' utterances does not logically entail (as is usually believed) that the learner's interlanguage must be following a restructuring continuum (see above). It is a matter of some interest to discover what principles the learner is following in his guessing and borrowing strategies. It has been suggested that we all have certain notions about the language-specific characteristics of our mother tongue (Kellerman, 1977) which inhibit our borrowing these features when attempting to communicate, because we believe it will be unsuccessful or lead to error. It has also been suggested that we all have notions about the degree of difference between other commonly studied languages in our culture and our own mother tongue—what we may call perceptions of language distance—and that these perceptions or beliefs may determine whether we adopt a basically restructuring or recreating strategy of learning. If we believe that another language is only distantly related structurally to our own (e.g., Chinese-English) we may opt for a recreative strategy, starting from scratch, on the grounds that the path to the target will be shorter, while if we believe that the target is closely related, (e.g., Danish-English) we may prefer a restructuring strategy as being more economical.

I have spoken about strategies that are available to learners both in order to learn—to develop their interlanguage—and in order to communicate, and how these may be related. What is implicit in what I have said is that these represent options, not, of course, normally conscious options, but a set of alternatives nonetheless. The moment we introduce the notion of alternatives we must necessarily abandon the idea that we are all programmed to learn in the same way, and it becomes relevant to enquire into the circumstances that incline us to adopt one or another strategy. In discussing, for example, the notion of language distance as a factor in causing learners to adopt one rather than another strategy of learning, we may ask where does the concept of language distance come from? Or, in the case of borrowing, where does the concept of language-specific or unique features come from? We can suppose that there are several possibilities—the learner's experience of learning the language, the stereotyped attitudes of the community, or the beliefs of his teachers. When it comes to selecting a risk-avoiding strategy of communication as against a risk-taking strategy, this may be determined by the nature of the interaction the speaker is engaged in—whether he is more concerned at the moment in maintaining contact with his interlocutor than with passing on some piece of information he has available, i.e., whether the *interpersonal* function of language prevails over the *ideational* function on a particular occasion (Halliday, 1973). It may also have to do with personality factors: is he a risk-taker or not? What seems certain is that we can discern in the speech of individuals distinct personal preferences for certain communicative strategies. We may also suppose that age, social background, linguistic sophistication, attitudes toward the culture related to the language, and so on may all play a part in determining the strategies of learning and communication adopted by interlanguage speakers. These affective and social factors which influence learning are poorly understood, but may all be expected to account for the variability we may find both in terms of sequence and speed of movement which overlays the basic pattern of interlanguage development which I referred to earlier (cf. Schumann, 1975).

VARIABILITY

I have drawn attention to the variability of interlanguage as one of the stumbling blocks in conceptualizing it as a language in the same way as we conceptualize pidgins, creoles, and child language as languages. I suggested that we could locate any individual or group of interlanguage speakers along some sort of continuum of approximation toward the target language. But there is another sort of variability which we must deal with, not just the variability found within interlanguage because of its dynamic nature, but variability found in the performance of any one particular interlanguage speaker.

A distressing experience that most teachers suffer is to find that their pupils sometimes appear to go backwards and to forget what they have learned. At one moment they seem to have acquired some form and at the next to have lost it. They are apparently inconsistent in their behavior. How can it be that having achieved some piece of learning they can promptly forget it, reverting to earlier forms derived from a previous stage of their interlanguage grammar? Inconsistency is another name for variability. It was this inconsistency in learners' behavior which was used as the principal argument against the validity of the concept of interlanguage as a coherent and regular language system underlying learners' speech. These arguments, however, overlooked the well-established fact that we are all variable in our use of our mother tongue. This variability is not random, but patterned and related to the social context of speech activity. It is principled variation (cf. Labov, 1970). We range over some area of variation which we call a verbal repertoire. This variability has been shown to correlate with the amount of attention we are giving to how we are speaking in contrast to our attention to the content of our speech. Is there any reason, we may ask, why a learner should not attempt to exploit his admittedly more restricted repertoire for the same social ends? In fact, quite young children show variability in their speech in precisely the same way as adults. Systematic variability in speech is learned early and is all-pervasive.

It is now clear that, at least at the phonological level, language learners also vary their speech in a similar way (Dickerson, 1975). They utilize the more advanced level of their interlanguage development in formal spoken and written communication and regress to earlier levels in their casual and informal spoken language. They vary their speech by moving up and down the continuum of their own development. This is one reason why, if we wish to obtain an adequate account of the current state of a learner's interlanguage, we must not confine ourselves to data elicited from one type of performance, e.g., tests and written exercises, but must sample his performance over a range of different types of discourse.

The difference between native speakers and learners is that native speakers have a far larger room for maneuver; they can vary their performance in at least two dimensions, i.e., across a *lectal* continuum of equal complexity, and by using certain *simplified registers*—baby talk, foreigner talk, headlines, telegraphese, etc. The interlanguage speaker has only one effective option: to move up and down the scale of complexity represented by his own interlanguage development. His informal style will be simpler, representing an earlier stage of his development, than his more formal spoken or written style. Variability of this sort is not a sign of forgetting or backsliding but is an exploitation of his restricted resources to convey social meanings, e.g., attitudes toward his interlocutor, and should thus be no cause of concern to the teacher.

SIMPLIFIED REGISTERS AND THE
LEARNER'S STARTING POINT

I have just said that native speakers of a language can vary their performance by moving up and down a scale of complexity and mentioned what have been called simplified registers (Ferguson, 1971). It appears that all of us have available, for certain types of discourse, codes which are linguistically simpler than the fully complex code with which we operate most of the time. These simplified registers are stereotyped in language communities and can be plotted according to the degree of their structural complexity along a development-like continuum. Thus, the language of instructions, telegraphese, and headlinese show only a moderate degree of structural simplification, e.g., omission of articles and omission of the copula, while baby talk and foreigner talk show a much greater degree of simplification, e.g., omission of all morphological marking, fixed word order, reduced vocabulary, etc. There are probably many other intermediate stages of simplification between these two which regularly occur, but which have not become institutionalized and thus received recognition and a name. There is still a great field of research into the variability of performance which involves movement up and down a scale of complexity in native speaker's speech.

What is clear is that from a very early age all of us regularly exploit this range of variability. Jakobson (1968) reports on quite young children using baby talk to their younger brothers and sisters; children regularly use foreigner talk to represent or make fun of undifferentiated foreigners speaking their language, sometimes without ever having met a foreigner. All of us then have access to registers or codes which are linguistically extremely simple. When we come to analyze these codes linguistically we find that they have striking formal resemblances to pidgin languages and to the earliest stages in the interlanguage continuum and of child language acquisition. This can scarcely be accidental.

It is commonly assumed that we learn these simplified registers of our mother tongue by hearing them spoken around us, as we might pick up other dialect forms of our language in early youth. An alternative and equally if not more plausible hypothesis is that these registers are remembered stages in our own linguistic development to which we can revert or regress on socially approved occasions. In other words, we do not kick away the ladder of our own linguistic development, but keep it available for climbing up and down, all our lives.

As I have said, whether we learn these simplified registers or not, we do have available in our repertoire a range of linguistic systems of varying degrees of complexity and, furthermore, the further down the scale of simplicity we go the more similar these systems appear to be in different languages. It has been suggested that they may represent something we can call an approximation to some basic universal linguistic system or *natural semantax*. As Elizabeth Traugott (1973) speculates in relation to the development of pidgins:

> Does it not involve the acquisition of lexical items so typical of adult innovation, combined with a return to earlier processes especially syntactic ones, that have in the speaker's native language been partially or wholly suppressed? This would make sense if we

wish to relate pidgin simplification to the general ability we all have to simplify in various ways when talking to foreigners, babies—and, I may add, stupid people. Even small children seem to do this . . . and do so largely by reverting to structures similar to their own earlier ones.

Ervin-Tripp (1974) has also observed that children acquiring a second language "regress to a processing strategy still available to them for use under certain conditions." The effect is that they regularly produce utterances which show no specific structural resemblance either to their mother tongue or the target language.

We can now return to the question I raised on page 78, that there may be some hypothesis about the nature of the interlanguage continuum intermediate between the restructuring and the recreation hypothesis, namely, that second language learning may be *both* a process of restructuring *and* a process of progressive complexification. We now have a candidate for the starting point for a complexification process, which at the same time is partly a restructuring process. We do not, in learning a second language perhaps start from scratch, but neither do we start from the fully complex code of our mother tongue. Our starting point may be some simple register of our mother tongue, some basic linguistic system, some natural semantactic system from which all language development starts, mother tongue, pidgin, creole, or interlanguage which, as Bickerton (1974) has suggested, may be innate, not in a Chomskyan sense of being language specific, but in the sense that it is the product of the innate cognitive and perceptual processes of the human mind. One could, however, add this qualification: just how far down the scale of simplification one moves before starting to build up again (recomplexify) will depend upon the relatedness of the mother tongue to the target language; this is our old friend, the notion of perceived language distance. In other words, economy of effort suggests that we do not necessarily always have to strip down to bare essentials, but only so far as to reach a point at which the two languages begin to diverge structurally. In the case of such closely related languages as Danish this may not be very far down, but in the case of Chinese and English it may involve a good deal of simplification. It is one of the strategies of learning to find out just how far down the scale it is going to be necessary to go before starting to build up again.

REFERENCES

Bailey, C. J. N. *Variation and Linguistic Theory.* Washington: Center for Applied Linguistics, 1973.

Bailey, N., S. D. Krashen, and C. Madden. "Is there a 'Natural Sequence' in Adult Second Language Learning?" *Language Learning, 24*.2, 1974, 235-243.

Bickerton, D. "Creolization, Linguistic Universals, Natural Semantax and the Brain," *Working Papers, 6*, No. 3, 1974, Dept. of Linguistics, University of Hawaii.

———. *Dynamics of a Creole System.* Cambridge: Cambridge University Press, 1975.

Brown, R. *A First Language.* London: Allen and Unwin, 1973.

Corder, S. P. "The Significance of Learners' Errors," *IRAL, 5*.4. Reprinted in Richards, J. C., ed., *Error Analysis,* 1974.

Dickerson, L. J. "The Learner's Interlanguage as a System of Variable Rules," *TESOL Quarterly, 9*.4, 1975, 401-408.

Dulay, H., and M. Burt. "Errors and Strategies in Child Second Language Acquisition," *TESOL Quarterly, 8*.2, 1974, 129-136.

Ervin-Tripp, S. "Is Second Language Learning like the First?" *TESOL Quarterly, 8*.2, 1974, 111-128.

Ferguson, C. A. "Absence of the Copula and the Notion of Simplicity," in Hymes, D., ed., *Pidginization and Creolization of Languages,* Cambridge: Cambridge University Press, 1971.

Hatch, E. "Discourse Analysis and Second Language Acquisition," in Hatch, E., ed., *Second Language Acquisition: A Book of Readings.* Rowley, Mass.: Newbury House, 1978.

Halliday, M. A. K. *Explorations in the Function of Language.* London: Edward Arnold, 1973.

Holley, F., and J. K. King. "Imitation and Correction in Foreign Language Learning," in Schumann, J. H., and N. Stenson, eds., *New Frontiers,* 1975.

Jakobson, R. *Child Language, Aphasia and Phonological Universals.* New York: Humanities Press, 1968.

Kellerman, E. "Towards a Characterization of the Strategy of Transfer in Second Language Learning," Utretcht: *Interlanguage Studies Bulletin, 2*, No. 1, 1977, 58-145.

Labov, W. "The Study of Language in its Social Context," *Studium Generale, 23.* Reprinted in Labov, *Sociolinguistic Patterns.* Philadelphia: Univ. of Pennsylvania Press, 1970.

Nemser, W. "Approximative Systems of Foreign Language Learners," *IRAL, 9.2.* Reprinted in Richards, J. C., *Error Analysis,* 1974.

Richards, J. C., ed. *Error Analysis; Perspectives on Second Language Acquisition.* London: Longman, 1974.

Sankoff, G., and S. Laberge. "On the Acquisition of Native Speakers by a Language," KIVUNG, *6*.1, 1973.

Schumann, J. H. "Implications of Pidginization and Creolization in the Study of Adult Second Language," in Schumann and Stenson, eds., *New Frontiers,* 1974.

Schumann, J. H. "Affective Factors and the Problem of Age in Second Language Acquisition," *Language Learning, 25*.2, 1975, 209-236.

Schumann, J. H., and N. Stenson, eds. *New Frontiers in Second Language Learning.* Rowley, Mass.: Newbury House, 1974.

Selinker, L. "Interlanguage," *IRAL, 10*.3. Reprinted in Richards, J. C., *Error Analysis,* 1974.

Snow, C., and C. A. Ferguson, eds. *Talking to Children.* Cambridge: Cambridge University Press, 1977.

Tarone, E. "Some Influences on Interlanguage Phonology," *Working Papers in Bilingualism*, No. 8, 1976, 87-111.

Todd, L. *Pidgins and Creoles.* London: Routledge & Kegan Paul, 1974.

Traugott, E. "Some Thoughts on Natural Syntactic Processes," in Bailey, C-J. and R. W. Shuy, eds., *New Ways of Analyzing Variation in English*. Washington: Georgetown University Press, 1973.

Valdman, A. "On the Relevance of Pidginization and Creolization Model for Second Language Learning," Proceedings of the 6th Neuchatel Colloquium, 1978.

Varadi, T. "Strategies of Target Language Learners' Communication: Message Adjustment," paper presented to the 6th Conference of the Romanian-English Linguistic Project, May 1973.

STUDY AND DISCUSSION QUESTIONS

(1) Make a list of the languages taught in schools and colleges or spoken by foreigners in your community in their order of difficulty to learn. Compare your list with that of other members of your class or group. Discuss the differences between your orderings. Where did you get your notions of language difficulty/distance?

(2) Make a list of about ten idiomatic expressions in English. Which of these are likely to have, in your opinion, a more or less literal equivalent in the foreign languages you know about? Check in a dictionary whether you are right. What about languages you don't know? Can you give any account of why you thought a particular idiom was or was not transferable?

(3) Try telling your favorite funny story to the members of your class/group in some foreign language known to you all. Then discuss with them the problems you encounter. Is it possible to adopt a risk-avoiding strategy when telling a joke?

(4) Select an anecdote from a book or collection of anecdotes. Rewrite it in foreigner talk as best you can. Compare your version with that of the other members of your class/group. Try and see if you can together agree on an authentic foreigner talk version.

(5) Choose a comic strip. Have a member of your class/group tell the story it depicts as s/he would to a class of beginner learners or to a foreigner who doesn't know the language well. Tape record the performance. Record another member telling the same story as s/he would to fellow native speakers. Transcribe both recordings and compare them with respect to such rhetorical features as range of vocabulary, length of utterances, repetitions, use of pronouns, speed of delivery, etc.

(6) Studies have shown that native-speaking teachers of a language ignore, tolerate, or correct a different set of nontarget forms (errors) in their students' interlanguage speech from nonnative speaking teachers. Discuss why this might be. What are your own criteria as a teacher for dealing with students' errors?

(7) Discuss what elicitation methods you could use to tell whether some mother tongue feature in a learner's interlanguage speech is the result of transfer or of borrowing.

(8) It has been suggested in this chapter that what appears in a learner's speech to be evidence of regression may not be a case of forgetting what has been learned, but a principled use of alternative forms for communicative purposes. Does this rule out the possibility that there are genuine cases of forgetting once-learned rules?

(9) Perceived communicative needs and access to the linguistic data are necessary conditions for learning a second language. Are they sufficient conditions? What is the role of the teacher in creating these conditions?

(10) Discuss the statement, "Classroom texts and exercises are an inadequate device for discovering the nature of a learner's interlanguage."

5

MODELS OF LANGUAGE USE AND LANGUAGE LEARNING

Jack C. Richards

Learner-language data can be viewed from a number of perspectives, depending on whether one's primary interest is in learning principles and strategies, communication strategies, or some other dimension. I want to begin from a consideration of the concept of proficiency in a foreign or second language and to consider what models of proficiency are appropriate for different circumstances for the use of language. Most of my examples will be drawn from English; however, the analysis offered can be applied equally to the learning and use of other second or foreign languages. Four aspects of proficiency will be considered in relation to models for the use and learning of English: grammatical well formedness, speech act rules, functional elaboration, and code diversity. I want to consider how these concepts apply to interlanguage data, and relate particular models for the development of interlanguage phenomenon to the dynamics of second and foreign language communication.

GRAMMATICAL WELL FORMEDNESS

As Hatch points out in her review of research into the development of syntax in a second or foreign language, study of the development of interlanguage syntax has occupied a dominant position in recent research on second language learning. For many researchers and teachers, learning a second or foreign language is primarily a question of learning grammar, of learning the rules by which sentences are constructed in the target language. There has been detailed discussion of the formal grammatical characteristics of interlanguage and considerable research into such questions as sequences of grammatical development, the relationship between first and second language developmental sequences, and the invariance of the order in which grammatical rules are said to develop across language learners with different language backgrounds (Wode, 1976; Hatch, this volume).

Research directed to such questions has led to syntactic measures of proficiency (Burt, Dulay and Hernandez, 1975). There has also been an attempt to determine an index of second language development comparable to, say, the mean length of utterance used in first language studies. This would be an objective linguistic measure which could be used to determine the degree of proficiency of a second or foreign language user (Larsen-Freeman and Strom, 1977). For our purposes here it is sufficient to note that second language users are sometimes compared for evidence of differing degrees of mastery of the rules of the target language. Terms made use of in the literature to refer to differing degrees of grammatical development include on the one hand, *redundancy reduced, simplified, pidginized,* and on the other, *elaborated, expanded, complexified, creolized,* and so on (Corder, 1975; Valdman and Phillips, 1975).

SPEECH-ACT RULES

An alternative or complementary view of second and foreign language learning is to consider the learner's primary task as not merely the acquisition of the grammatical rules for the production of well-formed sentences in the target language, but rather the ability to use language appropriately for the realization of specific intentions and for the performance of particular speech acts (cf. Fraser, 1977; Platt and Platt, 1975; Austin, 1962; Searle, 1969; and Kennedy, this volume). For example, the intention *Request person to close window* might be realized by a request, "Please close the window," or by a statement from which the addressee will infer the intent, "Isn't it cold in here." What are the rules by which intentions are realized as speech acts? This is the focus of an area of second language research which goes by the rubric of pragmatics and discourse analysis. We can relate proficiency in a second or foreign language to the degree to which the language user has acquired the speech-act rules of the target language.

Searle states that there are over 1000 verbs in English, such as *state, assert, describe, warn, remark, comment, order, request, approve, criticize, apologize, censure, welcome, promise, express approval, express disapproval,* etc., which mark speech acts. Communication conflict and communication breakdown can result from the transfer of speech-act rules from one language to another, or from misinterpretation of speech-act rules in the target language (Clyne, 1975a).

The ways in which speech-act rules differ from one culture to another are sometimes dramatic, yet extremely subtle. For example, the anthropologist Geertz describes how, when he studied Javanese, he was also taught that in Javanese culture one has to acquire a rigidly formal way of doing things which conceals one's feelings. Geertz describes a typical situation that his language teachers employed in the model conversations they used to teach him Javanese:

> Two men are speaking. One wants something from the other (a loan, a service, his company in going somewhere) and both know it. The petitioner does not want to put his petition directly for fear of angering the petitioned; and the petitioned does not want to state his refusal directly for fear of frustrating the petitioner too severely. Both are very concerned with the other's emotional reactions because ultimately they will effect their own. As a result they go through a long series of formal speech patterns, courtesy forms, complex indirections, and mutual protestations of purity of motive, arriving only slowly at the point of the conversation so that no one is taken slowly by surprise.
>
> —Geertz, 1960

American businessmen doing business in Japan encounter similar examples of different speech-act rules, formalized almost to the degree of ritual, involved, for example, in negotiating a business contract. The American is frustrated by the inability of his Japanese counterpart to get to the point. The Japanese finds the American aggressive and in too much of a hurry. One particular type of speech event—the telephone conversation—has been discussed from the point of view of different speech-act rules, particularly from the viewpoint of sequencing and turn taking. Schmidt has discussed the considerable differences between the openings of a typical American telephone conversation and a typical Egyptian telephone conversation. One of the differences is that there is "a strong reticence on the part of both callers and answerers in Egypt to give self-identification on the telephone before ascertaining the identity of the other ... repeated hellos are an attempt to ascertain identities through the channel of voice. If this device is unsuccessful, Egyptian callers demand identification by the answerer far more frequently than do American callers" (Schmidt, 1975). Hence foreigners living in Egypt commonly feel that there are no rules for telephone conversations in

Egypt. They interpret the Egyptian ritualized organization of the speech events as being disorderly, due to differences between the way American and Egyptian telephone conversations are handled.

Different cultures may have institutionalized functions for particular speech acts. In one society, as Clyne points out, persuasion may be realized by the promise of a bribe or by a threat of a complaint to a higher authority. Danet, quoted by Clyne, in her study of Israeli's communication with bureaucrats, concluded that Israeli-born and European migrants stress more their status and occupation, while the near Eastern migrants appeal more by recourse to their family occupations (Clyne, 1975a). Apologizing and joking are also areas where there are often marked cross-cultural differences of this sort. The domain of speech-act rules has been much less researched than that of grammatical development in second language learning, yet clarification of the role of speech-act rules is vital to our understanding of second and foreign language proficiency.

FUNCTIONAL ELABORATION

Several approaches to analyzing language from a functional perspective have been proposed (Halliday, 1973; Robinson, 1972). A problem with functional approaches is that language is normally used multifunctionally, and the question of the validation of taxonomies remains unresolved. In considering proficiency from a functional perspective the focus is on the ways in which the functions assumed by the target language for the language user determine the form of the interlanguage. "In initial stages of second language learning, the target language serves only a narrowly communicative function; as a consequence, it is acquired in a highly deviant form that exhibits all the characteristic features of pidginization; emphasis on content words, invariable word order, elimination of functors, etc. As the target language's range of functions increases the learner's interlanguage progressively expands and complexifies" (Valdman, 1977). Rivers (1977) adapts a functional model proposed by Halliday (1973) to provide for nine language functions:

(1) instrumental: manipulating and controlling the environment

(2) regulatory: exercising control over others—the language of rules and instructions

(3) interactional: language defining and consolidating the group

(4) personal: language enabling the users to identify and realize their own personality

(5) heuristic: language as a means of learning about things

(6) imaginative: using language to create one's own environment

(7) representation or informative: language used to convey messages about the real world

(8) ludic: rhyming and making up nonsense words; trying out the possibilities of language as it is being acquired

(9) ritual: language defining the social group; language as good manners

Valdman compares two dimensions along which language learning may be compared, the grammatical and the functional. He proposes that "the key to interlanguage development lies in an understanding of the relationship between the two systems" (Valdman, 1977). In one situation, for example, the interlanguage may be relatively well-formed grammatically, but have a low degree of functional elaboration. This may be particularly true of classroom-acquired foreign languages, where the emphasis is often on grammatical correctness; on form, rather than on content, or on what Widdowson calls rules of use rather than rules of usage (Widdowson, 1975; compare also Krashen, 1977). Other learners, such as immigrant workers (Clyne, 1975b), may acquire a language primarily as a functional tool in a nonclassroom setting. Their interlanguage may be relatively efficient functionally, but lack grammatical well formedness. Alternatively a language learner may progress in a balanced way along several directions of proficiency: the grammatical, the speech act, and the functional. Valdman, considering just the grammatical and functional dimensions, illustrates three different models of development for an interlanguage (Figs. 5-1, 5-2, and 5-3).

The degree of functional elaboration and development also affects a related dimension, that of topic and content diversity of the interlanguage, which can be measured by type token density, availability (Mackey, 1965), lexical density (Linnarud, 1975), and related measures. A language user's interlanguage may be relatively well developed grammatically, but deficient in the range of topics which he or she can talk comfortably about. This may lead to topic avoidance, paraphrase, and other strategies of communication which shape the interlanguage in particular ways. Where there is a functional differentiation between languages in bilingual communities, certain topics may generally be discussed in one language (business, politics, education) and other topics in a different language (home life, religion). Ervin-Tripp (1968) studied changes in the content of conversations according to language shift of the participants. When bilingual subjects were interviewed in Japanese, they gave different responses to word association and sentence completion tests than they gave to the same stimuli when interviewed in English. Thus in sentence completion tests, a subject completed a sentence

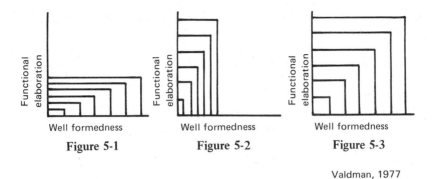

| Figure 5-1 | Figure 5-2 | Figure 5-3 |

Valdman, 1977

beginning *when my wishes conflict with my family* with *it is a time of great unhappiness* when answering in Japanese, and with *I do what I want*, when answering in English.

CODE DIVERSITY

In addition to proficiency being defined in terms of grammatical and speech act well formedness and range of functional elaboration, the degree to which the interlanguage reflects code distinctions must be accounted for. This refers to whether variation is possible in the interlanguage along formal-informal, standard-colloquial, written-spoken dimensions, and whether the learner possesses rules allowing for variation in the interlanguage according to participant-role and setting factors. Speaker-receiver roles for example, reflect dimensions such as age, sex, social proximity, and occupation. Studies of native-language communication have attested the importance of role factors on the form of speech events (Hymes, 1968). Observations of mother talk to young children have demonstrated that mother talk is different from adult-directed language (Snow, 1972). Mother talk is more explicit and relies more on the immediate observable environment than adult talk. Even young children use different speech styles according to the age of the addressee (Sach and Devin, 1976). However, the speech of foreign language users, even when quite a high degree of grammatical competence has been achieved, may be relatively inflexible in terms of code variation. This inability to adjust for role factors may be a cause of frustration and anxiety among second and foreign language users.

Segalowitz (1976) investigated the effect of a nonfluent language user attempting to adjust his or her interlanguage when a casual style of French was required. The hypothesis he investigated was that the

Anglophone subjects would show considerable discomfort when casual French was required compared to a situation where careful French was called for, since they were most familiar with a careful classroom register of French. It was also hypothesized that the subjects would handle their discomfort in the casual speech condition by downgrading the personality of the interlocutor and by believing that the interlocutor formed a bad impression. The results of the study supported this hypothesis.

Certain roles require specific types of speech acts. For example, a nurse is in a superordinate position in relation to a patient in a hospital, and may be required to comfort or console the patient. However, she herself is in a subordinate position in her relationship with the doctor. Herman (1968) reports that an immigrant nurse in Israel described how much more confidently she used her halting Hebrew when she was speaking to patients under her care than when she used it with other people. Children of immigrant workers in Australia also have been observed to switch from a type of worker-pidgin when they speak to their parents to a dialect of English closer to standard Australian-English when speaking to their peers. Here the child would appear to be adjusting his or her speech in the case of child-adult talk, so as not to downgrade the parent's status by a demonstration of superior language ability, and to vary his or her speech repertoire toward standard English when speaking to a peer, so as not to downgrade the child's own status vis-à-vis a peer.

In foreign language classes, the student's productive use of the target language may vary according to the role the child is required to play within the classroom learning situation. When the teacher is the instigator of communication, asking questions, instructing, demonstrating, etc., the learner may appear to be a nonfluent language user. However, when the classroom activity changes to that of a peer-teaching situation, the learner now takes on the role of teacher and may become a more fluent language user. This is the rationale of some individualized language-teaching activities.

Setting factors may also influence the foreign- or second-language code. Sampson has noted how phonological features in immigrants' English vary according to whether the setting is the classroom or the playground (Sampson, 1971). Likewise a public rather than a private setting may require a different code in the foreign language. A foreign student in France, for example, would need to know both formal French, and the informal "argot" spoken by students on the campus. Knowledge of only formal French would not enable the student to communicate effectively with other students. Similarly a foreigner learning Indonesian for use in Jakarta would need to acquire three distinct repertoires in Indonesian. Formal Indonesian would be required for such settings as talking to a government officer; informal Indonesian would be needed for talking to mixed company at a party, or when talking to Indonesian colleagues in the office. The third variety of Indonesian, the so-called Jakarta dialect, would be useful for contacts with a broad range of Indonesians in very informal settings.

MODELS OF PROFICIENCY AND MODELS OF LANGUAGE

What I have suggested is that in looking at language-learner data, we can view it according to at least four different but related dimensions of variability, encompassing linguistic, communicative, functional, and code factors in the speech event. The analysis could be pursued to show how each factor contributes in different ways to our understanding of language proficiency. However convenient such taxonomies of factors affecting second or foreign language use may turn out to be, we need to note that they are all defined with reference to a norm-oriented understanding of the target of learning English, French, or whatever the particular language may be. But while it may be plausible to view certain models of language acquisition in this way, as moving toward a single norm, it is not the only model for language learning. It may work quite well in the case of the child acquiring his or her mother tongue, or an adult studying a language like Thai or Polish. Yet it is not always an appropriate model for English. What is needed in accounting for the learning of English as a second or foreign language, are models that take account of different contexts for the use and learning of English. It is models intended for this function which I wish to consider now.

When I speak of a *model* of language, I mean the purposes, roles and characteristics of a language when it is used as a foreign or second language. It is the "who speaks what to whom and why?" I wish to consider four basic models of language that are needed to characterize the different contexts around the world where English is used.

MODELS OF LANGUAGE AND SPEECH EVENTS

The four basic models of language are what can be called *instrumental, intergroup, integrative,* and *interactional,* adapting terminology and even definitions from other sources for language models (Halliday, 1973; Schumann, 1975). They are defined as follows:

(1) instrumental: language for the transmission of referential denotative information; language for communication; language for manipulating and controlling the environment

(2) intergroup: language to communicate with someone who is not a member of our group

(3) integrative: language to mark affirmation and/or solidarity with another group; language to show similarity with another group; language as good manners

(4) interactional: language for intragroup functions; language to define and consolidate a group; language to mark membership of a group

All uses of English can be regarded as instrumental. Particular contexts for the use of English vary as to their intergroup, integrative, or interactional functions. Let us consider these functions or models for language in turn.

English for intergroup functions

Intergroup English speech events may be of two types: English used between speakers with different mother tongues or English used between two speakers, one with English as a mother tongue and the other without. The term *lingua franca* is commonly applied to the first situation, and *foreign language* to the second (Rice, 1962). These two contexts for intergroup uses of English need to be considered separately since they represent quite different communication networks.

Samarin observes that when a natural language becomes a lingua franca, it often loses some of its vocabulary or its syntax (Samarin, 1962). *Pidginization* is the constant reduction of the functions of language both in its grammar and use (Hymes, 1971). A *pidgin* is a special case of pidginization. Since a pidginized form of English, that is, a form of English where auxiliary, tense, and plural inflexion is often omitted, and with reduced syntactic and lexical complexity, can still perform instrumental functions quite satisfactorily, other models of language need to be posited when the interlanguage proceeds beyond the pidginized level to become closer to the target language in terms of grammatical and speech act well formedness, functional elaboration, and code diversity. In such cases we need to refer to the integrative model of language.

English for integrative functions

Both a lingua franca and a foreign language may be spoken with varying degrees of proficiency, as defined above. The integrative function for language by definition relates language proficiency to attitudinal factors such as self esteem, lack of ethnocentricism, empathy with the target language community, etc. (Gardner and Lambert, 1972; Schumann, this volume). In the case of a pidginized interlanguage, despite opportunity for further language development we would posit not necessarily the absence of such attitudinal factors as constitute the integrative function, but a failure to relate them to language proficiency. The integrative function is not necessarily related to the physical proximity of speakers of the target language. It might be assumed, for instance, that lingua francas, in the absence of native speakers of English, are more likely to show fossilized pidginization than foreign languages, yet one finds examples of language users *within* an English-speaking country using heavily pidginized interlanguages, and language users physically remote from native speakers of English who have managed to acquire an elaborated nonpidginized code. Schumann relates the former situation to degrees of social dominance, assimilation, acculturation, enclosure, etc. (Schumann, this volume).

Whinnom introduces the term *hybridization* in describing different contexts for linguistic change. He talks of *primary, secondary,* and *tertiary* hybridization. Primary hybridization is the development of dialects in a language. Secondary hybridization is the process of interaction between a native speaker and a nonnative speaker of a language. Tertiary hybridization is the case when the target language is withdrawn, as for example, with a pidgin (Whinnom, 1971). Whinnom discusses the case of Cocoliche, a variety of Spanish once extensively spoken by Italian immigrants in Argentina. This represented a continuum of interlanguage varieties of Spanish, renewed at one end of the continuum by the arrival of new immigrants from Italy, and brought into gradual approximation to Spanish at the other by social assimilation with the dominant community. Since the interlanguage had no institutionalized role within the immigrant community it was an individual rather than group phenomenon:

> Cocoliche was completely "unstable" in given individuals, since there was almost invariably continuing improvement in performance in achieving communication with Spanish speakers (and the succeeding generation acquired native Spanish). Furthermore the acquisition of lexical, phonological, morphological, and syntactic material must with each individual speaker have been subject to chance, so that the speech of no two individual cocoliche-speakers was ever quite identical (this is a consistent phenomenon with secondary hybridization). Nevertheless, the system as a whole, however ephemeral in given individuals, and however broad a series of spectra it encompassed, was fairly clearly *predictable* and was continuously renewed in recognizable and labellable form from year to year and from generation of immigrant to generation of immigrant.
>
> —Whinnom, 1971

We may regard the learning of English as a foreign language as a case of secondary hybridization (gradual movement toward the target language). The different learner-varieties of English thus observed in particular individuals, resulting from pidginized to native speaker-like, depending on the presence or absence of the integrative model of language, can be regarded as forming a *language learning developmental continuum*. The differences between the way individual learners speak English in Japan, Norway, Germany, etc., are hence illustrative of particular stages in the language learning developmental continuum which encompasses varying degrees of language mastery. Individual learners can be placed at different stages along this continuum of knowledge of target language rules. In each particular case, the learner is viewed as being in a transitional stage of learning. Further use, practice and exposure will enable the learner to gradually approximate closer and closer to the target language norm. Where the integrative function is absent, learning will fossilize at an arbitrary transitional stage, resulting in a pidginized variety of English.

In the case of lingua francas, either tertiary hybridization (movement further and further *away* from the target language norm) or secondary hybridization may take place, according to the proficiency and motivation of the participants.

English for interactional functions

An interactional model for language is a nonnative language used for intragroup, rather than intergroup functions, and which derives from this function the role of defining and consolidating the group or nation and to mark membership of it. Since English is the most widely used language with this special function, we will consider briefly the circumstances where this situation has arisen. Two different types of historical contexts for interactional uses of English need to be considered. The first is situations where linguistic and social interaction between speakers of English and other languages has resulted in radical tertiary hybridization and the consequent formation of English-based pidgins. These have in some instances disappeared (e.g., China-coast pidgin English); elsewhere they may have been adopted and institutionalized for more widespread use (e.g., New Guinea or Papua pidgin English), or they may have undergone creolization and decreolization (e.g., Jamaican creole and Jamaican English (Todd, 1974)). The second type of situation is instances where pidgins have not arisen or stabilized, but where *indigenization* of English has taken place. By indigenization I mean the evolution of distinct varieties of English as a result of the widespread use of English in new social and cultural contexts (Kachru, 1965, 1969,

1976; Richards, 1972, 1977; Tongue, 1974; Moag and Moag, 1977). This is the situation of immigrant minority dialects of English in many countries and of indigenous minority dialects (Puerto Rican-English in the United States, Mexican-American English, Italian-English in Australia, Black English, Aboriginal English, Maori English, etc.; cf. Richards, 1972, for extensive discussion). Indigenization can also be used to describe the processes which account for the new varieties of English which have emerged in Singapore, India, the Philippines, and so on. It is indigenization with reference to the latter contexts that is the particular focus here.

The question of the precise relationship between social and linguistic interaction which produces radical linguistic change resulting in pidgin languages remains an unresolved issue in the history of these languages. Grimshaw asks, "What is it about the differential experience of language contact sites that has sometimes resulted in pidginization (variously culminating in creolization, in the maintenance and continued renewal of the pidgin, in the disappearance of the pidgin) . . . and in other cases produced no special contact language at all?" (Grimshaw, 1971). He sees three factors as crucial in accounting for pidgins: the patterns of conflict relations, the industrial or commercial context, and the disproportionate numbers of speakers of English compared with the speakers of other languages involved.

In contexts where indigenization of English at a national level has been the outcome of language/social contact, we are generally dealing with the following circumstances:

(a) countries which were formerly under Colonial American or British administration

(b) countries characterized by multilingualism and multiethnicism. Such a degree of multilingualism was the principal reason for initially promoting the use of English in schools, rather than a local language

(c) the existence of an elite schooled in English, which has promoted the use of English as a working language in parliament, the courts, the post and telegraph, and most government departments

(d) a linguistic conflict exists as to the relative position of local languages such that promotion of the one local language might be resisted by members of different ethnic groups

(e) lack of a dominant national language to serve as a rallying point for the nation

(f) a consequent widespread use of English in the school system.

—Rice, 1962

A major difference between conditions for the development of a pidgin in one context and for the indigenization of English in another is that in the pidgin case, the contact situation provided neither the opportunity nor the environment for the learning of English. The disproportion between English- and non-English-speaking groups, the servile or semiservile economic and political status of the non-English speakers, resulted in limited interaction networks with English speakers (Reinecke, 1969). Occupational, racial, and social stratification meant that there was no solidarity between English- and non-English speakers. English was not therefore considered to be a target for learning. By contrast in contexts where English has indigenized, there is continued opportunity for the learning of English and access to important societal positions for a wide section of the community (Richards, 1972).

The evolution of these distinctive varieties of English is seen as the reflection of a universal need in situations where English is used interactionally, for both a formal and an informal model for English. In the case of countries where English has second language status, a local standard variety of English provides a model for formal uses of English and a local colloquial variety provides the model for informal uses. In situations where indigenous or immigrant minorities use English for interactional functions, a regional standard variety of English may be the model for formal uses of English, but a colloquial immigrant or indigenous minority variety of English might be used for informal communication in English. "Generally speaking, languages or varieties used for formal purposes tend to have high prestige, while those used for informal purposes fall somewhere on a scale between neutral and substandard, depending on conditions. Another general rule is that formal varieties, or languages, tend to mark social distance whereas informal ones signal closeness and intimacy" (Moag and Moag, 1977).

What distinguishes most contexts where English has indigenized and has developed interactional functions is that what began historically as a situation involving simultaneous secondary and tertiary hybridization but operating differentially according to the socioeconomic background of members of the community has now stabilized into a situation where *basilectal* (low), *mesolectal* (middle or neutral), and *acrolectal* (high) varieties of English have emerged (Bickerton, 1975). The difference between these situations and the Cocoliche example described by Whinnom is that through taking on intragroup or interactional functions, English comes to be institutionalized within a new cultural environment, and in so doing is required to exhibit variability according to such dimensions as educational background, economic standing, social distance, region, ethnic group, and so on, in much the same way as do native varieties of English. Let us now consider some of these new interactional functions for English.

Since in the multilingual countries where English has interactional functions, no single language of the country serves adequately as a vehicle for the expression of national sentiments, this role has to some extent been assumed by English, with ethnic identity being largely expressed through the use of the mother tongues. The situation is comparable to that in Indonesia in that there national identity is expressed through Bahasa Indonesia, a second language for most of the population, and ethnic identity is expressed through the use of Balinese, Javanese, Sundanese, etc. Singapore's representative to the United Nations captured this feature of English when he said:

> When one is abroad, in a bus or train or aeroplane, and when one overhears someone speaking, one can immediately say, this is someone from Malaysia or Singapore. And I should hope that when I'm speaking abroad my countrymen will have no doubt recognizing that I'm a Singaporean.
>
> —Tongue, 1974

Feelings of national loyalty are thus identified through the use of this interactional model of English, which would appear to be largely identifiable at the level of phonology. Thus if a Singaporean, an Indian, or a Filipino were to reject this model of English in favor of British or American-English, he or she would be regarded as presumptuous and affected. There is no motivation to model one's speech on a foreign pattern, any more than there is in Australia, New Zealand, or Canada. A different cluster of attitudinal factors operate from those present in the integrative foreign language model, leading in this case to the rejection of the foreign model and affirmation of a local norm.

Other interactional functions lead to distinct codes within the speech community, marking variation according to participant-role, setting, and social factors. While ethnic identity may be expressed through the mother tongue, there may still be a need to mark this dimension in interethnic communication. English may be spoken in Singapore with features that distinguish Malay, Chinese, or Tamil speakers. In the Philippines a Tagalog or Ilocano speaker can be identified by a characteristic accent in English which there is no attempt or desire to eradicate. This confirms Samarin's observation that "an inescapable aspect of language use is that it is more than a communication code; it also serves among other things to mark ethos identification and prestige" (Samarin, 1962). In interethnic communication, ethnic identity is hence one of several ethos identification dimensions. Formal versus informal registers will also be needed to mark different participant roles.

The process of indigenization of English can be seen to influence the four dimensions of language we noted above, encompassing rules for grammatical well formedness, speech acts, functional distribution, and code marking.

In Singapore English, variability with regard to a number of phonological, lexical, and grammatical features is used to mark a number of factors in the speech event. One such feature is a sentence particle *la*, borrowed originally from Hokkien, but used in Singapore English to mark intimacy, familiarity, and solidarity between participants in the speech event in addition to having emphatic function. The following extract illustrates the use of this particle, and is part of a telephone conversation in which two youths are discussing the purchase of a car:

Last time have (car). Now no have. Using motorcycle. My friend give it me la. Why you laugh? . . . Hey! Bernard ask me bring you along with me . . . to Lorong 7. I meet you after 4 at Orchard . . . four thirty . . . can . . . that day he ask me to go and enjoy . . . he got relative down there . . . I don't want . . . he is not there already la . . . not there la . . . no that day I meet him, I ask him about the car . . . he want one thousand man. I said I pay him 8 la . . . 8 or you want more a bit, I don't mind la . . . I told Bernard like that . . . I told him, I pay you more a bit la. He want one thousand no less la!

—Richards and Tay, 1977

The sample also illustrates some of the grammatical characteristics of the basilect.

Setting is also a factor which influences choice of English or another language from the participant's repertoire, though topic and proficiency may also influence code choice. For example, a restaurant is a typical setting for the use of Cantonese in Singapore; traveling in a bus, for the use of Hokkien; the school, for English and Mandarin; and the market, for Malay.

New speech-act rules are also developed as the result of the merging of speech-act rules from other languages, and as the result of different functional requirements for English. Stratton comments, "New conditions governing the appropriateness of speech acts are imposed. E. M. Forster makes good use of this fact in *A Passage to India*, where what an Indian couple intends as polite conversation is misinterpreted as a sincere invitation by Miss Quested and Mrs. Moore" (Stratton, 1977). Foreigners visiting Singapore likewise experience different speech-act rules for such transactions as shopping and using the telephone. They sometimes

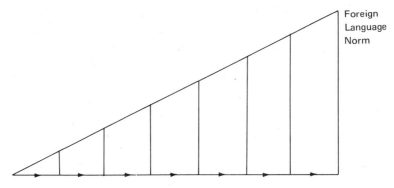

Foreign
Language
Norm

Figure 5-4   Language Learning seen as Movement Along a
Developmental Continuum

interpret differences between their own speech-act rules and Singapore-English speech-act rules as indicating a lack of politeness, where no such intention may have been present on the part of the speaker.

Difference between interactional and intergroup models

I will now attempt to summarize the basic differences between the different models of English discussed above:

(1) When English is used for intergroup functions, variation in individual proficiency is seen to reflect different stages of a developmental continuum that encompasses norm-oriented British or American rules of grammatical well formedness, speech act rules, functional elaboration, and code diversity. The developmental continuum may be thought of as a process of *recreation*, or of progressive complexification, and can be illustrated by the diagram in Fig. 5-4. The vertical lines represent differing degrees of progress along the continuum of development, which culminates in mastery of the target language norms.

(2) When English is used for interactional functions we may speak of a *nondevelopmental lectal continuum* (Corder, 1977). Different lects can be described in terms of rules for basilectal, mesolectal and acrolectal speech varieties, each with their own rules for grammatical well formedness, speech acts, functional requirements and code marking.

Movement along the continuum is not seen as a process of recreation, but of *restructuring*, and the different lects are not regarded as progressively more complex or elaborate but as functionally differentiated. Acquisition of the acrolect is thus not related to length of exposure or motivation but depends on the degree to which the speakers socioeconomic position and occupation requires him or her to use the basilectal, mesolectal or acrolectal variety. This may be represented by the following diagram, Fig. 5-5. The two contrasting models may thus be illustrated in Fig. 5-6. The differences between the four different language models discussed above, and the differing types of language learning they produce can be seen in Fig. 5-7.

GOALS FOR ENGLISH TEACHING

Two different sets of factors operate with respect to determining goals for English teaching. Where English is being taught for ultimate intergroup functions, either for use with speakers of other languages (lingua franca) or with native speakers of English, the choice of norm is made by the learner, who may select either an integrative or a nonintegrative model. There are no societal functions for particular norms or for particular levels of proficiency. While the model for *teaching* is usually the native speaker's model as proficient language user, the *learner's model* will be located at one or the other end of the interlanguage developmental continuum according to the presence or absence of an integrative language model and according to individual motivation, aptitude, exposure, practice opportunities, etc. Since within an educational system catering for all segments of society, there is no way of knowing which *learning model* individual learners will adopt, a *teaching model* must at present be based on the native speaker's norms. However, at the same time, we must recognize the fact that an integrative model for *language learning* is not true of all language learners, and that not all communication between nonnative and nonnative speaker in English or between native speaker and nonnative speaker, requires an integrative model of English. Very little research has been done in the area of what *learner models* constitute appropriate *communication models* for particular types of interaction. Further research is needed in the area of what has been called error gravity (Johansson, 1975; James, 1974) to determine which learner models function as the most effective communication models. Such research will have to go beyond the investigation simply of grammatical and phonological variables, and examine the communicative effect of violation of speech-act rules, language-function rules and code-marking rules. Hence the need for research into the ethnography of second and foreign language communication. Until a great deal more research has been done in this area the degree to which teaching models can be identified with learning models remains a question of speculation and opinion (cf. George, 1972, where teaching models and learning models are not sufficiently separated).

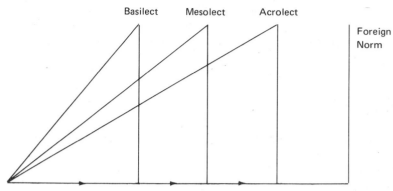

Figure 5-5   Language Learning as a Nondevelopmental Lectal Continuum

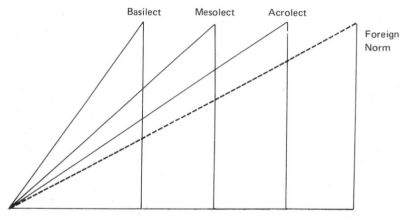

Figure 5-6   An Interactional and Intergroup Model Compared

	Language Model			
Product	instrumental	integrative	interactional	intergroup
Pidgin	+	—	—	+
Creole	+	—	+	—
Basilect	+	—	+	—
Acrolect	+	(+)	+	—
Pidginized FL	+	—	—	+
Nonpidginized FL	+	+	—	+

Figure 5-7   Language Models Compared

Where English has indigenized and taken on interactional functions, communication models for English have been institutionalized for different types of interaction in the community, and basilectal, mesolectal, and acrolectal speech varieties can be recognized for different types of interaction. The goals of English teaching in such settings is not to improve proficiency or to eradicate errors, but to develop fluency in the different lectal norms of the community according to rules for their sociolinguistic appropriateness. The school and the classroom are only one source of input to the learning process in such contexts, and may be seen as a primary factor in establishing the acrolectal functions of English. English language teaching has here the goal of lectal addition and expansion.

CONCLUSIONS

Several distinct models for the use of English have been discussed in an attempt to account for the different motivational, social, cultural, interactional, and situational factors which provide different contexts for the use and learning of English as a second and foreign language. In situations where students speak a basilect and are exposed to an acrolectal variety of English in schools, it would be quite counterproductive to consider the basilectal variety as characterized by poor learning, broken syntax, etc.; rather it is necessary to acknowledge the subtle and vital functions fulfilled by the informal variety of English and to regard the teaching of the acrolect as a case of dialect addition rather than dialect replacement. By considering differences between instrumental, intergroup, integrative, and interactional models for language use, we are able to characterize and, hence, to better understand the dynamics and dimensions of the varying uses of English as a second and foreign language around the world.

REFERENCES

Austin, J. L. *How To Do Things With Words.* Oxford: Clarendon Press, 1962.

Bickerton, Derek. *Dynamics of a Creole System.* London: Cambridge University Press, 1975.

Burt, M. K., H. C. Dulay, and Chavez E. Hernandez. *Bilingual Syntax Measure.* New York: Harcourt-Brace Jovanovich, 1975.

Clyne, Michael. "Intercultural Communication Breakdown and Communication Conflict: Towards a Linguistic Model and its Exemplification," paper read at the annual meeting of the Linguistic Society of Australia, Sydney, 1975a.

———. "German and English Working Pidgins," paper presented at the International Congress on Pidgins and Creoles, Honolulu, Hawaii, 1975b.

Corder, S. P. "The Significance of Learner's Errors," in Richards, 1974, pp. 19-27.

———. "Simple Codes and the Source of the Second Language Learners Initial Heuristic Hypothesis," *Colloque, Theoretical Models in Applied Linguistics*, IV, Université de Neuchatel, 1975.

———. "Language Continua and the Interlanguage Hypothesis," *Colloque: The Notion of Simplification*, Université de Neuchatel, 1976.

Crewe, William, ed. *The English Language in Singapore*. Singapore: Eastern Universities Press, 1977.

Ervin-Tripp, S. "An Analysis of the Interaction of Language, Topic and Listener," in Fishman, 1968, 192-211.

Ferguson, Charles A. "Towards a Characterization of English Foreigner Talk," *Anthropological Linguistics, 17,* 1975, 1-14.

Fishman, Joshua A. *Readings in the Sociology of Language*. The Hague: Mouton, 1968.

Fraser, Bruce. *On Requesting*, manuscript, 1977.

Gardner, R. C. and W. E. Lambert. *Attitudes and Motivation in Second-Language Learning*. Rowley, Mass.: Newbury House, 1972.

Geertz, Clifford. *The Religion of Java*. New York: The Free Press, 1960.

George, H. V. *Common Errors in Language Learning*. Rowley, Mass.: Newbury House, 1972.

Grimshaw, Allen D. "Some Social Functions of Pidgin and Creole Languages," in Hymes, 1971, 427-446.

Halliday, M. A. K. *Explorations in the Functions of Language*. London: Edward Arnold, 1973.

Henning, Carol A., ed. *Proceedings of the Los Angeles Second Language Research Forum*. Los Angeles: UCLA, 1977.

Herman, Simon R. "Explorations in the Social Psychology of Language Choice," in Fishman, 1968, 492-510.

Hymes, Dell. "The Ethnography of Speaking," in Fishman, 1968, 99-138.

———, ed. *Pidginization and Creolization of Languages*. Cambridge: Cambridge University Press, 1971.

James, Carl. "Linguistic Measures for Error Gravity," *Audio-Visual Journal, 12,* 1, 1974, 3-9.

Johansson, Stig. "Problems in Studying the Communicative Effect of Learner's Errors," *Colloque, Theoretical Models in Applied Linguistics*, IV, Université de Neuchatel, 1975.

Kachru, Braj B. "The Indianness in Indian English," *Word, 21,* 1965, 391-410.

———. "English in South Asia," in Thomas A. Sebeok, ed., *Current Trends in Linguistics, 5,* 1969, 627-678.

———. "Models of English for the Third World: White Man's Linguistic Burden or Language Pragmatics," *TESOL Quarterly, 10,* 2, 1976, 221-239.

Katz, Joel T. "Foreigner Talk Input in Child Second Language Acquisition," in Henning, 1977.

Krashen, S. D. et al. "Testing the Monitor Model," paper presented at the 1977 TESOL Convention, Miami, Fla.

Larsen-Freeman, Diane, and Virginia Strom. "The Construction of a Second Language Acquisition Index of Development," in Henning, 1977, 180-190.

Linnarud, M. *Lexis in Free Production: An Analysis of the Lexical Texture of Swedish Students' Written Work*. Swedish-English Contrastive Studies, Report No. 6, Lund University, 1975.

Mackey, W. F. *Language Teaching Analysis*. London: Longman, 1965.

Moag, Rodney F., and Louisa B. Moag. "English in Fiji: Some Perspectives and the Need for Language Planning," *Fiji English Teachers Journal, 13*, 1977, 2-25.

Platt, John T. "The Singapore English Speech Continuum and its Basilect 'Singlish' as a 'Creoloid,'" *Anthropological Linguistics, 17, 7*, 1975, 363-374.

———. "The Sub-Varieties of Singapore English: Their Sociolectal and Functional Status," in Crewe, 1977, 83-95.

Platt, John T., and K. K. Platt. *The Social Significance of Speech*. Amsterdam: North-Holland, 1975.

Quirk, Randolph, Sidney Greenbaum, Geoffrey Leech, and Jan Svartik. *A Grammar of Contemporary English*. London: Longman, 1972.

Reinecke, John. *Language and Dialect in Hawaii*. Honolulu: University of Hawaii Press, 1969.

Rice, Frank A. *Study of the Role of Second Languages in Asia, Africa and Latin America*. Washington: Center for Applied Linguistics, 1972.

Richards, Jack C. "Social Factors, Interlanguage, and Language Learning," *Language Learning, 22*, No. 2, 1972, 159-188.

———, ed. *Error Analysis: Perspectives on Second Language Acquisition*. London: Longman, 1974.

———. "Variation in Singapore English," in Crewe, 1977, 68-83.

Richards, Jack C., and Graeme Kennedy. "Interlanguage: A Review and a Preview," *RELC Journal, 8*, 1, 1977, 13-28.

Richards, Jack C., and Mary W. J. Tay, "The La Particle in Singapore English," in Crewe, 1977, 141-157.

Rivers, W. M. "The Natural and the Normal in Language Teaching: Where's the Difference," in Schulz, R., ed. *Personalizing Foreign Language Instruction: Learning Styles and Teaching Options*. Skokie, Ill.: National Textbook Co., 1977, 101-108.

Robinson, W. P. *Language and Social Behaviour*. Harmondsworth: Penguin, 1972.

Sach, S. J., and J. Devin. "Young Children's Use of Age-Appropriate Speech Styles in Social Interaction and Role-Playing," *Journal of Child Language, 3*, 1, 1976, 81-98.

Samarin, William J. "Lingua Francas, with Special Reference to Africa," in Rice, 1962, 54-64.

Sampson, Gloria P. "The Strategies of Cantonese Speakers Learning English," in Regna Darnell, ed., *Linguistic Diversity in Canadian Society*. Edmonton: Linguistic Research Inc., 1971.

Schmidt, Richard W. "Sociolinguistic Rules and Foreign Language Teaching," paper presented at the Symposium on Sociolinguistics and Applied Anthropology, Amsterdam, March 18-23, 1975.

Schumann, John H. *Second Language Acquisition: The Pidginization Hypothesis*. Thesis, Harvard University, 1975.

———. "The Implication of Interlanguage, Pidginization and Creolization for the Study of Adult Second Language Acquisition," in Schumann, J. H., and N. Stenson, eds., *New Frontiers in Second Language Learning*. Rowley, Mass.: Newbury House, 1976, 137-152.

Searle, J. *Speech Acts: An Essay in the Philosophy of Language*. Cambridge: Cambridge University Press, 1969.

Segalowitz, Norman. "Communicative Incompetence and the Nonfluent Bilingual," *Canadian Journal of Behavioural Science, 8*, 1976, 122-131.

Selinker, L. "Interlanguage," reprinted in Richards, 1974.

Snow, Catherine E. "Mothers' Speech to Children Learning Language," *Child Development*, 43, 1977, 549-565.

Stratton, Florence. "Putting the Communicative Syllabus in Its Place," *TESOL Quarterly*, 11, 2, 1977, 131-141.

Todd, L. *Pidgins and Creoles*. London: Routledge Kegan Paul, 1974.

Tongue, R. K. *The English of Singapore and Malaysia*. Singapore: Eastern Universities Press, 1974.

Valdman, Albert. "On the Relevance of the Pidginization-Creolization Model for Second Language Learning," *Colloque, Theoretical Models in Applied Linguistics*, VI. Université de Neuchatel, 1977.

Valdman, Albert, and John S. Phillips. "Pidginization, Creolization and the Elaboration of Learner Systems," *Colloque: Theoretical Models in Applied Linguistics*, IV. Université de Neuchatel, 1975.

Whinnom, Keith. "Linguistic Hybridization and the 'Special case' of Pidgins and Creoles," in Hymes, 1971, 91-115.

Widdowson, H. G. "The Significance of Simplification," *Colloque: The Notion of Simplification*. Université de Neuchatel, 1976.

Wode, Henning. "Developmental Sequences in Naturalistic L2 Acquisition," Englisches Seminar der Universität Kiel, 1976.

STUDY AND DISCUSSION QUESTIONS

(1) Examine Halliday's list of language functions on page 97. To what degree can this list be applied to the issue of functions in second and foreign language learning? Identify language functions likely to be needed by (a) an adult studying a foreign language, and (b) a young child studying a foreign language in a classroom setting.

(2) Listen to a tape recording of any sample of continuous unrehearsed language (e.g., a classroom lesson, a radio interview, etc.). Try to classify each utterance using a taxonomy of speech functions such as that of Halliday. What problems does this raise and what does it suggest about the complexity of the functions of speech?

(3) Discuss the four models of language proposed on page 101. To what degree do you agree or disagree with this classification?

(4) Can you explain the observation made by Samarin, that when natural languages become lingua francas, they tend to be simplified by language users? Is this always true? Can you find exceptions?

(5) Can you find examples of other languages apart from English which have indigenized? Explain the factors which account for this process in contexts you are familiar with.

(6) Are you familiar with situations where English is used for interactional functions, among immigrants, minority groups, or others? Discuss the concept of interactional functions for English with respect to instances you are familiar with and identify the salient interactional functions for English in those settings.

(7) In what ways might the appropriate expression of such speech functions as disagreement, doubt, approval, disapproval, pleasure, annoyance, etc., differ from one speech community to another? In what ways can second and foreign language learners be provided with opportunities to express such speech functions within the constraints of classroom interaction?

(8) Can you find examples of differences between speech-act rules in English and any other language you are familiar with? Compare the list in D. A. Wilkins, *Notional Syllabuses*, Oxford University Press, 1976.

(9) Discuss the concept of code diversity as it applies to the interlanguage of foreign and second language learners. Which should be taught first, a formal or an informal variety of a language? Suggest ways in which such distinctions can be taught.

(10) Knowing how to ask questions appropriately in different social situations is an important part of language learning. Suggest ways in which the second or foreign language teacher can provide opportunities for learners to acquire different ways of asking questions.

6

CONCEPTUAL ASPECTS
OF LANGUAGE LEARNING

G. D. Kennedy

A thirteen-year-old learner of English as a second language who was asked to read a paragraph of her history text and to underline words or phrases she didn't understand underlined the following constructions in four sentences:

> ... *not quite half* of the population were affected by the epidemic. ... In the villages, the inhabitants were to be found sick and dying *in the open*. ... It stayed that way *for days*. ... The control of the disease was *beyond them.*

Her problem is a familiar one for language teachers. While the meanings of unfamiliar individual words can be located in a dictionary, it is just as often *familiar* words in constructions in particular contexts which prove more intractable. In the past, constructions such as those underlined, expressing concepts of quantity, space, and time, were often treated as idioms or idiosyncratic constructions which had to be learned like individual lexical items. In recent years, however, so-called notional analyses have begun to broaden our understanding of the semantic dimensions of the second language learner's task and to provide stimulating new insights for organizing some of the items for language-teaching programs.

This recent renewed interest in the semantic dimensions of second language learning has become most well known through the work of Wilkins (1973, 1976) and his associates in accounts of functional and

117

notional syllabuses for language teaching designed for adult learners in Europe. This semantic focus parallels developments in linguistic theory, cognitive psychology, psycholinguistics, sociolinguistics, and the philosophy of language in the 1970s but also reiterates an intermittent but recurring concern with semantics by theoretical and applied linguistics over a much longer period. While it has always been recognized that both form and function must be acquired by a language learner, there has been a tendency in the history of language teaching to use one rather than both of these factors as the basis of teaching. Although Wilkins has emphasized the importance of both form and function, it has been one of his basic premises that "what people want to do through language is more important than the mastery of language as an unapplied system" (Wilkins, 1973). The strength of this statement is in part a reaction against the prevailing tendency to view second language learning as discrete point grammar and vocabulary learning even if tempered by learning structure and vocabulary in situations. "In drawing up a notional syllabus instead of asking how speakers of the language express themselves, or when and where they use the language, we ask what it is they communicate through language" (Wilkins 1976). That is, instead of a grammatical or situational basis for the organization of second language teaching materials, the emphasis moves to content.

The content of utterances can be considered in terms of two major types of meaning. Austin (1962) made a fundamental distinction between the propositional or conceptual meaning of an utterance and its illocutionary force. The conceptual meaning expresses our perception of *events, entities, states, processes, quantities, causes, location, time,* etc., and includes grammatical functions such as *agent, instrument,* and *object.* The illocutionary force of an utterance expresses its functional meaning: whether it functions in a particular context as a *command, request, denial, approval,* and so on. There is a growing literature on the functional meaning of utterances both in terms of speech acts, e.g., Austin (1962), Searle (1969), and in terms of speech functions, e.g., Jakobson (1960), Hymes (1968), Firth (1957), Halliday (1973). Halliday (1975) has even gone so far as to suggest that the environment "does not consist of things or even of processes and relations; it consists of human interaction, from which the things derive their meaning." Halliday admits the obvious overstatement, but the important point remains that conceptual meaning as the expression of thought is only part of the picture.

The distinction between conceptual meaning and functional meaning may be illustrated with the following sentence spoken by a guest in a friend's house. *It's been a little cooler these last few days, hasn't it?* The conceptual meaning includes reference to the weather at a particular place for a period of time including the moment the utterance is made. The functional meaning here may be covert and be a request for an extra blanket on the guest's bed, or an inquiry as to whether the heating in the house can be increased.

Notional syllabuses are attempts to incorporate both conceptual and functional meaning in language-teaching programs. Wilkins, in fact, distinguishes three categories of meaning. "Semantico-grammatical categories" include aspects of conceptual meaning; "categories of modal meaning" include, for example, expressions of attitude, degree of likelihood, and obligation; "categories of communicative function" cover the expression of functional meaning.

There has been a tendency in recent discussions of semantic approaches to language teaching to concentrate on functional categories, e.g., Johnson (1977), Allen (1977), and even Wilkins (1976) has suggested that his treatment of functional meaning is more innovative if "largely ad hoc." This emphasis on functional meaning is understandable, not only because proper recognition of the importance of the use of language is long overdue in language-teaching programs, but also because of the rich insights which the fields of sociolinguistics and the philosophy of language have provided in recent years.

It would be unfortunate however, if, with the current focus on functional meaning, the role of conceptual meaning were to be underestimated in semantic approaches to language learning and teaching. This paper therefore reviews attempts to describe categories of conceptual meaning in natural language, and explores aspects of the language-learning task in conceptual category rather than functional terms. The focus is on categories of concepts and their linguistic manifestations rather than on the learning of individual concepts and their word labels as vocabulary items, which has traditionally been properly recognized as an important part of language learning.

There is a long tradition of attempts to describe and classify the conceptual categories or propositional content of natural languages. Aristotle, in "The Categories" suggested ten fundamental categories: substance, place, time, relation, quantity, quality, position, state, action, and affection. These were clearly related to grammatical categories in Greek. Much later, Kant added to his basic categories of space and time a set of twelve categories classified into four groups:

(1) quantity: unity, plurality, totality
(2) quality: reality, negation, limitation
(3) relation: substance-and-accidence, causality, reciprocity
(4) modality: possibility, existence, necessity

In more recent times, there have been a variety of claims made about conceptual categories. For example Cassirer (1953) wrote ". . . it becomes evident that concepts of space, time and number are the essential framework of objective intuition as it develops in language."

At a conference called to examine the Sapir-Whorf hypothesis of linguistic relativity, it was even suggested by a conference participant that it was not the categories themselves which were difficult to define but their importance relative to each other. "I will not argue about the definition of a 'conceptual category.' On the common sense level I think we all know what it means. Take a category like 'time': obviously time is handled in the morphology of a language in different ways in different languages . . . To stay at the grammatical level is obviously not enough. But suppose we ask the question: How many and what kind of time words are there?" (Hoijer, 1954).

Similarly, some of Piaget's followers have taken for granted that the kinds of categories he has explored have self-evident validity. Flavell (1963), referring to them as "these grand and fundamental categories of experience," lists such categories as number, space, time, classes, and relation. Inhelder (1962) simply refers to them as "the categories and concepts of established science." Carroll (1964), as examples of fundamental conceptual categories, included identity, similarity, comparison of magnitudes, spatial position, temporal sequences, and causation.

A more systematic and apparently less arbitrary approach to conceptual categories may be seen in the work of Garvin, Brewer, and Mathiot (1967), who proposed using actual utterances as a basis for the analysis of propositions into a large number of semantic types, e.g., statement of sequence (A is followed by B), statement of source (A comes from B).

Perhaps the best source of information for devising a taxonomy of conceptual categories, however, has been that provided by lexicographers. Roget's *Thesaurus of English Words and Phrases,* first published over a century ago, was organized according to conceptual categories rather than the standard principle of alphabetical order. More recently, at The Seventh International Congress of Linguists a section of the Congress was devoted to the topic of concept dictionaries.

Mezger (1952) outlined a basis for a dictionary of conceptual categories. It included, in a section on Man and the World, existence, relation, time, space, area, position, shape, form, quantity, size, degree, number, and motion. More detailed taxonomies have appeared as the basis for concept dictionaries of German (Dornseiff, 1959) and French (Hallig and Von Wartburg, 1952).

As part of explorations of the problem of semantic representation within contemporary linguistic theory, similar problems concerning the classification of what it is we talk about when we use language have received attention. One of the most notable has been that of Fillmore (1968), who developed the notion of case into a set of partially covert deep case grammatical relations existing between noun phrases, some of which may lack obvious morphemic marking. It may be equally fruitful to use a similar approach to covert conceptual categories such as time, and to summarize the surface variety of devices for expressing, say, simultaneity by means of an underlying common representation.

Indeed, Jackendoff (1976) has attempted something like such an analysis and argued that insight into the semantics of natural language is to be found "in the study of the innate conception of the physical world and the way in which conceptual structures generalize to ever wider more abstract domains." The five primitive functions he describes relate to motion, point in time, duration, cause, and permission.

Bierwisch (1970) and Chafe (1970) are among those linguists who have explored the problem of semantic primitives from different viewpoints, with Bierwisch suggesting that "semantic structures might finally be reduced to components representing the basic dispositions of the cognitive and perceptual structure of the human organism."

The relation between perception and the semantics of natural language has been the subject of a major study by Miller and Johnson-Laird (1976). They suggest that ". . . time and space provide the basic coordinate system within which all experience can be located, and much of the machinery of language is devoted to making such localizations communicable." An example of the complexity of temporal organization is discussed later in this paper. According to Miller and Johnson-Laird, fundamental perceptual predicates (e.g., adjacent, cause, place, shape, size, touch, top) in association with what are called "psychological predicates" (feel, intend, know, perceive, remember) form the basis of a conceptual system of incredible complexity which in turn intervenes between the physical world and word labels. In a natural language, of course, the lexicon (and possibly the syntax) is constantly being stretched and modified to cover a changing conceptual system.

Kitagawa (1974), in a discussion of linguistic devices in English for expressing the conceptual category of purpose, provides an indication of how fruitful this semantic approach to linguistic analysis can be.

Two important manifestations of this persistent interest in the theoretical foundations of semantics have been, first, the reorientation of language acquisition studies in the 1970s, away from a preoccupation with the forms of language and toward the study of the acquisition of the semantic system as part of cognitive development in general and, second, the appearance of communication grammars.

The work of Brown and others studying language development in terms of the acquisition of basic semantic relations has influenced many researchers (Brown, 1974). Brown has studied the early stages of language acquisition, focusing on the kinds of semantic variables discussed by Chafe and Fillmore.

Communication grammars such as those by Close (1964) and Leech and Svartvik (1975) contain descriptions and classifications of conceptual categories. Leech and Svartvik include 19 main categories and many further subcategories, but there is room for further description of the semantic and structural richness of many of the categories. Motion, for example, is discussed largely in terms of prepositions, but not in such a way that *continued at a fast rate* or *came to a stop* or *slow down* are covered. Any learner of English who wished to understand quite basic uses of the language of motion could be expected to meet constructions where motion is expressed lexically (continued, came, fast rate, slow) as well as through grammatical constructions. There is thus room for considerable development from the promising start which communication grammars have made.

Among language teachers there has been a similar recurring reference to conceptual category analyses of the language-learning task. This has not been restricted to any one kind of method of language teaching. Thus, Brooks (1960) as an advocate of audiolingual methodology provided in a checklist of types of utterances such now-familiar categories as time, place, quantity, and cause. He also includes such functional categories as obligation, command, and request. Hodgson (1958) described the use of Cuisenaire rods for the teaching of the language associated with such conceptual categories as quantity, comparison, and positions in space and time. Close (1963) produced a course book for English as a second language which made use of a conceptual organization of grammar, while Pittman (1960, 1970) organized within a situational approach to English both lexical and grammatical devices to teach selected conceptual categories, arguing that description, definition, measurement, degree, proportion, development, and processes are fundamental categories for scientific and technical education. Finally, Bull (1968), a consistent advocate of semantically based approaches to language teaching over at least two decades, used the category of relationship of entities in space to illustrate an often-overlooked dimension of the language-learning task.

All this is suggestive rather than taxonomic. Many writers, from a variety of theoretical and applied linguistic fields, have stressed the importance of different conceptual categories in language learning and language use. But we have no definitive descriptions of the categories. We know they exist but we do not know which of them are empirically of greatest significance, and we have no obvious methodology for ensuring a comprehensive taxonomy of the categories or which need teaching. Further, recent research suggests that any attempt to draw up a taxonomy might be quixotic. Certainly we are in no position to base complete language teaching syllabuses on discrete categories. In part, this is because some of the apparently major categories such as space, time, cause, and intent are simply too important to be confined to any one category. "They are organizers. They impose patterns of meaning on other concepts and determine the internal structure of semantic fields, but they do not provide nuclei around which semantic fields can be organised" (Miller and Johnson-Laird, 1976).

From the second language teacher's point of view, West (1951) issued an important pedagogical warning on the organization of teaching materials according to categories. Language use occurs in specific circumstances. We should provide opportunities for the learning of relevant material avoiding at all costs teaching neat comprehensive lists which exhaust the range of linguistic devices which the language makes available for the communication of a category. Exhaustiveness is the aim of the theoretician, not the teacher. Selection is crucial.

While it is easy to criticize semantic approaches in terms of conceptual categories as being unduly subjective, vague, and amounting to little more than personal opinion, there nevertheless appears to be something of psycholinguistic significance in the approach which deserves further exploration.

If we do not yet have available a satisfactory comprehensive list of the major categories and their subcategories (let alone a description of the linguistic devices used to express each of them), we can at least at this point list some of the categories which can be classified as major, if only by virtue of being repeatedly mentioned by a wide variety of scholars in various disciplines. Such a list would include at least the following general categories whose subcategories find expression in various lexical and grammatical ways:

    entities
    states
    events
    attributes
    classes of entities, attributes, events
    parts of entities
    quantity, number, degree, proportion

similarity and difference
spatial position and order of entities
motion, direction
time—order of events, sequence, simultaneity, intervals, duration,
    frequency, change, processes, points in time
causation
spatial, temporal, quantitative relations

Such a list illustrates the kinds of categories to be considered. It is one thing to have such a list of categories, but that is only the beginning. How can the linguistic devices which a language evolves to communicate such concepts be classified. It is simply not possible to classify linguistic devices and predict what their function will be out of context for there is no one-to-one relationship between form and function. The same point has been made by Labov (1969) with respect to functional meaning and sentence forms. *Jack will be at the party* can be a warning, a prediction, or a promise, depending on the context. Similarly, constructions with *when* can sometimes refer to simultaneous events, and sometimes to sequential events.

He left in a hurry when he heard the news (sequence).
He was weeding his garden when he heard the news (simultaneity).

Examination of the linguistic devices used to communicate conceptive categories within authentic texts can serve a most useful purpose in demonstrating some of the semantic dimensions of the language learner's task.

TEMPORAL RELATIONS

The following example is from the first few sentences of a popular children's story, classified as suitable for 6-8 year olds, and is the kind of story which has been read to a class containing learners of English as a second language. It contains a number of temporal concepts, which are listed at the end of the extract.

(Once upon a time there lived a family of dragons. They were a horrible bunch of beasts)[1] (who traveled about from country to country)[2] (stirring up trouble)[3] (wherever they went.)[4] (One day on a trip to some faraway land the dragon family flew into a dense fog)[5] and (Droofus, the youngest of the dragons, lost track of the others.)[6] (Droofus kept circling about in the endless grey cloud,)[7] (calling and calling in a squeaky small voice)[8] (until at last he was too weary (to flap his wings.)[9])[10] (Then the little dragon gave up)[11] (and)[12] (went gliding down)[13] (to land on a mountainside)[14] (and)[15] (crawled into a cave)[16] (where)[17] (he curled up in a corner)[18] (to sleep for the night.)[19]

(Droofus awoke the next morning)[20] (feeling very lonely and ever so hungry.)[21] (So)[22] (he left his cave to find something for breakfast.)[23] (Droofus was just four years old,)[24] and (at that age)[25] (dragons feed on small things like grasshoppers and beetles.)[26] (As he was searching the tall grass near the cave, he came across a grasshopper struggling helplessly in a spider web.)[27] (The spider was all set to pounce)[28] (when)[29] (suddenly Droofus snatched the grasshopper out of the web.)[30] (For a long while,)[31] (Droofus held the grasshopper by one leg wondering what to do.)[32] (How could he eat someone just after saving his life?)[33] (It didn't seem right,)[34] (so)[35] (he finally set the grasshopper free.)[36] (After that)[37] (Droofus gave up eating grasshoppers and beetles and all other things (that hopped or crept or crawled.)[38])[39] As much as he disliked it (the young dragon took to eating grass.)[40] ("It tastes awful," he said after one mouthful,)[41] "but (I'll just have to get used to it.")[42] And sure enough, (the more grass he ate the better he liked it.)[43] (Pretty soon)[44] (Droofus found the grass so tasty)[45] (he was stuffing it down by the fistful.)[46] (And)[47] (in a surprisingly short time)[48] (the grass-eating dragon grew into a giant of a monster,)[49] a huge scaly brute with a long pointed tail and big leathery bat wings. (From *How Droofus the Dragon Lost His Head*, W. B. Peet, published by André Deutsch, 1971)

Temporal concepts contained in the passage

   (1) State in past
   (2) Repeated activity in past
   (3) Repeated activity in past
        (note different verb forms for similar concepts in (2) and (3))
   (4) Repeated activity in past
   (5) Single event in past
   (6) Single event in past, occurring as a result of (5)
   (7) Repeated activity in past
   (8) Repeated activity in past
   (9) Repeated activity in past, not continuing into future
 (10) End of previous repeated activities (7, 8, 9)
 (11) Event in past
 (12) Sequence marker
 (13) Activity in past
 (14) Single event in past
 (15) Sequence marker
 (16) Event in past
 (17) Sequence marker?
 (18) Event in past
 (19) Duration

(20) Event at specific point in past subsequent to previous events described
(21) State in past
(22) Sequence marker
(23) Event in past, beginning new activity
(24) State in past
(25) Point in time
(26) Habitual activity
(27) Two simultaneous activities in past (searching and struggling) and a single event (came across)
(28) State in past
(29) Sequence marker
(30) Rapidly occurring event in past
(31) Nonspecific duration in past
(32) Two simultaneous activities in past
(33) Two hypothetical sequential events, with the order of mention reversing the actual order of events
(34) State in past
(35) Sequence marker
(36) Event in past occurring in sequence after (32)
(37) Sequence marker
(38) Habitual generic activity
(39) End of habitual activity in past
(40) Beginning of habitual activity in past
(41) Sequential events (eating and speaking) with the order of mention reversing the actual order of events
(42) Habitual state/duration in past
(43) Sequence
(44) Nonspecific point in time in past following previous activities and states
(45) State in past
(46) Repeated activity in past
(47) Sequence marker
(48) Nonspecific duration in past
(49) Change over period of time in past

This analysis of the different temporal concepts and relationships in the text is by no means exhaustive, but it should serve to exemplify the semantic complexity and the rapid changes of temporal perspective involved in learning and using a language. It is even more remarkable that the reader or listener may be aware of nothing more than that the story is about a dragon. The importance of grammatical knowledge for comprehension and the learner's obvious need to know the meanings of individual words (e.g., *dense, four, right, awful,* and so on) have, of course, been left aside.

It is worthwhile to consider just how complex the temporal relations are, how the same relations can be expressed in a number of different ways, and how temporal information can be given both grammatically and lexically through most parts of speech. The following sentences from the text illustrate some of these points. *The spider was all set to pounce when suddenly Droofus snatched the grasshopper out of the web. For a long while, Droofus held the grasshopper by one leg wondering what to do.* States, events, duration, sequentiality, and simultaneity are all juxtaposed.

CAUSALITY

The following passage has been chosen to illustrate some of the ways in which various linguistic devices in English communicate relational concepts, especially aspects of the conceptual category of causality. It is taken from part of a handout prepared for a class of high school geography students.

> The type and condition of the soil *play a large part in determining* the possible yield of crops. These qualities *are a result of the action* of the weather and *the management* of man; either *can be helpful,* either *can be harmful,* although no agricultural system can continue for long if natural conditions are hostile and man's management is incompetent. There is *a very close connection* between the soil and the type of vegetation which grows naturally upon it. The soil *exercises a control* on the vegetation, and the vegetation *affects* the soil. For example, forest soils tend to be deficient in fertility in the upper layers. The trees obtain their nutrients from the lower soil layers. The forests occur in areas where rainfall exceeds water use. The excess rain *influences* the soil by washing the chemical constituents from the surface layers towards the lower layers as it percolates downward—a process known as leaching.

In addition to the relationships expressed lexically or grammatically in the italicized constructions in the text, causality is expressed by the juxtaposition of sentences, leaving a causal relation implied. For example, the reader is intended to interpret the sentence *The trees obtain their nutrients from the lower soil layers* as resulting from the stated deficiency in the upper layers expressed in the previous sentence which in turn is caused by the leaching process described in the following sentence.

A third example illustrates the language of physical motion used metaphorically to describe economic activities at a level which an adult advanced learner of English may need to comprehend.

Though production generally *advanced* in 1961, the year was not noticeable for *the vigour of its upward thrust. Recovery* from the *recession* in North America *got under way* towards the end of the first quarter of 1961, but this did not *raise output* for the year as a whole much above the level of 1960. In W. Europe and Japan, the *upswing* in economic *activity,* which *had begun* in 1958, *paused* temporarily *in the course of* 1961 and *the rate of increase* for the year as a whole was considerably below that of a year earlier. In face of the mixed *trends* in industrial countries, *exports* of the primary producing countries *rose* only moderately while prices of primary commodities *entering* international trade *under-went* a further *decline.* In most of the centrally-planned economies, though total *output* continued to *increase at a high rate, the pace of advance slackened*; industrial *output rose* at a somewhat *slower rate* while agricultural production either *fell* absolutely, or *in-creased* only slightly, owing mainly to adverse weather conditions. In mainland China, agricultural production, which had *fallen* substantially in 1960, failed to *recover* to any significant degree in 1961; largely because of the agricultural situation, industrial expansion was also *brought to a halt.* (From *World Economic Survey,* pub. by the U.N., 1961.)

It is of course possible to reanalyze the text in terms of other categories such as spatial location or degree. It should be clear from the italicized constructions that the category of motion, however, is a basic, organizing category for the expression of the economic phenomena in the text.

The three passages have been chosen to illustrate the presence of certain conceptual categories in textual material at levels appropriate for different language learners and users. The categories rarely occur in isolation. Indeed several may occur in the same sentence, e.g., *Would you mind helping me move the piano a metre or so to the right.* This sentence contains manifestations of spatial position, approximation, quantity, and motion, as well as having the illocutionary force of being a request. Further, the categories frequently are found in metaphorical uses, e.g., the use of spatial language in *The control of the disease was beyond them,* or the use of the language of physical motion to describe economic processes.

Whether the major categories are universals, as perhaps part of a "cognitive deep structure which is common to the first and second language" (Allen, 1977) cannot be resolved at the present time. Whether we need to highlight the conceptual categories for learners or concentrate on the linguistic devices which express them remains unknown. There are possibly important cultural differences as to whether there is a tendency for particular categories to be obligatorily expressed. Temporal reference in English is a case in point.

The pedagogical implications of the conceptual categories and their linguistic manifestations as part of the language-learning task are not easy to assess. It is perhaps significant that Wilkins, the leading protagonist of notional approaches to language teaching incorporating both conceptual and functional categories, has urged restraint and has suggested that it may be premature to *base* syllabuses on such categories. Rather, the value of notional approaches to language lies initially in deepening our understanding of the dimensions of the language learner's task. With increasing emphasis being placed on second-language learning through the curriculum as in immersion programs or in communicative contexts, it is particularly important that teachers recognize as fully as possible the nature of the learning task, including phonological, grammatical, lexical, conceptual, and functional aspects.

Where the learning situation demands a more structured presentation of a second or foreign language to learners, usually for reasons of economy of time, notional insights can profitably inform the syllabus, however. A syllabus is a manifestation of the principles of selection and control, i.e., what to expose the learner to. Even the most grammatically based courses have never entirely neglected semantic factors. Rather, they have not attempted to cover systematically conceptual or functional factors to the same extent as they have the grammar. Semantics has not been the major organizing principle for course design. With the growing awareness that learning a language involves learning vocabulary and grammar as well as how to perform or interpret various speech acts in situationally appropriate meaningful discourse has come a parallel recognition that grammatical and lexical bases, informed by awareness of the major conceptual categories, may still be the most appropriate for initial language instruction. Functional factors as a basis for syllabus organization may perhaps be best left for more advanced stages of language instruction (Johnson, 1977). That is, the most suitable pedagogical progression might be seen as moving from grammatical and conceptual acceptability to stylistic appropriateness.

A major problem which faces teachers of language who wish to incorporate systematically into a syllabus linguistic devices to communicate major conceptual categories is what to select and how to sequence. For example, it is neither feasible nor desirable to attempt to teach all the linguistic devices the language makes available for expressing duration all at once. However, as Wilkins's (1976) excellent discussion of the functional category of "ways of seeking permission" illustrates, adequate descriptions of the rules of situationally appropriate variation are simply not yet available.

Whether the criteria for selection is difficulty for the learner, frequency, range, or usefulness, the problem remains that it is not easy to decide which linguistic devices to select within a conceptual category. For example, if it is conceded that ways of expressing indefinite quantities are relevant for the learner, the teacher may have difficulty deciding even which uses of *some* should be selected and how to order their presentation. For example:

I want *some help.*
I waited for *some time.*
I read for *some of the time.*

Notional approaches need not be linked to any particular method of language teaching. Successful methods of language teaching or learning are often restricted to particular learning situations and are not exportable. What succeeds with adults learning English as a second language as a means to higher education in an English-speaking environment may not be successful in other contexts. Similarly, immersion programs which have succeeded so impressively with young children have yet to prove themselves with adults beginning a second language, where cognitive and attitudinal factors and available time for learning may differ. Thus methods appropriate for second language or foreign language situations, adults or children, listening comprehension or reading, may all incorporate notional variables.

Learners' needs differ and it is simply not possible to predict what each learner will need to be able to understand unless he is led through material which he knows he will meet. To discover that learners of English as a second language, for example, may interpret the quantitative expression *not quite half* as meaning either more or less than half when it normally can mean only less than half is to become aware of a characteristic comprehension problem in understanding just one of the linguistic manifestations of the conceptual category of quantity. There would thus seem to be a case for considering some emphasis on conceptual categories where the major learning aim is listening, or particularly reading comprehension.

For the productive use of a language, we cannot predict what the learner will need to do with the second or foreign language—and he may not be able to predict, either. In a restaurant, he may find he wishes to praise the cook, or complain, to ask for permission to use the phone, to deny he has not paid for his meal, or to flatter a companion. Such uncertainty, combined with the present lack of adequate descriptions, tends to reinforce the opinion expressed earlier that insights about conceptual and functional categories should be of value in informing us primarily of the nature of the problems facing the learner, particularly in the comprehension of authentic (rather than pedagogically organized) materials. This may be the case especially with older beginning learners of a second or foreign language and learners attempting to understand so-called "advanced" uses of language.

REFERENCES

Allen, J. P. B. "Structural and Functional Models in Language Teaching," *TESL Talk*, 1977, *8*, (1), 5-15.

Austin, J. L. *How to do Things with Words.* London: Oxford University Press, 1962.

Bierwisch, M. "Semantics," in J. Lyons, ed., *New Horizons in Linguistics.* Harmondsworth: Penguin, 1970.

Brooks, N. *Language and Language Learning.* New York: Harcourt, Brace and Co., 1960.

Brown, R. *A First Language.* Cambridge, Mass.: Harvard University Press, 1974.

Bull, W. E. "We Need a Communications Grammar." *Glossa*, 1968, *2*, (2), 213-228.

Carroll, John B. *Language and Thought.* New Jersey: Prentice-Hall, 1964.

Cassirer, E. *The Philosophy of Symbolic Forms.* New Haven: Yale University Press, 1953.

Chafe, W. *Meaning and the Structure of Language.* Chicago: University of Chicago Press, 1970.

Close, R. A. *English as a Foreign Language.* London: Allen and Unwin, 1963.

———. *The New English Grammar.* London: Allen and Unwin, 1964.

Dornseiff, F. *Der Deutsch Wortschatz nach Sachgruppen.* Berlin, 1959.

Fillmore, C. J. "The Case for Case," in E. Bach and R. T. Harms, eds., *Universals in Linguistic Theory.* New York: Holt, Rinehart and Winston, 1968.

Firth, J. R. *Papers in Linguistics 1934-1957.* London: Oxford University Press, 1957.

Flavell, J. H. *The Developmental Psychology of Jean Piaget.* Princeton: Van Nostrand, 1963.

Garvin, P. L., J. Brewer, and M. Mathiot. "Predication-Typing: A Pilot Study in Semantic Analysis," supplement to *Language*, 1967, 43.

Halliday, M. A. K. *Explorations in the Functions of Language.* London: Arnold, 1973.

———. *Learning How to Mean.* London: Arnold, 1975.

Hallig, R., and W. Von Wartburg. *Begriffssystem als Grundlage für die Lexikographie.* Abhandlungen der deutschen Akademie der Wissenschaften zu Berlin, Heft 4, 1952.

Hodgson, F. M. "Language Learning Material," *English Language Teaching*, 1958, *12*, 131-137.

Hoijer, H., ed. *Language in Culture*. Chicago: University of Chicago Press, 1954.

Hymes, D. "The Ethnography of Speaking," in J. A. Fishman, ed., *Readings in the Sociology of Language*. The Hague: Mouton, 1968.

Inhelder, B. "Some Aspects of Piaget's Genetic Approach to Cognition," in Kessen and Kuhlman, eds., *Thought in the Young Child*. Monograph of Society for Research in Child Development, 1962, 83.

Jackendoff, R. "Toward an Explanatory Semantic Representation," *Linguistic Inquiry*, 1976 (1), 89-150.

Jakobson, R. "Linguistics and Poetics," in T. A. Sebeok, ed., *Style and Language*. Cambridge, Mass.: MIT Press, 1960.

Johnson, K. "The Adoption of Functional Syllabuses for General Language Teaching Courses," *Canadian Modern Language Review*, 1977, *33*, (5).

Kitagawa, C. "Purpose Expressions in English," *Lingua*, 1974, *34*, 31-46.

Labov, W. "A Study of Non-Standard English," ERIC Document ED024053. Washington, D.C., 1969.

Leech, G., and J. Svartvik. *A Communicative Grammar of English*. London: Longman, 1975.

Mezger, H. In *Proceedings of the Seventh International Congress of Linguists*. The Hague: Mouton, 1952.

Miller, G. A., and P. N. Johnson-Laird. *Language and Perception*. Cambridge, Mass.: Harvard University Press, 1976.

Pittman, G. A. *Preparatory Technical English*. London: Longman, 1960.

———. "Advanced Vocabulary Development: The Bring-Come Nexus," *English Language Teaching*, 1970, *24*, 147-154.

Searle, J. R. *Speech Acts*. London: Cambridge University Press, 1969.

West, M. P. "Catenizing," *English Language Teaching*, 1951, *5*, 147-151.

Wilkins, D. A. "The Linguistic and Situational Concept of the Common Core in a Unit Credit System," in *Systems Development in Adult Language Learning*. Strasbourg: Council of Europe, 1973.

———. *Notional Syllabuses*. London: Oxford University Press, 1976.

STUDY AND DISCUSSION QUESTIONS

(1) Select five pages of a book considered suitable for reading to young children beginning school. List the linguistic devices used for expressing one or more of these conceptual categories:

    (a) nonspecific quantity (e.g., quite a few)

    (b) duration (e.g., lasted all night)

    (c) motion (e.g., picked up speed)

    (d) parts of entities 'e.g., the rest of the family)

    (e) purpose (e.g., she shut the window to keep out the rain)

    (f) sequentiality (e.g., he lit a fire when he realized how cold it was)

    (g) comparison (e.g., The river was deeper than I had expected)

(2) What criteria should be used in sequencing the pedagogical presentation of the linguistic devices within a category?

(3) Make a comparison of some of the ways young children and adults express one of the categories in English or any other language.

(4) What evidence is there that conceptual categories are cognitive universals which receive different emphasis in different languages?

(5) Analyze the language of a chapter of a textbook in a college subject (e.g., physics, zoology, economics, politics, geography, psychology). Do any conceptual categories appear to assume particular importance in the way the subject matter is expressed?

(6) What evidence can you find to support the statement of Miller and Johnson-Laird that "time and space provide the basic coordinate system within which all experience can be located, and much of the machinery of language is devoted to making such localisations communicable."

7

SOCIOLINGUISTIC COMPETENCE
IN THE CLASSROOM

J. Holmes

Part of the task facing any language learner is that of acquiring sociolinguistic competence: learning how to use language appropriately for a variety of functions in a wide range of different situations. Children begin to demonstrate sociolinguistic ability at a very early age. Infants, for example, often vary the amount of "speech" they produce in the presence of familiar and unfamiliar listeners. Two-year-olds vary the form of their speech when talking to babies by using baby talk intonation (Ervin-Tripp, 1972). Similarly children of three and four have been observed using shorter, grammatically less complex utterances to younger listeners (Sachs and Devin, 1976). This process of learning to use language appropriately continues throughout life, developing as new situations and new sociolinguistic demands are encountered.

The first few months at school are particularly demanding in this respect. School is generally the child's first encounter with a formal setting in which he is expected to be a full participant. This article sets out to examine some of the sociolinguistic constraints governing the more formal classroom interactions in which children are involved. Examples are then provided of ways in which these constraints may inhibit the participation of children from minority linguistic and cultural groups. Finally some suggestions are made for alleviating such problems and for developing sociolinguistic competence in a second language.

THE CLASSROOM: A FORMAL SITUATION

The variety of language which is used for much of the time in classrooms, especially in secondary and higher education, is generally considered to be a rather formal standard variety. This use of a relatively formal code in educational institutions seems to characterize a wide range of speech communities, whether monolingual, bilingual, or multilingual. A child in Egypt, for example, is expected to learn to comprehend, and eventually to produce, an extremely formal variety of Arabic in the school context (Ferguson, 1959). In Switzerland and Norway schoolchildren are taught the standard forms of the regional dialects they speak at home (Fishman and Lueders-Salmon, 1972; Blom and Gumperz, 1972). Many children are educated in a completely different language from their mother tongue for a variety of social, economic, and political reasons; the language of the school is always the "superposed variety," the more socially prestigious language associated with formality in the community.

The reasons for the use of a formal language variety in many classrooms are almost certainly social, rather than pedagogical:

It's acquisition marks a social rather than a cognitive change in the learners and is a test of their acculturation.
—Edwards, 1976

The most general function of the school is usually considered to be to instruct children, to transmit to them facts, opinions, and skills. There is no convincing evidence to suggest that such instruction cannot be adequately carried out in a nonstandard dialect, a minority group language, or even in a less formal style of a language. The use of formal varieties in the school can be seen then as a reflection of social features of the situation, nonlinguistic constraints, which in turn reflect the values and beliefs of the society concerning education and the ways in which it is appropriately transmitted.

It is useful to consider some of the nonlinguistic components of the classroom situation as a basis for and background to an analysis of classroom interaction. Taking the lesson as a unit of analysis, five components of the situation seem particularly relevant: the setting, the participants, the topic, the medium, and the function of the interaction (Ervin-Tripp, 1964; Hymes, 1964 and 1967).

Setting　In traditional "chalk and talk" classrooms, the physical layout of the room—the arrangement of space—identifies the classroom as a formal setting. The teacher's desk is at the front separated by some distance from the rows of desks at which pupils sit. The teacher is thus physically the natural focus of attention and pupils' communications are most naturally directed to him or her rather than to fellow pupils. This traditional layout of the classroom "both reinforces and symbolizes a definition of learning as dependent on one teacher with many children, engaged in a highly organized sequence of activities" (Edwards, 1976). It also results, in most cases, in the use of a relatively formal variety of language and formal rules for speaking.

In some schools especially at the primary level there have been moves away from this traditional layout to open-plan arrangements which allow pupils much greater freedom of movement. One finds in these classrooms a greater degree of pupil-pupil interaction and a corresponding decrease in the formality of the language and the rules for speaking. Individual teacher-pupil interactions also increase in number and decrease in formality, both verbally and nonverbally. There are still occasions, however, when the teacher interacts with the whole class, and in such interactions other components of the situation are more significant influences on language use.

Participants   The role-relationship between the teacher and pupils in the classroom is an asymmetrical one: the teacher is older and more knowledgeable than the pupils. He or she is therefore regarded as being of superior status and is expected to maintain an appropriate social distance from the pupils. Waller (1932) described the teacher as a "paid agent of cultural diffusion," whose status was ascribed by virtue of this role, and he regarded the impersonality and formality of speech in the classroom as a means of preserving an appropriate social distance between teacher and pupils. Another contributing factor is simply the ratio of pupils to each teacher in any one classroom. Hence, even in open-plan classrooms communications from the teacher to the class as a whole are generally characterized by the linguistic formality associated with traditional classrooms.

Topic   The official content or topics of classroom communication are gradually narrowed down and more explicitly prescribed as pupils progress from primary to secondary school. They increasingly correspond to traditionally recognized "subject-areas" with a consequent increase in the use of technical terminology and "specialist language" (Barnes, 1969). It is often assumed that the discussion of a particular topic or subject inevitably involves the use of a particular "register," character- ized by specialist terminology and distinctive grammatical constructions. It is certainly true that an analysis of the textbooks written on a particular topic may identify linguistic features which occur with relatively high frequency (see, for example, Barber, 1962). The extent to which the teacher's spoken language reflects the language of the textbooks, however, is a relatively unresearched area. Barnes (1969) provides some suggestive examples of teachers who seem unable to escape from the jargon of their subject; e.g.,

T. If we did it using a different method actually . . . where we heat up the grass with acetone actually . . . heating it under, er . . . an enclosed system, except . . . I'll have to show using a diagram on that . . . well er . . . under reflux conditions so that we didn't lose the acetone . . .

Part of learning a subject presumably involves learning the technical terminology, and insofar as this is explicitly taught it is unlikely to cause severe comprehension problems for learners. More problematic for pupils (and particularly second language learners) are perhaps those linguistic features of the school register which are not specific to any particular subject but which "pupils would not normally hear or use in speech" (Barnes, 1969). Barnes (1969) provides the following examples from recorded transcripts: "developed," "tend to," "supported themselves," "complete in themselves," "the position of . . . in relation to . . ."

It is only possible to hypothesize about the extent to which teachers might use colloquial or informal language to discuss particular topics in the classroom since the bulk of research to date provides very few examples. Whether the predominance of formal styles and rules for speaking is due in part to the constraints of the topic per se, or whether it can more accurately be traced to convention, tradition, or the overriding influence of the setting and the participant relationships, is an interesting question.

Medium   It was suggested above that the language of textbooks, in some subject areas at least, may be distinctive to the subject matter being presented. Rosen (1967), discussing the language of textbooks in relation to the writing of the pupils who use them, comments on the formality of the style in which many textbooks are written, and the inaccessability of this style to the majority of pupils. The written medium has established its own conventions, and textbooks, often the most frequently encountered samples of written language in the classroom, exemplify the more impersonal and formal tendencies of these conventions. The written medium is therefore a component which contributes to some extent to the formality of classroom language. It is worth pointing out how culture-specific is the identification of the curriculum content with material from books. Many cultural groups, including, for example, the Maori people of New Zealand, do not share this view of what should be taught by one generation to the next. This point will be discussed in more detail in relation to norms for spoken interaction in a later section. In the examination of classroom interaction in the next section the focus will be on the medium of speech rather than on writing.

Function   The function or purpose of classroom interaction, as mentioned above, is generally considered to be to instruct and inform. The relationship between this aim and the way it is realized in many educational institutions reflects the beliefs of white middle-class society about the ways in which children should learn. Many educationalists have recently begun to question these beliefs[1] (see, for example, Barnes, 1969 and 1976; Britton, 1970; Jackson, 1968; Postman and Weingartner, 1971). From a sociolinguistic viewpoint, however, leaving aside their relative merits for the moment, it is possible to examine the ways in which these beliefs about the aims of education and the proper methods of achieving them influence the kind of interaction considered appropriate in the classroom. In this sense, then, "function" is a relevant contributory factor to the formality of classroom interaction.

A more detailed analysis of the functions of classroom interaction might be achieved by examining the functions of language in the classroom. Taxonomies of the functions of language have been attempted by a number of researchers including Halliday (1973 and 1975), Hymes (1964 and 1967), and Jakobson (1960); but no completely satisfactory theory has yet been developed and, to a large extent, attempts to devise a universal set of categories are "at the stage of what has been called botanising—the pretheoretical or natural history stage in the development of a science . . . we are still concerned with 'ethnography of speaking' " (Corder, in press). Sinclair and Coulthard (1975) approached the problem of identifying language functions from a somewhat different point of view. They were concerned with identifying the function of utterances in discourse. In their analysis of classroom interaction the function of an utterance is consistently defined in relation to the discourse structure in which it occurs. (Some examples of the categories they established will be provided in the analysis below.)

The relationship between the function and form of classroom interaction is clearly a complex one. Theoretically, language functions such as expressive, directive, phatic, metalinguistic, referential, and so on (Hymes, 1964) may be realized in any code, and in a variety of forms within any code. In practice, for cultural reasons, such functions tend to be expressed in the classroom using a relatively formal variety of language, and a rather narrow range of forms, as Sinclair and Coulthard (1975) demonstrate.

Rules for speaking in the classroom
In this section an example is provided of how an examination of classroom discourse can suggest the kinds of sociolinguistic competence

children are expected to acquire in order to behave appropriately in the classroom. Using Merton's (1957) distinction between manifest and latent function, the focus will be predominantly on the underlying social meaning of classroom interaction, rather than its overt or manifest function. Barnes (1973) makes a similar distinction:

> Language performs two functions at once: it conveys the overt message and at the same time sets up or confirms the social identity and relationships of the people who are speaking or writing to one another.

In particular, by examining some of the ways in which teachers *control* classroom discourse in interactions with the class as a whole, some light may be shed on how children learn to perform their roles as pupils and come to recognize the situational constraints on this contribution to the discourse.

> The classroom is a socializing context where children are expected to learn about "something" and at the same time to learn certain rules of proper and appropriate behaviour.
>
> —Mishler, 1972

The social roles of teacher and pupil are to a large extent established and maintained through the functions and structure of classroom discourse. It is in interactions with pupils as members of the class as a whole, in public, that the nonlinguistic constraints discussed above operate most powerfully, resulting in the use of a formal language variety and formal rules for speaking. It is these uses of language which are most likely to be unfamiliar to the child and which will require a further development of his sociolinguistic competence. I have chosen to concentrate on the rules for speaking rather than on linguistic features of the variety used, since comments on the former have been shown to apply much more widely than could any precise description of the phonological, grammatical, and lexical characteristics of the language used in the classroom of one particular geographical area. Four different aspects of the rules for speaking are considered: amount of talk, turn-taking, questions, and the relationship between form and function.

Amount of talk   The most obvious way in which teachers control classroom discourse is by talking more than anyone else. In all types of classrooms, including both traditional and open-plan, in a variety of different countries, teachers dominate 70% of the talking-time available. Delamont (1976) points out that "research reported from all over the world shows a similar pattern: in India, Belgium, Iraq, South America and New Zealand the teacher keeps on talking. Britain is no exception."

A gross assessment of how this time is distributed suggests that about 50% is devoted to lecturing and questioning pupils about the content of the lesson; the other 50% includes "explicit disciplinary and management moves and much of her reaction to pupil's contributions" (Delamont, 1976). Even in primary schools it has been found that many of the teacher's utterances are directed at the whole class: e.g., about 25% of all teacher-talk is spent on organization and discipline (Boydell, 1974). One strategy that the teacher uses for controlling classroom discourse, then, is to "hold the floor" for longer than his pupils.

Turn-taking   Native speakers acquire rules for turn-taking in different speech events by experience over a number of years. By the age of three, children have been observed "to sustain a coherent dialogue over a number of turns" (Keenan, 1974). Informal conversations between adults involve complex and subtle signals for taking turns at speaking (see, for example, Burton and Stubbs, 1975; Schegloff, 1968; Schegloff and Sacks, 1973; Sacks, Schegloff, and Jefferson, 1974). No one participant has the *right* to direct the discourse to select the topic, to dominate the speaking time or to insist the others contribute. Speakers often self-select at "points of possible completion" (Sacks ms. quoted in Coulthard, 1975). In formal speech events, however, the rules for speaking are often different. At a political meeting, for example, the chairman has the right to direct the discourse, speaking whenever he wishes, allocating the right to speak to others present, interrupting other speakers to comment on the relevance of their contribution to the topic he has introduced, deciding when sufficient discussion has taken place, and so on.

Classroom discourse often resembles the second example: the rules for turn-taking in the classroom are much more similar to those of a formal meeting than to those of casual conversation. The teacher's role is similar to that of the chairman. While he is speaking to the whole class, pupils are expected to listen or at least not to interrupt. Hence, during the time he is lecturing, organizing, and disciplining pupils, he controls the discourse by retaining the speaking role. When he is questioning pupils and discussing a topic with them, however, he expects them to contribute to the discourse. Here the situational constraints discussed above are relevant to an understanding of the turn-taking rules.

Some "linguistic etiquette" is clearly necessary to ensure orderly communication in any group where there are large numbers of participants. In the classroom the teacher's role and status give him the right to assign speaking turns to individual pupils. The most commonly used method of giving a child the right to speak is by "nominating" him, or using his name.[2] Teachers often nominate particular pupils to respond to a question they are posing, e.g.,

Which part do you actually see with Julia?
What do you think we could compare it to? Ashfaq.[3]

Pupils who are thus nominated are expected to respond, though they do not do so in every case. In most classrooms a failure to respond is interpreted by all present as an indication that the pupil does not know the correct response. In some cases, however, pupils who do not respond are considered to be uncooperative and may even be accused of deliberately disruptive behavior (some examples are discussed in a later section). If the teacher asks a question without nominating a particular pupil to respond, then pupils are generally expected to "bid" to be nominated. Bidding is also appropriate if a pupil fails to respond or responds incorrectly to a teacher's question, or if a pupil wishes to volunteer information which has not been specifically requested: i.e., bidding is the way in which pupils request the right to contribute to the discourse; nominating is one way in which they are given that right.

These turn-taking rules have to be explicitly taught in primary-school classrooms since children generally have no experience of the rules for speaking in such a formal situation before they start school. The teacher frequently gives the children a "cue" to bid: "Hands up." This is to be interpreted not as a directive for every child to raise his hand, but as "put your hand up if you know" (Sinclair and Coulthard, 1975). It is often some time before children learn to interpret this correctly, as observations in primary schools reveal. Children often raise their hands whether they think they can respond or not, as revealed by their subsequent confusion when they are nominated by the teacher. They misinterpret "hands up" as a directive to the whole class, not realizing that the teacher will interpret their response as demonstrating willingness to contribute to the discourse. A second implication of "hands up" is that the teacher requires that only one pupil should respond at a time, and intends to nominate the respondent: self-selection by calling out a response is not permitted. Many children find this difficult to perform, although they know the rule in the sense that they can verbalize it if asked to do so. Observations of eight- to nine-year-olds in classrooms provide abundant evidence that, even after three or four years of primary schooling, children still have difficulty in refraining from calling out responses to teachers' questions, e.g.,

T. Can you remember anybody what the black bit is called?
Several voices call out: Pupil, pupil.
T. Hands up. Now, please don't shout out.

Although this teacher apparently addresses the question to "anybody," it is clear from her reproof that pupils are expected to bid for the right to respond by raising their hands. Despite consistent reminders, the pupil's desire to demonstrate that he knows the correct answer leads to frequent infringements of this particular rule. Rules of classroom etiquette, and especially the unstated implications discussed, may provide even greater difficulties for children from minority cultural groups. Coulthard (1974) provides an example from a school with 72% West Indian and Asian immigrant children in Britain:

T: (elicit) What do we do with a saw?
P: (response) Cut wood.
T: (feedback) Yes, YOU'RE SHOUTING OUT THOUGH.
T: (elicit) What else would you use?
P: (response) Icing.
T: (feedback) CAN'T HEAR YOU IF YOU SHOUT OUT.[4]

The rules for allocating speaking turns and obtaining permission to speak provide one very clear example of how teachers control classroom interaction, and of the sociolinguistic competence children must acquire in order to understand and produce appropriate behavior in the classroom.

Another less immediately obvious way in which teachers keep control of classroom discourse during question sessions (and for many teachers these include what they label "discussions") can be revealed by examining the structure of teacher-pupil "exchanges." These typically consist of three "moves": (a) the teacher asks a question; (b) a pupil responds; (c) the teacher provides evaluative feedback; e.g.,

T. What was that program that we just watched really about? In one word what was it about? Just one word. Dominic.
P. An owl.
T. No, it wasn't about an owl.

(See also examples of teacher-pupil interaction above.) The initial and final moves are the teacher's prerogative; in this way he or she "retains the conversational initiative" (Burton and Stubbs, 1975).[5] The pupil's response is sandwiched between the teacher's utterances. Unsolicited contributions from pupils are often cut off or ignored; the teacher alone has the right to decide which pupil utterances may contribute to the discourse and which may not, which are relevant and which are not. This is further exemplified by the fact that when unsolicited contributions are accepted, they are often evaluated by the teacher in the same way as pupils' responses, e.g.,

P. All babies have blue eyes.
T. Clever girl. Did the rest of you know that?

Or the pupils' topic is occasionally taken over by the teacher; e.g.,

P. What were Popes?
T. Still have Popes. The Pope's the Head of the Catholic Church.
P. Mm. Oh.
T. Where does he live?

P. Rome.

T. Rome, yes. Do you know which part of Rome?

—Sinclair and Coulthard, 1975

The three-part structure thus clearly illustrates a further means by which the teacher maintains his or her role as director of the discourse. This method of teaching, by asking "test" questions, is remarkably stable and pervasive: it has been stable over the past fifty years and across different countries (Stubbs, 1976). And the orderly structure is " 'typical' in Firth's sense of being repeatedly observable because of a 'constellation' of constraints on what is said and how it is said" (Edwards, 1976).

Questions   The popularity of questioning as a teaching technique reflects another aspect of the teacher's control on the discourse; questioning is a very effective way of controlling the form and content of pupils' responses. Barnes (1969) make a distinction between "open" and "closed" questions:

Closed questions have only one acceptable answer; whereas to *open* questions a number of different answers would be acceptable.

In the lessons he analyzed at the secondary school level he found that entirely open questions hardly ever occurred. Most questions resembled those in the examples above, in that they required a short one-word label or a short statement of fact as an appropriate response. The value which many teachers attach to brevity in the form of pupils' responses is made quite explicit in the example quoted above, on page 142. Clearly the form of teachers' questions limits the form of pupils' responses.[6]

When only one answer will be accepted as correct then the content of pupils' responses is equally controlled by the teacher's questions. Such questions are not genuine requests for information:

The teacher rarely asks a question because he wants to know the answer; he asks a question because he wants to know whether a pupil knows the answer.

—Sinclair and Coulthard, 1975

Often questions which, on the basis of their form might be considered open, are in fact closed, as the teacher's response to pupils' contributions indicates. Barnes calls such questions "pseudo-questions," and he provides an excellent example from a secondary school classroom which illustrates the skill with which children learn to recognize such questions:

T. What can you tell me about a bunsen burner, Alan?

P. A luminous and nonluminous flame.

T. A luminous and nonluminous flame.

—Barnes, 1969

A great many of the teacher's questions are aimed, then, at getting children to display what they know. How do children learn to recognize that this is what is required?

Willes (1975) suggests, on the basis of her observations in preschool and primary classrooms, that teachers often teach children how to provide appropriate responses by behaving as if the children already knew how to respond appropriately:

> If they did not get an expected and acceptable response, they would interpret a look, a gesture, or silence *as if it* were at least an attempted response, and evaluate it. If the response were noise, they would impose on it a prompt, or even an answer. Given that children need, and want, adult approval, and that this desire is strong and compelling, this is a very effective way of indicating what is expected.
>
> —Willes, 1975

The occasional mistakes are quickly rectified, but they are suggestive to the observer. In the following exchanges for example, the children's responses suggest they are using their knowledge of the sociolinguistic rules for speaking in informal conversation in the school context where it is inappropriate:

> T. Can anybody remember a song?
> Pupils. Yes . . . yes . . . yes . . .
>
> —Willes, 1975

The expected response is a song title selected from the repertoire known to the teacher. The responses show the children are treating the question as a genuine yes/no question.

> T. Who rides on a pony? Who rides on a pony?
> There is a chorus of "me!" . . . the teacher prompts:
> In the song who rides on a pony?
> Nothing but a renewed babble of voices, so she tries again:
> Who *can* ride on a pony?
> On the ensuing noise the *teacher* imposes the answer she wants, "A cowboy!" and at her signal the children sing, "On my pony see me ride."
>
> —Willes, 1975

The teacher's first question in this exchange is a pseudo-question. Although it looks at first as if there is a wide range of possible responses, the question is in fact a veiled hint or prompt for the *particular* song title which she has in mind.

Stubbs (1976a) suggests that some children get practice in answering closed or test questions in the home. He provides this example of an interchange between a four-year-old and his mother:

> Mother: Right, now what do you think the next instruction is because that's what I've got to do?
> Child: Put it in the baking tin.

Mother: Yes.
Well, first of all we've got to grease it though—why do you think?
why do you grease it Tommy?
Child: So the pastry doesn't stick.
Mother: Right.

—Stubbs, 1976

The child is learning rules for responding which will clearly serve him well when he reaches school.[7] Stubbs suggests that there may be specific ways, such as the use of the same discourse structures, in which the culture of home and school may be continuous for some children. This needs researching, but it suggests another way in which the transition from home to school may be easier for some children than for others. Some children may be exposed in the home to aspects of the sociolinguistic competence they will be required to demonstrate in the classroom. It is very likely that such children will belong to the middle-class majority group, where the values of the society concerning what is worth learning and how children should learn are most firmly established.

Form and function   Linguists have frequently pointed out that there is no one-to-one relationship between form and function in language. Many different linguistic forms may be used to fulfill the same basic function and vice versa. The correct interpretation of the function of an utterance often depends on social constraints, such as the setting and the relationship between the participants. Labov (1969) points out, for example, that for an utterance to be heard as a command, it is necessary that the addressee believes that the speaker believes:

a. X should be done.
b. The addressee has the obligation to do X.
c. The addressee has the ability to do X.
d. The speaker has the right to request that the addressee do X.

—Labov, 1969

In the classroom, the teacher-pupil relationship is such that the teacher clearly has the right to give orders to his pupils. A variety of forms may serve this function since the preconditions are all fulfilled. Part of learning to perform the role of pupil involves learning to accurately interpret the function of the teacher's utterances without being misled by the range of forms in which they may be expressed. Edwards (1976) provides the following example of a group of utterances which serve the same function of invoking one of the rules for speaking in the classroom:

Direct statement of the rule   "You must not talk when I am
                                  talking."

Statement of deviant behavior (rule implied)	"you are talking."
Attention-drawer	"Jones." "3B"
Direct command	"Shut up." "Stop talking."
Command in the form of a question	"Do I have to tell you again?"
Warning (implied serious short-term consequences)	"I'm going to lose my temper with you."
Warning (long-term consequences)	"You won't pass the exam, acting like that."
Evaluative labeling of conduct	"That is very silly."
Evaluative labeling of pupil	"You are very silly."

—Edwards, 1976

The meaning of many of these utterances is retrievable only from the social context. Another example is provided by Sinclair and Coulthard (1975) who point out that "yes" with a fall-rise intonation means "no" when uttered by a teacher providing evaluative feedback in the classroom. Pupils learn to interpret the implications of such utterances by experience of the social situation in which they are produced. Members of minority cultural groups and second language learners whose cultural values differ from those of the school may find it difficult to correctly interpret the functions of such remarks; this is a point which will be taken up in the next section.

A number of ways in which teachers control the behavior of pupils have been examined in order to illustrate some of the sociolinguistic demands made on pupils in the classroom. There are obviously many other means by which teachers retain *"conversational control* over the topic, over the relevance or correctness of what pupils say, and over when and how much pupils may speak" (Stubbs, 1976a).[8] This brief discussion will serve, however, as a basis for an examination of some of the implications of sociolinguistic research on classroom interaction for minority group children and second-language learners.

Minority group children[9]

Analysis of the cultural norms and values reflected in the classroom behavior of children and teachers can suggest potential areas of difficulty for the minority group child. Hymes (1972a) refers to the possibility of "sociolinguistic interference" between sociolinguistic systems:

When a child from one developmental matrix enters a situation in which the communicative expectations are defined in terms of another, misperception and misanalysis may occur at every level.

When information on the sociolinguistic system of the child's speech community is available, it may be possible to predict areas where sociolinguistic interference might occur. This point can be exemplified in relation to some of the characteristics of classroom interaction discussed above.

Many majority group cultures tend to identify both teaching and learning with *talking*. The amount of teacher-talk and the structure of teacher-pupil interaction in classrooms provide evidence of this belief that educational knowledge should be primarily conveyed through language. Stubbs (1976a) points out that educationalists who criticize the extent to which the teacher dominates classroom talk are equally culture-bound when they advocate replacing teacher-talk with pupil-talk. Many educationists "take it for granted that it is a good thing if pupils can be encouraged simply to talk *more* in lessons" (Stubbs, 1976a). Moreover, the structure of teacher-pupil interchange examined earlier demonstrates the teacher's "concern to elicit talk from pupils, to get them to answer questions at appropriate moments" (Stubbs, 1976a).

All cultures do not equate learning and talking in this way.

There are a number of sociolinguistic descriptions of American-Indian cultures, for example, which suggest that speech is not always regarded as the most appropriate means of learning in some of these speech communities (Basso, 1970; Dumont, 1972; Philips, 1972). Children from such groups are frequently silent in the classroom; they often refuse to respond to their teachers' questions, although outside the classroom they are observed to be "noisy, bold, daring and insatiably curious," and highly verbal (Dumont, 1972). Their "uncooperativeness," and apparent unwillingness to behave appropriately in the classroom, can be at least partly accounted for by examining the rather different sociolinguistic systems of the cultures of which they are members. Philips (1972), for example, describes appropriate methods of learning in the Warm Springs Indian culture. The crucial differences from the ways of learning which dominate most classrooms seem to be, first, a relatively long period of silent listening and watching; second, cooperation with and supervision by an older relative in carrying out small segments of a task; and third, self-initiated testing, unsupervised and in private, until the child feels ready to demonstrate the acquired skill to others. Very little speech is involved in this learning process. In the classroom, however, the child is required to demonstrate knowledge from the start by answering the teacher's questions, before being given any opportunity to observe others performing successfully or any time for private practice:

the assumption is that one will learn, and learn more effectively, through making mistakes in front of others.   —Philips, 1972

The Warm Springs children were much more willing contributors in group activities, and were also observed to initiate private interactions with the teacher during periods of independent work by pupils.

There is some evidence that Polynesian children, too, find it difficult to cope with the demand that they respond to questions in public before they are confident that they know the right answer.

One of the biggest hurdles which has to be overcome by most island children, in a school situation, is their own fear of being the object of laughter or of making mistakes.

—*A Handbook for Teachers of Pacific Island Children,* 1977

And Boggs (1972) observed that Hawaiian children would respond to questions addressed to the whole class, but refused to answer if questioned individually: i.e., where responses were voluntary children volunteered frequently; it was to the use of the coercive nominating technique that they seemed to react so negatively.

Basso's (1970) research suggests a different reason for the reluctance of the Apache Indian to speak in certain social situations. He points out that silence is an appropriate cultural response for Apaches in situations where the individuals involved perceive the relationship to be uncertain, unpredictable, or ambiguous in some way. He says "the critical factor in the Apache's decision to speak or keep silent seems always to be the nature of his relationships to other people" (Basso, 1970). Other features of the situation are only relevant "to the extent that they influence the perception of status and role."

The normal response to criticism, for example, by an Apache is silence rather than self-vindication. Similar observations have been made about Maori people in New Zealand: they are often silent when criticized or accused of wrongdoing, whether guilty or not. In the dominant white culture, silence in the face of criticism or an accusation of wrongdoing is usually interpreted as an acknowledgment of guilt. Clearly cross-cultural misunderstanding of the meaning of silence as a response can cause difficulties for the minority group in the classroom.

A child's refusal to participate in the structure of classroom discourse may be traced in some cases to different norms for participation in speech events. Philips (1972) describes two sociolinguistic features of most social events in the Warm Springs community which differ markedly from those of many other cultures. First, no one person has the right to direct activities by virtue of holding a particular position in the community; anyone who feels himself qualified may speak for as long as he wishes and can retain his audience's attention; if he is respected, people may follow his suggestions and participate in activities he organizes. Second, every individual is free to participate or not in any activity, and may choose the degree of his participation at every point in the proceedings. Children from this culture obviously bring to the classroom a set of rules for speaking which conflict with those they will encounter there. The teacher directs activities, as discussed earlier, by virtue of his or her role and ascribed status rather than as a result of the individual pupils' choices to follow his suggestions or directions:

> This difference helps to account for the Indian children's frequent indifference to the directions, orders and requests for compliance with classroom social rules that the teacher issues.
>
> —Philips, 1972

Pupils are expected to pay attention when the teacher is speaking, to bid for the right to respond to teacher's questions or for permission to speak before volunteering information, and there is a further expectation that they will respond to teacher's questions when directed to them as individuals. This is rather different from the self-selection apparent in many of the social events in the Warm Springs community, and provides a possible explanation for the children's failure to comply with the sociolinguistic norms of classroom interaction as described by Philips:

> They do not remember to raise their hands and wait to be called on before speaking, they wander to parts of the room other than the one in which the teacher is conducting a session, and they talk to other students while the teacher is talking.
>
> —Philips, 1972

Some of the children discussed in these examples are ESL learners; others use a nonstandard variety of English outside the classroom. Yet the explanations suggested for their failure to conform to the rules for speaking in the classroom are based not on linguistic differences but on sociolinguistic ones: their perceptions of the relationship between the participants and the setting on the one hand, and the rules for verbal interaction on the other, derive from the sociolinguistic norms of their own speech communities which are different from those of the majority culture.

Further examples of the kind of difficulties which may confront children from minority ethnic groups in the classroom are provided by sociolinguistic research on Black American speech behavior. Black American children often speak a nonstandard dialect of English, yet there is abundant evidence to suggest that it is sociolinguistic rather than linguistic differences which underlie many of the communicative misunderstandings between these children and their teachers:

> Those brought together in classrooms, even though having the language of the classroom in common, may not be wholly members of the same speech community. They may share a speech situation,

but bring to it different modes of using its language and of interpreting the speech that goes on there.

—Hymes, 1972b

One well-researched area, for example, is that of the distinctive verbal games which characterize much Black speech, and particularly the speech of Black male adolescents. Abrahams (1974) and Kochman (1972), for example, describe a vast repertoire of such speech events as jiving, signifying, sounding, running it down, and rapping. The point that emerges very clearly is that children who have been described as nonverbal, uncooperative, and unresponsive in the classroom place an extremely high value on verbal ability outside the classroom where the setting and audience are different. The sociolinguistic competence of these adolescents reflects their ethnic background and is distinctive to the Black male speech community. In middle-class schools, faced often by a White female teacher, many of them refuse to conform to the sociolinguistic norms of classroom interaction. Kochman (1972) further suggests that some Black children may evaluate the school setting as less formal than do White middle-class children, and cites as evidence their use of profanity in the classroom.

Another point of potential sociolinguistic conflict, discussed by both Kochman (1972) and Abrahams and Gay (1972), is the different discourse rules evident in many Black children's interactions. Among themselves, Black children gain the floor by speaking on top of other voices and repeating the same utterance until they get a response from someone, or until someone else catches their attention. When someone speaks he *expects* an overlap of voices as a sign that others are listening and reacting:

If the presentation is stimulating the audience will take an active part, becoming vocally and physically involved in the interchange, if only by murmuring and moving about in their seats. *Complete silence is a sure sign of boredom.*

—Abrahams and Gay, 1972

As pointed out earlier, there are prescribed rules for turn-taking in the classroom which directly conflict with these sociolinguistic norms. Turns are assigned by the teacher, interruptions are regarded as rude, and the child who talked loudly over the top of the teacher's voice would not receive enthusiastic approval in most classrooms! Teacher's complaints about the silence and lack of participation of minority group children in the classroom are often a reflection of the prescribed and restricted opportunities allowed for such contributions within the sociolinguistic norms of much classroom interaction. In different speech events, in different participant relationships, these children contribute freely to the discourse.

A final example of how sociolinguistic interference can cause misunderstandings in the classroom is provided by Lein's (unpublished) discussion of the response of the Black-American children she observed to commands given by parents. She distinguished between two kinds of response:

"Reasonable" commands, such as "You can't go outside now, it's dark," are immediately obeyed. But commands without obvious justification, like "Wipe that smile off your face," or "Come stand over here by me," are treated differently. The children understand the latter quite correctly as invitations to engage in a routinized verbal game in which the children resist, the adults repeat, with escalating insistence until the adults appeal to higher status members of the family or community to enforce the command. The game often lasts fifteen to twenty minutes, and everyone understands it as such.

—Lein, quoted in Cazden, 1975

In school, predictably, Lein found that the children frequently misinterpreted teachers' commands: they would resist playfully when their teachers gave them commands for which they could see no obvious justification. The teachers naturally labeled the children "defiant," not realizing that they were transferring to the school setting rules for speaking which were not appropriate there.

Knowledge of the sociolinguistic norms of the children one is teaching is always an advantage. For the second language teacher such information can be an invaluable asset in avoiding unnecessary conflicts and problems. It can also be extremely useful in devising teaching material and techniques which take account of the sociolinguistic skills the children already possess, while providing ways of extending their sociolinguistic competence which do not conflict with the norms and values of the children's cultural background.

Second language teaching

In this section some suggestions are provided for alternatives to the traditional question-and-answer sessions which characterize so many classrooms and of ways in which some of the sociolinguistic conflicts experienced by many minority group children in such classrooms may be alleviated. These alternatives may not, however, be useful or appropriate to all groups. The need for teachers to match teaching material and techniques to the interests and sociolinguistic norms of the particular children they are teaching cannot be overemphasized. Some children, for example, seem to thrive in a highly formal teaching environment. There is no perfect solution to the teacher's problems, no one "best" method.

The suggestions in this section are also aimed at extending the sociolinguistic competence of second language learners in particular.[10]

The focus is therefore on ways of learning how to speak appropriately in different situations, and how to interpret the social meaning of utterances, rather than on the skills required for, say, reading and writing or for interpreting the referential functions of language. Hence, much of what follows is most relevant to the second language teacher, although some of the suggestions may also be of use to the foreign language teacher, depending on the needs of his students and the purposes for which the language is required.

While awareness of the culture-specific nature of the equation of learning with talking may be useful in avoiding the misinterpretation of the behavior of many minority group children in the classroom, it cannot be allowed to inhibit the second language teacher's methods. It is clear that, given unlimited time and exposure, and adequate motivation, second language learning presents few problems, and third and fourth languages may be acquired well into adulthood. Sorensen (1972), for example, reports of the Indian tribes in the Northwest Amazon:

> As an individual goes through adolescence, he actively and almost suddenly learns to speak these additional languages to which he has been exposed, and his linguistic repertoire is elaborated. In adulthood he may acquire more languages; as he approaches old age, field observation indicates, he will go on to perfect his knowledge of all the languages at his disposal.

The second language teacher, however, is committed to teaching students as much as possible within the limitations imposed by the time-table and the classroom context. How can these constraints be minimized?

Perhaps the simplest way in which the teacher can provide sociolinguistic diversity for pupils is to change some aspects of the classroom situation. The second language teacher can often change the setting completely, by moving out of the classroom for visits to places of interest to students, involving them in community work, weekend camps, and so on, thus exposing students to "natural language use" in a variety of situations as suggested by Rivers (1976). Such experiences are very valuable, but they cannot form the whole of the syllabus for any class, and are obviously impossible for foreign language teachers. Role-plays or "classroom mockups" of situations are sometimes suggested as alternatives to such excursions, but however useful these may be in "stimulating the learner's interest," they can never be completely satisfactory as a means of teaching *communicative* uses of language, as Criper and Widdowson (1975) point out. There are, however, other components of the situation which can be altered within the classroom setting, without abandoning the aim of using language in genuinely communicative ways. One can, for example, alter the participant relationships and the kind of tasks set in order to increase pupils' opportunities for developing sociolinguistic skills.

Pupil-pupil interactions in small groups or in a one-to-one situation (dyad) offer a number of advantages to second language learners, particularly from a sociolinguistic point of view. For many children such "participant-structures" provide a more culturally congenial means of interacting, permitting cooperative learning as opposed to the competitiveness which often characterizes full class interactions (see, for example, Graves and Graves, 1973, for research with Maori children; Lucker, Rosenfield, Sikes, and Aronson, 1976, for research with Mexican-American and Black children; Philips, 1972, for observation of American-Indian children). Such interactions also provide an opportunity for learners to use a more colloquial variety of language in the classroom, a variety which is more appropriate for the expression of solidarity than the formal standard generally used for full class interactions, which reflects the status differences and the social distance between teacher and pupils. Pupil-pupil discussion, moreover, seems likely to provide an escape from the three-part structure and predominantly closed questions which also characterize so much of teacher-pupil interaction. Tarrant (1977), for example, comparing six small discussion groups—three led by teachers, three involving only pupils—found that in all groups, incidence of the three-part structure was low, but it was highest in the teacher-led groups; pupils used significantly fewer closed questions than did teachers; and teachers used markedly more complex ways of eliciting pupil responses than did pupil group leaders. In addition, small-group interactions obviously provide an opportunity for pupils to use language for a much wider range of speech functions than is possible in full class interaction. Many educationalists, for example, have pointed to the advantages of small-group work in allowing pupils to explore ideas and to interpret information, rather than to receive it passively (see, for example, Barnes 1969, 1973, 1976; Britton, 1970; Postman and Weingartner, 1971). From a sociolinguistic viewpoint one can add that pupils get little opportunity in full class interaction to hypothesize, evaluate, argue, challenge, disagree, express approval, appreciation, etc., or to use language in the tentative, speculative, or exploratory way which is appropriate in small group discussions, for example. Wilkins (1973) lists a great variety of such communicative functions which second language learners may need to express. There are very few which *pupils* can appropriately use in full class discussions.

Second language teachers in a school which includes native speakers of the language being taught can further extend the advantages of pupil-pupil interactions by making judicious use of native speakers as tutors. There is an extensive literature on the benefits to both tutor and pupil of peer-peer and different age tutoring (Allen, 1976). Improvements in attitudes and self-esteem have been reported, as well as in social development and the amount of material mastered or skills acquired. In an article comparing adult and child teaching strategies, Gumperz and Herasimchuk (1972) demonstrate that the adult and the child use different means of communicating with their pupils, and research by Allen and Feldman (1975) suggests that children are more sensitive than adults to nonverbal cues indicating understanding and nonunderstanding. At the very least, such interactions expose the learner to a more colloquial variety of the second language produced by a native speaker and, given an interesting task, provide a natural motivation to understand and be understood.

There is an increasing awareness of the need for material aimed at developing sociolinguistic competence in a second language, which takes account of the sociolinguistic norms of the particular pupils being taught and their specific requirements in this area. The earlier discussion of classroom interaction suggests that some minority group children, for example, might benefit from exercises which are aimed at sensitizing them to the implications of utterances, and at focusing their attention on the social as well as the referential or manifest meaning of language (see, for example, Holmes and Brown, 1976; Mortimer, 1974). Acquiring new listening and interpretative skills, particularly skills in recognizing the social meaning of utterances, is clearly important for any minority group child in the classroom, but these skills are also important and often underestimated aspects of sociolinguistic competence for the second language learner. Children need to recognize the functions of such questions as "who's making that noise?" in the classroom situation, or the implications of "I hope I won't have to remind you again" in any similarly status-differentiated role relationship (see Brown and Holmes, 1977, for further examples).

Turning to productive rather than receptive sociolinguistic skills, Labov (1973), discussing conflicting sociolinguistic rules for refusing to comply with a request, suggests some minority group children may benefit from an opportunity to acquire "those verbal routines of mitigation which would make it possible for him to object and refuse without a major confrontation." He suggests that, in response to a demand that work be repeated because it is "sloppy," a child might reply acceptably with such forms as:

"It's not that sloppy is it?" or
"If it's right it doesn't have to be pretty does it?"

—Labov, 1973

Much clearly depends on the intonation and paralinguistic features of these responses, and also on the teacher-pupil relationship. In some classrooms, however, such utterances, as they stand, might be considered insolent. Forms serving this speech function clearly need to be selected with care, and attention must be given to intonation. Other language functions which second language learners could usefully learn to express are ways of responding appropriately to a false accusation or refusing a request for assistance. In both cases it is usually appropriate to provide a suitable excuse or supportive evidence for one's claim: e.g.,

To an accusation:
No, it wasn't me. I was (outside)
(asleep)
(working)

To a request for assistance:
No, I'm sorry but (I'm too (tired) right now   )
((busy)   )
(I have to (finish this) first   )
((see Mary)   )
((wash my hands)   )

Clearly such examples could be multiplied. Research is needed to establish the various ways in which such functions are expressed in different situations before second language teachers can hope to select appropriate forms on a principled basis to teach their pupils. Criper and Widdowson (1975) also suggest that learners need to know which form to select in a given context and recommend that teachers should make available forms at "one or two different points on a scale of mitigation and politeness."[11] Learners need to be able to assess the relative importance of different social features in a situation in order to produce appropriate forms. Status differences, for example, may be based on different attributes in different cultures. Selecting appropriately polite or deferential forms depends on developing skills in accurately assessing such factors as one's relationship to one's addressee, the formality of the setting, and so on. More research is needed, however, to provide a basis for teaching such skills.

The predominantly passive role of pupils in classrooms suggests another area where the second language teacher might usefully "turn the tables" in second language lessons. Pupils rarely get an opportunity to initiate interactions in full class discussion. Yet this is an area where foreign language learners in particular need a great deal of practice and encouragement:

Many foreign students lack the confidence to initiate or contribute anything substantial to a conversation. The native speaker is often expected to carry the conversational load while the foreign student replies to his questions with the minimum of information thus providing him with little encouragement to continue the conversation.

—Holmes and Brown, 1976

Many second language teaching textbooks include exercises which can be used or adapted to give the learners more opportunity to contribute genuinely to interactions. By using them between pupils rather than between teacher and pupil there is greater opportunity for a real exchange of new information and more realistic alternation of the initiating role. Communication games, such as those suggested in the *Concept 7-9* material (Wight, Norris, and Worsley, 1972), developed for native speakers as well as for immigrant children, and by Nation (1977), provide further examples of exercises which give pupils the opportunity to share the role of initiator more effectively than is ever possible in teacher-pupil interactions.

If the emphasis in this section has fallen on the advantages of small group and one-to-one interaction, this is an accurate reflection of the ways in which I believe many *sociolinguistic* skills can best be developed. Even where participants are nonnative speakers, carefully devised materials can help them interpret social meaning and develop sociolinguistic skills in the second language, in a situation where the communication is meaningful to all participants. Full class interactions offer adequate opportunities for hearing a formal standard variety of the language and learning the rules for speaking in a formal situation. A necessary complement can be provided by small-group work where less formal language is appropriate, and where the equal status of the participants results in a more symmetrical distribution of speaking turns and the opportunity to interpret and convey very different kinds of social meanings.

The tacit values and expectations concerning appropriate pupil behavior, about what comprises knowledge and how it should be transmitted have been labeled "the hidden curriculum" (Jackson, 1968). The diagram below, taken from Barnes (1976), neatly summarizes those aspects of the hidden curriculum which most obviously constrain the sociolinguistic behavior of pupils in the classroom, and limit the kinds of sociolinguistic competence they can acquire there. In the absence of an adequate description of the sociolinguistic norms of the particular group to which one's pupils belong, it provides a useful guide for taking account of these limitations and constraints, and heightening awareness of the problems which second-language learners may face in acquiring sociolinguistic competence. Finally those who still doubt the force of the

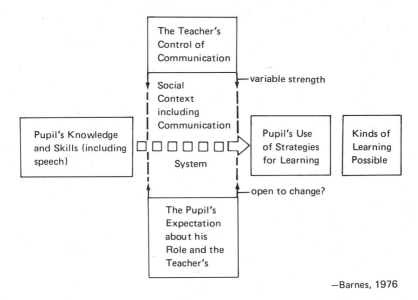

—Barnes, 1976

constraints on classroom interaction might like to consider how odd this interchange would sound in any other context:

A. Where do you live, Tony?
B. Wellington.
A. Good boy. Who else can tell me where they live?

NOTES

1. The content of the curriculum is, of course, equally culture-bound and this too is being questioned by educationalists. This aspect will not, however, be pursued here.

2. The terms "nominate," "bid," "cue," "exchange," and "move," used in this discussion, are technical terms introduced by Sinclair, Forsyth, Coulthard, and Ashby (1972) and further discussed by Sinclair and Coulthard (1975).

3. All examples are taken from recorded classroom lessons. Where no reference is provided the examples are from my own recordings.

4. This interesting utterance makes great demands on the children's comprehension. At first sight it looks nonsensical. It presumably means "I can't hear any individual response if you all shout out together," but this meaning is not explicit and is only retrievable by those who have some experience of the situation in which it occurs.

5. See also Brazil (1976) on the role of intonation as a linguistic means by which teachers convey their right to reinitiate.

6. For an interesting and detailed discussion of a lesson in which "form" was an explicit focus of teaching, see Mehan (1974).

7. Wootton (1974) provides further evidence that this three-part structure is quite commonly used in play sessions between middle-class mothers and preschool children. This suggests the importance of the function "to instruct," as a dominant factor influencing the discourse patterns discussed.

8. For a more extensive discussion of how teachers maintain conversational control on classroom discourse, see Stubbs (1976b). For a detailed discussion of how social control and discipline are maintained in classrooms, see Torode (1976).

9. This term is intended to include children from both linguistic and cultural minority groups, i.e., those whose language and/or cultural values are different from those of the mainstream society.

10. The term "second language" refers here to a language which is spoken by the majority group, and is therefore a necessity for immigrants and minority group members who wish to participate in the wider community. The term "foreign language" is restricted to a language which is not *essential* for everyday communication in the society and which is in many senses therefore a "luxury."

11. For further discussion of the learner's need for a range of available stylistic variants see Holmes and Brown (1977).

REFERENCES

A Handbook for Teachers of Pacific Island Children. Auckland: Pacific Islanders' Educational Resource Centre, 1977.

Abrahams, R. D. "Black Talking on the Streets," in R. Bauman and J. Sherzer, eds., *Explorations in the Ethnography of Speaking.* London: Cambridge University Press, 1974.

Abrahams, R. D., and G. Gay. "Black Culture in the Classroom," in R. D. Abrahams and R. C. Troike, eds., *Language and Cultural Diversity in American Education.* Englewood Cliffs: Prentice-Hall, 1972.

Allen, V. L., ed. *Children as Teachers: Theory and Research on Tutoring.* New York: Academic Press, 1976.

Allen, V. L., and R. S. Feldman. *Decoding of Children's Nonverbal Responses.* Technical Report No. 365. Madison, Wisc.: Wisconsin Research and Development Centre for Cognitive Learning, 1975.

Barber, C. "Some Measurable Characteristics of Modern Scientific Prose," in F. Behre, ed., *Contributions to English Syntax and Philology.* Gothenburg University Press, 1962.

Barnes, D. "Language in the Secondary Classroom," in D. Barnes, J. Britton, Harold Rosen, and the L.A.T.E., *Language the Learner and the School.* Harmondsworth: Penguin Books, 1969.

———. *Language in the Classroom.* Bletchley: The Open University Press, 1973.

———. *From Communication to Curriculum.* Harmondsworth: Penguin Books, 1976.

Basso, K. H. " 'To Give up on Words': Silence in Western Apache Culture," in P. P. Giglioli, ed., 1972, *Language and Social Context.* Harmondsworth: Penguin Books, 1970.

Bellack, A., ed. *Studies in the Classroom Language.* New York: Teachers College Press, 1973.

Blom, J. P., and J. J. Gumperz. "Social Meaning in Linguistic Structures: Code-Switching in Norway," in J. J. Gumperz and D. Hymes, eds., *Directions in Sociolinguistics*. New York: Holt, Rinehart, and Winston, 1972.

Boggs, S. T. "The Meaning of Questions and Narratives to Hawaiian Children," in C. B. Cazden, V. P. John, and D. Hymes, eds., *Functions of Language in the Classroom*. New York: Teachers College Press, 1972.

Boydell, D. "Teacher-Pupil Contact in Junior Classrooms," *British Journal of Educational Psychology*, 1974, *44*, 313-318.

Brazil, D. "The Teacher's Use of Intonation," *Educational Review*, 1976, *28*, 180-189.

Britton, J. N. *Language and Learning*. Harmondsworth: Penguin Books, 1970.

Brown, D. F., and J. Holmes. "Practical Exercises for Fostering Communicative Competence in Adult Learners of English," *TEFL/TESL Newsletter*, 1977, *2, 4*, 28-37.

Burton, D., and M. Stubbs. "On Speaking Terms," *Journal of the Midlands Association for Linguistic Studies*, Sociolinguistics ed., 1975.

Cazden, C. B. "Problems for Education: Language as Curriculum Content and Learning Environment," in M. Bloomfield and E. Haugen, eds., *Language as a Human Problem*. London: Lutterworth Press, 1975.

Corder, S. P. "Some Problems in the Design of a Functional Syllabus," *Proceedings and Papers of the Eighteenth Congress of the Australasian Universities Language and Literature Association*. Wellington, in press.

Coulthard, R. M. "Approaches to the Analysis of Classroom Interaction," *Educational Review*, 1974, *26*, 229-240.

―――. "Discourse Analysis in English—A Short Review of the Literature," *Language Teaching and Linguistics Abstracts*, 1975, *8*, 73-89.

Criper, C., and H. G. Widdowson. "Sociolinguistics and Language Teaching," in J. P. B. Allen and S. P. Corder, eds., *Papers in Applied Linguistics*. The Edinburgh Course in Applied Linguistics, Volume 2. London: Oxford University Press, 1975.

Delamont, S. *Interaction in the Classroom*. London: Methuen, 1976.

Dumont, R. V. "Learning English and How to be Silent: Studies in Sioux and Cherokee Classrooms," in C. B. Cazden, V. P. John, and D. Hymes, eds., *Functions of Language in the Classroom*. New York: Teachers College Press, 1972.

Edwards, A. D. *Language in Culture and Class*. London: Heinemann Educational Books, 1976.

Ervin-Tripp, S. M. "An Analysis of the Interaction of Language, Topic and Listener," *American Anthropologist*, 1964, *66*, 6, part 2, 86-102.

―――. "Children's Sociolinguistic Competence and Dialect Diversity," in I. J. Gordon, ed., *Early Childhood Education: The Seventy-First Yearbook of the National Society for the Study of Education*. Chicago: University of Chicago Press, 1972.

Ferguson, C. A. "Diglossia," *Word*, 1959, *15*, 325-340.

Fishman, J. A., and E. Lueders-Salmon. "What Has the Sociology of Language to Say to the Teacher? On Teaching the Standard Variety to Speakers of Dialectal or Sociolectal Varieties," in C. B. Cazden, V. P. John, and D. Hymes, eds., *Functions of Language in the Classroom*. New York: Teachers College Press, 1972.

Graves, N. B., and T. D. Graves. "Inclusive Versus Exclusive Behaviour in New Zealand School Settings: Polynesian-Pakeha Contrasts in Adaptation," *Research Report to the Royal Society of New Zealand,* 1973.

Gumperz, J. J., and E. Herasimchuk. "The Conversational Analysis of Social Meaning: A Study of Classroom Interaction," *Monographs Series on Languages and Linguistics 25,* Washington, D.C.: Georgetown University Press, 1972.

Halliday, M. A. K. *Explorations in the Functions of Language.* London: Edward Arnold, 1973.

———. *Learning How to Mean: Explorations in the Development of Language.* London: Edward Arnold, 1975.

Holmes, J., and D. F. Brown. "Developing Sociolinguistic Competence and Second Language Learning," in R. W. Brislin and M. P. Mammett, eds., *Topics in Culture Learning,* 1977, 5, Honolulu: East-West Center.

Hymes, D. "Introduction: Towards Ethnographies of Communication," *American Anthropologist,* 1964, 66, 6, part 2, 1-34.

———. "Models of the Interaction of Language and Social Setting," *Journal of Social Issues,* 1967, 23, 2, 8-28.

———. "On Communicative Competence," in J. B. Pride and J. Holmes, eds., *Sociolinguistics.* Harmondsworth: Penguin Books, 1972a.

———. "Introduction," in C. B. Cazden, V. P. John, and D. Hymes, eds., *Functions of Language in the Classroom.* New York: Teachers College Press, 1972b.

Jackson, P. W. *Life in Classrooms.* New York: Holt, Rinehart and Winston, 1968.

Jackson, R. "Concluding Statement: Linguistics and Poetics," in T. A. Sebeok, ed., *Style in Language.* Cambridge, Mass.: The MIT Press, 1960.

Jakobson, R. "Linguistics and Poetics," in T. A. Sebeok, ed., *Style and Language.* Cambridge, Mass.: MIT Press, 1960.

Keenan, E. O. "Conversational Competence in Children," *Journal of Child Language,* 1974, 1, 163-183.

Kochman, T. "Black American Speech Events and a Language Program for the Classroom," in C. B. Cazden, V. P. John, and D. Hymes, eds., *Functions of Language in the Classroom.* New York: Teachers College Press, 1972.

Labov, W. "Contraction, Deletion, and Inherent Variability of the English Copula." *Language* 45: 715-762, 1969.

Labov, W. "Modes of Mitigation and Politeness," in J. S. DeStefano, ed., *Language, Society and Education: A Profile of Black English.* Worthington, Oh.: C. A. Jones Publishing Company, 1973.

Lucker, G. W., D. Rosenfield, J. Sikes, and E. Aronson. "Performance in the Interdependent Classroom: A Field Study," *American Educational Research Journal,* 1976, 13, 115-123.

Mehan, H. "Accomplishing Classroom Lessons," in A. V. Cicourel et al., *Language Use and School Performance.* New York: Academic Press, 1974.

Merton, R. *Social Theory and Social Structure.* New York: Free Press, 1957.

Mishler, E. G. "Implications of Teacher Strategies for Language and Cognition: Observations in First-Grade Classrooms," in C. B. Cazden, V. P. John, and D. Hymes, eds., *Functions of Language in the Classroom.* New York: Teachers College Press, 1972.

Mortimer, C. "Developing Language Skills Through Seeking Implications," *English Teaching Forum,* 1974, 12, 2, 22-24.

Nation, I. S. P. "The Combining Arrangement: Some Techniques," *The Modern Language Journal,* 1977, 61, 89-94.

Philips, S. U. "Participant Structures and Communicative Competence: Warm Springs Children in Community and Classroom," in C. B. Cazden, V. P. John, and D. Hymes, eds., *Functions of Language in the Classroom*. New York: Teachers College Press, 1972.

Postman, N., and C. Weingartner. *Teaching as a Subversive Activity*. Harmondsworth: Penguin Books, 1971.

Rivers, W. M. "The Natural and the Normal in Language Learning," *Language Learning*. Special Issue, 1976, no. 4, 1-8.

Rosen, H. "The Language of Textbooks," in J. N. Britton, ed., *Talking and Writing*. London: Methuen, 1967.

Sachs, J., and J. Devin. "Young Children's Use of Age-Appropriate Speech Styles in Social Interaction and Role-Playing," *Journal of Child Language*, 1976, 3, 81-98.

Sacks, H., E. A. Schegloff, and G. Jefferson. "A Simplest Systematics for the Organisation of Turn-Taking for Conversation," *Language*, 1974, 50, 696-735.

Schegloff, E. A. "Sequencing in Conversational Openings." *American Anthropologist*, 1968, 70. 1075-1095.

Schegloff, E. A., and H. Sacks. "Opening Up Closings," *Semiotica*, 1973, 11, 109-122.

Sinclair, J. McH., and R. M. Coulthard. *Towards an Analysis of Discourse*. London: Oxford University Press, 1975.

Sinclair, J. McH., I. J. Forsyth, R. M. Coulthard, and M. C. Ashby. *The English Used by Teachers and Pupils*, final report to S.S.R.C., Birmingham: University of Birmingham, Dept. of English. Mimeo, 1972.

Sorenson, A. P. "Multilingualism in the Northeast Amazon," in J. B. Pride and J. Holmes, eds., *Sociolinguistics*. Harmondsworth: Penguin Books, 1972.

Stubbs, M. *Language, Schools and Classrooms*. London: Methuen, 1976a.

———. "Keeping in Touch: Some Functions of Teacher-Talk," in M. Stubbs and S. Delamont, eds., *Explorations in Classroom Observation*. London: Wiley, 1976b.

Tarrant, J. "Teacher and Pupil Elicitations in Small Group Discourse," unpublished term paper. Wellington: Victoria University, 1977.

Torode, B. "Teacher's Talk and Classroom Discipline," in M. Stubbs and S. Delamont, eds., *Explorations in Classroom Observation*. London: Wiley, 1976.

Waller. *The Sociology of Talking*. London: Wiley, 1965. (Reprint of 1932 edition.)

Wight, J., R. Norris, and F. J. Worsley. *Concept 7-9*. Leeds: Edward Arnold, 1972.

Wilkins, D. A. "The Linguistic and Situational Content of the Common Core in a Unit/Credit System," in *Systems Development in Adult Language Learning*. Strasbourg: Council for Cultural Cooperation, Council of Europe, 1973.

Willes, M. "Early Lessons Learned Too Well?" Birmingham: University of Birmingham, Dept. of English. Mimeo, 1975.

Wootton, A. "Talk in the Homes of Young Children," *Sociology*, 1974, 8, 277-295.

STUDY AND DISCUSSION QUESTIONS

(1) In what ways do the nonlinguistic components of the situation mentioned in this article influence the variety of language used, and the rules for speaking appropriately, in the following situations: playground interaction, an interview with the headmaster, a woodwork lesson, school assembly, a play rehearsal?

(2) Tests and interviews designed to elicit information about a child's (socio)linguistic competence often resemble full class interactions in a number of ways: e.g., they require children to "display what they know." For what reasons does this article suggest that such tests may provide an inadequate picture of the child's abilities?

(3) Is there a place for practice in using closed questions in the second language learning classroom? Consider the extent to which they occur naturally in situations which the second language learner is likely to encounter.

(4) The term "communicative competence" (Hymes, 1972) includes nonverbal aspects of communication such as body movement, gesture, facial expression, etc. Are there rules governing appropriate and acceptable nonverbal behavior in the classroom? Consider, for example, how one signals attentive listening or difficulty in following the discourse. Is nonverbal communicative behavior culture-specific?

(5) Do you agree that classroom mockups and role-plays are only useful for stimulating the learner's interest? Is this an unimportant factor in second language learning?

(6) Record a preschool child working with a parent on a task. Examine the interaction for evidence that the rules for speaking in this situation are similar to those described in this article for classroom interaction.

(7) Record a preschool child in a play situation with a friend and talking to an unfamiliar adult. Is there any evidence that the child uses different turn-taking rules in these situations?

(8) Observe a full class interaction (a) in the first year of primary school and (b) in the first year of secondary school. Compare how teachers deal with unsolicited contributions from pupils. Is there any evidence of a change in the rules for speaking as pupils get older? If so, what does this imply about the influence of the age of pupils on the ways of learning regarded as appropriate in their community?

(9) In some cultures it is considered impolite to display knowledge in front of others, since such behavior is interpreted as an attempt to "put them down" or "show them up." In what ways could a teacher avoid cultural conflict for children from such groups in the classroom situation?

(10) Observe several consecutive lessons conducted by a second language teacher. How does he or she vary the nonlinguistic components of the situation discussed in this article? What kind of sociolinguistic skills are likely to be acquired by pupils in these classes?

$$=========\ 8\ =========$$

SOCIAL AND PSYCHOLOGICAL FACTORS IN
SECOND LANGUAGE ACQUISITION

John H. Schumann

For the past several years researchers (Schumann, 1975b, 1976a; Swain, 1977; Tucker, 1977) in second language acquisition have been developing taxonomies of factors that are involved in the second language learning process. Oversimplifying a bit, we can say that the first two factors identified were instruction and interference. Later, aptitude, attitude, and motivation were added. Now the list includes social, affective, personality, cognitive, biological, aptitude, personal, input, and instructional factors. Table 8-1 attempts to provide an up-to-date taxonomy of these influences on the acquisition of a second language.

This paper will focus on social and psychological factors in second language learning and therefore will treat section I of Table 8-1 (social factors), section II (affective factors), section III (personality factors), section IV-C (cognitive style factors), and section VII (personal factors).

SOCIAL FACTORS

When we examine social factors that affect SLL we look at variables which involve the relationship between two social groups who are in a contact situation, but who speak different languages (see Schumann, 1976b and 1976c). One group is considered the second language learning group (2LL group) and the other the target language group (TL group). Certain social factors can either promote or inhibit contact between the

Table 8-1   Taxonomy of Factors Influencing
Second Language Acquisition

I. *Social Factors*
   A. Dominance
   B. Nondominance
   C. Subordination
   D. Assimilation
   E. Acculturation
   F. Preservation
   G. Enclosure
   H. Cohesiveness
   I. Size
   J. Congruence
   K. Attitude
   L. Intended length of
      residence in TL area

II. *Affective Factors*
   A. Language shock
   B. Culture shock
   C. Motivation

III. *Personality Factors*
   A. Tolerance for ambiguity
   B. Sensitivity to rejection
   C. Introversion/Extroversion
   D. Self-esteem

IV. *Cognitive Factors*
   A. Cognitive Development
   B. Cognitive processes
      1. Imitation
      2. Analogy
      3. Generalization
      4. Rote memorization
   C. Cognitive style
      1. Field dependence
      2. Category width
      3. Cognitive interference
      4. Monitoring

V. *Biological Factors*
   A. Lateralization
   B. Transfer
   C. Infrasystems

VI. *Aptitude Factors*
   A. Modern Language Aptitude
   B. I.Q.
   C. Strephosymbolia

VII. *Personal Factors*
   A. Nesting patterns
   B. Transition anxiety
   C. Reaction to teaching methods
   D. Choice of learning strategies

VIII. *Input Factors*
   A. Frequency
   B. Salience
   C. Complexity
   D. Type of interlocutor

IX. *Instructional Factors*
   A. Goals
   B. Teacher
   C. Method
   D. Text
   E. Time
   F. Intensity
   G. Means of evaluation

two groups and thus affect the degree to which the 2LL group learns the target language.

The first such factor involves social dominance patterns. If the 2LL group is politically, culturally, technically, or economically superior (dominant) to the TL group, it will tend not to learn the target language. For example, French colonists in Tunisia were potential learners of Arabic. But the French, as a group, because of their political, cultural, technical, and economic dominance, were socially distant from the Tunisians and felt very little need to acquire Arabic. If the 2LL group is inferior (subordinate) to the TL group, there will also be social distance between the two groups, and the 2LL group will tend to resist learning the target language. For example, American Indians living in the Southwest have traditionally been subordinate to the dominant Anglo group and have also resisted the acquisition of English. This situation is compounded by issues of enclosure, congruence, and attitude which will be mentioned below. If the 2LL group and the TL group are roughly equal in terms of political, cultural, technical, and economic status, then contact between the two groups is likely to be more extensive, and the acquisition of target language by the 2LL group will be enhanced.

The second social factor affecting second language learning involves three integration strategies: assimilation, preservation, and acculturation. If the 2LL group assimilates, then it gives up its own life style and values and adopts those of the target language group. This strategy maximizes contact between the two groups and enhances acquisition of the target language. If the 2LL group chooses preservation as its integration strategy then it maintains its own life style and values and rejects those of the TL group. This situation creates social distance between the two groups and makes it unlikely that the 2LL group will acquire the TL group's language. If the 2LL group acculturates, then it adapts to the life style and values of the TL group but maintains its own life style and values for the intragroup use. This particular integration strategy yields varying degrees of contact between the two groups and thus varying degrees of acquisition of the target language.

Enclosure is the third social factor that affects second language learning. Enclosure refers to the degree to which the 2LL group and the TL group share the same churches, schools, clubs, recreational facilities, crafts, professions, and trades. If the two groups share these social constructs, enclosure is said to be low, contact between the two groups is enhanced, and acquisition of the target language by the 2LL group is facilitated. However, if the two groups have different churches, schools, clubs, recreational facilities, crafts, professions, and trades, then enclosure is said to be high, contact between the two groups is limited, and opportunities for acquisition of the target language are reduced.

Cohesiveness and size are related social factors that also affect second language learning. If the 2LL group is cohesive, its members will tend to remain separate from the TL group, and if the 2LL group is large, intragroup contact will be more frequent than intergroup contact. Both these situations will reduce the opportunities for acquisition of the target language.

Congruence or similarity between the culture of the TL group and that of the 2LL group also affects the degree of contact between the two groups. If the two cultures are similar, then social contact is more likely and second language learning will be facilitated.

Attitude is another important social factor involved in second language learning. If the 2LL group and the TL group have positive attitudes toward each other, second language learning is more likely to occur than if they view each other negatively.

The final social factor to be considered is the 2LL group's intended length of residence in the target language area. If the 2LL group intends to remain for a long time in the target language area it is likely to develop more extensive contacts with the TL group. Therefore, an intended lengthy residence in the target language area would tend to promote second language learning.

Psychological factors   When discussing social factors we are concerned with language learning by groups of people. However, psychological variables relate to language learning by individuals. An individual may learn under social conditions which are not favorable for SLA and not learn under social conditions which appear to be favorable. The psychological variables affecting these individual learning patterns are such things as affective factors, personality factors, cognitive style factors, and personal factors.

AFFECTIVE FACTORS

Affective factors involve issues of language shock, culture shock, motivation, and ego permeability.

Language shock   In discussing what can be called language shock, Stengal (1937) points out that when learners attempt to speak a second language they often fear that they will appear comic. He compares the use of a second language with wearing fancy clothes. The adult learner may want to wear his fancy clothes, but he also fears criticism and ridicule. The child, however, sees language as a method of play and finds communication a source of pleasure. Thus, he doesn't fear his fancy clothes; he enjoys wearing them. Stengal states, "The adult will learn the new language more easily, the more of these infantile characteristics he has preserved." He also points out that adults speaking a second language are often haunted by doubts as to whether their words actually reflect their ideas. Children, he says, are less worried about this. The child is willing to use a word incorrectly and to form new words if necessary. Finally, learners often get a good deal of narcissistic gratification from their use of their native language, and in many cases, they use language to attract attention and praise. When speaking a second language in which they are much less proficient, they lose an important source of narcissistic gratification.

Culture shock   Culture shock can be defined as anxiety resulting from the disorientation encountered upon entering a new culture. The learner, when moving into a new culture, finds himself in a dependent state. The coping and problem-solving mechanisms that he has at his disposal often do not work in the new culture. As a result, activities which were routine in his native country require a great deal of energy in the new environment. This situation can cause disorientation, stress, anxiety, and fear. The resulting mental state can produce a powerful syndrome of rejection which diverts energy and attention from second language learning. The learner, in attempting to find a cause for his disorientation, may reject himself, his own culture, the organization for which he is working, and the people of the host country. Under such conditions the learner is unlikely to make the effort necessary to become bilingual.

Motivation   Motivation, the third affective factor, involves the learner's reasons for attempting to acquire the second language. Researchers (Gardner and Lambert, 1972) have identified two motivational orientations for second language learning—an integrative motivation and an instrumental motivation. An integratively oriented learner wants to learn the second language in order to meet with, talk to, find out about, and perhaps become like speakers of the target language whom he both values and admires. An instrumentally oriented learner is one who has little interest in the people who speak the target language but nevertheless wants to learn the language for more utilitarian reasons such as getting ahead in his occupation or gaining recognition from his own membership group. It has generally been thought that integrative motivation is the more powerful of the two because it implies a desire to integrate with speakers of the target language. A learner with an instrumental motivation would be expected to acquire the second language, only to the point where his instrumental goals were satisfied. If the learner merely wanted to be able to buy food and take public transportation, he could achieve these goals with a very low level of proficiency in the second language. If the learner had to use the target language in his professional life, his level of learning would be much higher. Recent research, however, seems to indicate that the motivational orientation associated with proficiency in the second language seems to vary according to setting. An integrative motivation appears to be more effective in settings where it is neither necessary nor an accepted fact of life that the second language be acquired. Such conditions obtain in the United States with regard to learning languages such as French, German, or Italian. On the other hand, in settings such as Iran and Saudi Arabia, learners may have very little integrative motivation to acquire English, but they may have a great deal of instrumental motivation to learn the language in order to be able to deal with English-speaking technical advisors, educators, and businessmen. Oller, Baca, and Vigil (1977) have even found that with colonized populations such as Mexican-Americans in the Southwest, proficiency in the second language (in this case English) is associated with an anti-integrative motivation. So, while instrumental and integrative motivations are useful ways to think about success in second language learning, they are complex constructs that interact with both the social variables discussed earlier and the other psychological variables which will be examined below.

Ego permeability   Guiora (1972), in attempting to explain the ability of some people to acquire native-like pronunciation in a second language, developed the notion of "language ego." He sees language ego as parallel to the Freudian construct, body ego. In the course of general ego development the child acquires body ego by which he becomes aware of the limits of his physical being and learns to distinguish himself from the object world around him. In a similar fashion, in the course of general ego development, the child acquires a sense of the boundaries of his language. The sounds, words, syntax, and morphology of his language become objectified and develop firm outlines and boundaries. In the early stages of development, language ego boundaries are permeable, but later they become fixed and rigid.

Guiora, Beit-Hallahmi, Brannon, Dull, and Scovel (1972) equated rigidity of ego boundaries with heightened levels of inhibition. They reasoned that if inhibition level could be lowered, ego rigidity would be reduced and ego permeability would be enhanced. To test this idea, they conducted an experiment in which they gave subjects varying amounts of alcohol (0, 1, 1.5, 2, or 3 ounces of ninety-proof liquor) and then tested their pronunciation in a second language. It was found that with the ingestion of one to one-and-one-half ounces of alcohol, pronunciation was better than in either the no-alcohol or the two- or three-ounce conditions. This experiment suggests that ego permeability is inducible and that perhaps the successful adult second language learner is an individual who has access to more childlike ego states in which greater ego permeability exists.

PERSONALITY FACTORS

Since 1974 at the Ontario Institute for Studies in Education, research has been conducted (Naiman, Frolich, and Stern, 1975; also reported in Cohen, 1977) in order to define the characteristics of a good language learner. In the course of this research several personality characteristics (tolerance for ambiguity, introversion and extroversion, empathy, and sensitivity to rejection) and cognitive style characteristics (field dependence, category width, and cognitive interference) have been examined.

The subjects in this research were English-speaking high school students studying French in English-speaking Canada. The students' personality and cognitive style traits were correlated with their performance on a listening comprehension task and a sentence imitation task. Similar research is also being conducted at the English Language Institute of the University of Michigan on college level students of English as a second language from various parts of the world (Brown, 1977).

Tolerance for ambiguity   Language learning is a very complex endeavor in which the learner often has to perform in highly ambiguous situations where the purpose of the activity, the topic of the conversation, and the appropriate response are unclear. Those learners who have a low tolerance for ambiguity might be expected to react to such situations with depression, dislike, or avoidance. Naiman et al. found that tolerance for ambiguity was significantly correlated with listening comprehension, but not with the imitation task. Cohen (1977) suggests these results indicate that students who are tolerant of ambiguity may be able to listen more attentively while those who are intolerant of ambiguity may become confused by the linguistic input and thus attend to it much less efficiently.

Extroversion   Popular mythology has it that extroverts are better language learners than introverts. However, Naiman et al. found no significant correlation between scores on an extroversion/introversion scale and performance on the listening comprehension or imitation tasks.

In an experiment on fifty twelfth-grade students of English as a second language, Rossier (1975) found that if he controlled for time spent studying in the United States, grade point average, general educational attainment, and I.Q., extroverts were better speakers of English than introverts. In other words, if everything else is equal, extroverts do better in speaking than introverts. However, in real life "everything else" is rarely equal. Thus we have to say that, to date, experimental evidence does not seem to support popular notions about the role of extroversion in second-language learning.

Empathy   In the previous section on affective factors, we discussed ego permeability, which is sometimes equated with empathy. The idea is that lowered inhibition induced by alcohol produces a state of ego permeability which is assumed to be the essential component of empathy. When empathy is considered as a personality factor, it is not viewed as inducible, but is seen as a stable characteristic that some people have and some people do not have.

In order to assess their subjects' empathic capacity (i.e., the students' psychological ability to put themselves in another person's place and modify their behavior in the direction of the other person), Naiman et al. administered the Hogan Empathy Scale. They then correlated the scores on this scale with the two criterion measures, listening comprehension and sentence imitation. However, in neither case was the correlation significant.

Sensitivity to rejection   In most modern language classes a student is expected to use the target language orally in various ways. He is asked to respond in drills, generate his own sentences in grammar exercises, role play, recite dialogues, and participate in communication games. In all these activities there is the possibility that the learner's performance will bring on negative reactions from the teacher or the other students. The learner who is sensitive to the negative reinforcing behaviors of others would be made particularly anxious in such situations. Naiman et al. hypothesized that this sensitivity to and expectation of rejection might make certain students avoid active participation in class for fear of being ridiculed by their classmates and/or the teacher. To test this idea the researchers correlated scores on a sensitivity to rejection scale with performance on the two criterion measures. However, no significant relationship was found.

Self-esteem   At the University of Michigan, Adelaide Heyde (1977) is investigating the relationship between self-esteem and the oral production of a second language. Self-esteem is the degree of value or worthiness which an individual ascribes to himself. There are three aspects of self-esteem: (1) global self-esteem, which is an individual's overall assessment of his worth; (2) specific self-esteem, which refers to self-valuation in various life situations (education, work, social interactions, sports) and various individual characteristics (personality, intelligence, and attractiveness); and (3) task self-esteem, which involves self-valuations in specific tasks (writing papers, driving a car, taking tests).

As of this writing, Heyde has only completed pilot research, but preliminary results seem to indicate the total self-esteem scores are predictive of both the best and the worst second language learners.

COGNITIVE STYLE FACTORS

Field dependence   Researchers have been attempting to determine whether field independent learners acquire second languages more readily than field dependent learners. A field independent learner is one who can perceive a visual or auditory field and detect subpatterns within that field. A learner who is field dependent gets lost in the totality of the visual or auditory stimulus and fails to detect relevant subpatterns and subsystems. In terms of second language learning we would expect a field independent learner to be able to focus upon the relevant grammatical items of a lesson or a conversation, whereas we would expect a field dependent learner to be distracted by less significant aspects of the linguistic interaction at hand. Naiman et al. found that measures of field independence correlated significantly with performance on both the listening comprehension task and the imitation task. In another experiment, Tucker, Hamayan, and Genesee (1975) found that a measure of field independence grouped with several attitudinal factors (ethnocentrism and French class anxiety) to predict performance on a test of French listening comprehension, speaking, grammar, and vocabulary.

These results offer some support for the hypothesis that field independent learners acquire second languages more easily than those who are field dependent. However, Brown (1977) points out that the field independent person is generally thought to be more analytical, precise, and affectively independent. On the other hand, the field dependent person is thought to be more empathic, open, and affectively and cognitively perceptive of total patterns. A conflict arises when we see that researchers have claimed that both analytical precision and empathic openness are important for second language learning. Brown believes that a resolution of this conflict may lie in the distinction between learning a language in a classroom through instruction and acquiring it in its natural environment through contact with native speakers. He speculates that field independence may be more important in the classroom setting where learning is measured by tests, and that field dependence may be more important in the natural setting where learning is measured by how well the learner can communicate with speakers of the target language.

Category width   Language teachers and researchers have long recognized that overgeneralization characterizes many aspects of second language learning. Learners often produce overgeneralized forms such as *He goed* or *I know where is he going.* Learners may also undergeneralize and fail to recognize that *Is he going?* and *Did he go?* are characterized by the same inversion rule. Thus, overgeneralizers risk including too many items in a particular category or rule and undergeneralizers risk creating more categories or rules than are necessary to handle the linguistic data confronting them. The extreme, but unlikely, form of an undergeneralizer would be the learner who felt it necessary to memorize every sentence of the language.

Naiman et al. hypothesized that the best language learners would be those students who neither generalized too much nor too little. To test this idea they administered Pettigrew's category-width scale to their subjects and then correlated the results with performance on the criterion measures. However, they found that this measure of the tendency to overgeneralize or undergeneralize did not correlate significantly with either listening comprehension or sentence imitation.

Cognitive interference   Since interference of native language habits on performance in the second language is a phenomenon commonly associated with second language learning, Naiman et al. hypothesized that successful second language learners would be those who could resist the intrusion of native language structures on their target language performance. To test this idea students were administered the Speed of Color Discrimination test, which assesses the subject's propensity to resist a stronger habit (reading color names on cards) by exercising a weaker habit (naming the color of the words on the cards). However, the researchers found no significant correlation between performance on this test and performance on the listening comprehension and imitation tasks.

Monitoring   Krashen (1976, 1977a, 1977b) has identified an aspect of cognitive style which he calls monitoring. He argues that there are two ways in which learners gain productive competence in a second language. The first is through *acquisition,* which is a nonconscious process fostered by exposure to and interaction with linguistic input in the natural environment. The second route is through *learning,* which results in the "conscious representation of pedagogical rules." Monitoring takes place when the learner uses his conscious knowledge of target language rules to modify his performance in the second language.

Monitoring can occur only when the learner has time to modify his performance (as in writing) and when he is focusing on correctness of grammatical form rather than communicative function.

Monitoring also seems to be limited to certain individuals, certain rules, and certain situations. There is evidence that some individuals do not monitor under any conditions and make judgments of correctness by "feel." In addition, there are rules such as those for article usage and inversion in yes/no questions which, because of their complexity, are not amenable to monitoring and are therefore acquired and not learned. Finally, due to the fact that monitoring is constrained by time and focus on form, it also becomes limited by situation. Monitoring is most likely to occur on grammar tests and is least likely to occur in free conversation. On compositions, monitoring seems to increase to some extent when there is time and motivation for editing.

Research on monitoring differs in two ways from that done on the other cognitive style factors discussed above. In monitoring research, no argument is made about which are the better learners, those who monitor or those who do not, and since no test of monitoring exists, researchers cannot simply generate monitoring scores and relate them to perform-ance on language tests. Instead, learners are asked to produce under conditions which allow monitoring and then their performance is compared with target language productions under conditions which do not permit monitoring. Another strategy is to ask learners to introspect about whether their production of certain grammatical forms was governed by the application of conscious grammatical rules or by an acquired feel for the item's correctness.

Of the nine personality and cognitive style factors discussed, only four—tolerance of ambiguity, self-esteem, field independence, and monitoring—have shown a relationship to second language learning. In addition, of the four factors which show a relationship, the self-esteem results were only based on pilot research and the monitoring results were generated in a research paradigm which did not directly relate measures of monitoring to measures of language performance.

There are several possible explanations for the nonsignificant out-comes. First, there may indeed be no relationship between these constructs and second language acquisition. Second, the personality and cognitive style scales may not be measuring what they purport to measure. In this regard, Naiman et al. report that students who were observed to be shy and reticent in the language classroom and who, in interviews, reported that they were embarrassed and feared ridicule scored no differently on the extroversion scale than those who demonstrated extroverted behavior in classrooms and who reported extroverted characteristics in interviews with the researchers. Hence, more valid ways of tapping personality and cognitive style may be needed.

Third, certain personality and cognitive style characteristics may be more important at different stages of the language learning process. For example, Naiman et al. report that field independence was the most important predictor of successful performance on the criterion measures for grade 12 students, but was not significant in either grade 8 or 10.

Finally, different results might be obtained if the personality and cognitive style measures were used in different settings with different subjects and different criterion measures. As research continues in Toronto and Michigan, additional light will be shed on these issues.

PERSONAL FACTORS

The final set of psychological factors to be examined are what Schumann and Schumann (1977) and Jones (1977) have called personal factors. These factors were derived from diary accounts of second language learners' sojourns in the target language environment. The diaries document the learners' reactions to the people, culture, and language instruction encountered in the foreign country. The personal factors that have been identified are such things as nesting patterns, transition anxiety, and reaction to pedagogical techniques.

Transition anxiety refers to the emotional discomfort that often accompanies travel from one's home country to the foreign country. It is generated by such tasks as working out itineraries, purchasing tickets, making banking arrangements, closing out one's house, arranging for storage, getting to airports, and negotiating customs, stopovers, and the arrival in the new country. This anxiety can be aggravated by changes in plans and unexpected problems.

During this transition period some learners psychologically embed themselves in the target culture and use their free time to study the target language so that they will be ahead of the game on arrival. Other learners handle transition anxiety by keeping themselves psychologically embedded in their native country. They do this by reading native language magazines, newspapers, books, and by avoiding study of the new language.

Nesting patterns refer to the way the learner settles into his dwelling in the target country. Some learners require that their household be in near perfect order before they can begin to concentrate on learning the language. Others find they can pursue language study regardless of their living conditions. These latter individuals have an advantage in those situations where it takes a good deal of time to locate and settle into new housing.

Another personal factor involves an individual's reaction to language teaching methods which he does not like. Some learners continue studying in the face of such a situation and in addition, attempt to augment the classroom instruction by seeking contact with native speakers or even by eliciting the aid of a tutor. On the other hand, the diary studies have shown that other learners react so negatively when they encounter teaching methods they do not like that they abandon language study completely.

Another way to look at personal factors is to consider them situational variables or "states." In contrast, personality and cognitive style factors might be considered stable "traits" that are part of an individual's psychological makeup and that are carried with him into every temporary situation or state. Future research will have to attempt to determine which are more influential in second language acquisition, trait factors or state factors.

CONCLUSION

Investigation into the sociology and psychology of second language acquisition is still in its infancy. Future work in this area will have to accomplish several things:

(1) it will have to identify and study additional social and psychological variables that have potential influence on second language learning;

(2) through continued experimentation, it will have to eliminate from the taxonomy those variables which are proven to be unimportant in second language learning;

(3) it will have to attempt to determine which are the independent variables and which are the intervening variables in the second language acquisition process. In other words, future research must identify those factors that are more important in that they *cause* second language acquisition and those which are less important in that they simply serve to modify the effects of the causal factors (Paulston, 1977).

To accomplish this, researchers in second language acquisition will have to be as much psychologists and sociologists as they are linguists and educators. The challenge in the field lies in achieving successful integration of these various disciplines.

REFERENCES

Brown, H. D. "Cognitive and Affective Characteristics of Good Language Learners," in C. A. Henning, ed., *Proceedings of the Los Angeles Second Language Research Forum.* Los Angeles: UCLA Department of English (TESL), 1977.

Cohen, A. "Successful Second-Language Speakers: A Review of Research Literature," *Balshanut Shimushit* (The Journal of the Israel Association for Applied Linguistics), 1977, *1*, 3-21.

Gardner, R. C., and W. E. Lambert. *Attitudes and Motivation in Second Language Learning.* Rowley, Mass.: Newbury House, 1972.

Guiora, A. "Construct Validity and Transpositional Research: Toward an Empirical Study of Psychoanalytic Concept," *Comprehensive Psychiatry,* 1972, *13*, 139-150.

Guiora, A., B. Beit-Hallahmi, R. Brannon, C. Dull, and T. Scovel. "The Effects of Experimentally Induced Changes in Ego States on Pronunciation Ability in a Second Language: An Exploratory Study," *Comprehensive Psychiatry,* 1972, *13*, 421-428.

Heyde, A. W. "The Relationship of Self-Esteem to the Oral Production of a Second Language," paper presented at the Eleventh Annual TESOL Convention, Miami Beach, Fla., April 26-May 1, 1977.

Jones, R. A. "Psychological, Social and Personal Factors in Second Language Acquisition," unpublished masters thesis, University of California at Los Angeles, 1977.

Krashen, S. "Formal and Informal Linguistic Environments in Language Learning and Language Acquisition," *TESOL Quarterly,* 1976, *10*, 157-168.

———. "The Monitor Model for Adult Second Language Performance," in M. Burt, H. Dulay, and M. Finocchiaro, eds., *Viewpoints on English as a Second Language.* New York: Regents, 1977a.

———. "Some Issues Relating to the Monitor Model," paper presented at the Eleventh Annual TESOL Convention, Miami Beach, Fla., April 26-May 1, 1977b.

Naiman, N., M. Frolich, and H. H. Stern. *The Good Language Learner.* Modern Language Center, Ontario Institute for Studies in Education, Toronto, Canada, 1978.

Oller, J., L. Baca, and F. Vigil. "Attitudes and Attained Proficiency in ESL: A Sociolinguistic Study of Mexican Americans in the Southwest," *TESOL Quarterly,* 1977, *11*, 173-183.

Paulston, C. B. "Theoretical Perspectives on Bilingual Education Programs," paper presented at the Conference on the Dimensions of Bilingual Education, National Institute of Education, Washington, D.C., Feb. 14-15, 1977.

Rossier, R. E. "Extroversion-introversion: A Significant Variable in the Learning of English as a Second Language," unpublished doctoral dissertation, University of Southern California, 1975.

Schumann, J. H. "Affective Factors and the Problem of Age in Second Language Acquisition," *Language Learning,* 1975a, *25*, 209-235.

———. "Second Language Acquisition: The Pidginization Hypothesis," doctoral dissertation, Harvard University; Rowley, Mass.: Newbury House (in press, 1978); 1975b.

Schumann, J. H. "Second Language Acquisition Research: Getting a More Global Look at the Learner," in H. D. Brown, ed., *Papers in Second Language Learning*. Ann Arbor, Michigan: *Language Learning*, 1976a, special issue no. 4, 15-28.

———. "Social Distance as a Factor in Second Language Acquisition," *Language Learning*, 1976b, *25*, 135-143.

———. "Second Language Acquisition: The Pidginization Hypothesis," *Language Learning*, 1976c, *26*, 391-408.

Schumann, F. M., and J. H. Schumann. "Diary of a Language Learner: An Introspective Study of Second Language Learning," in H. D. Brown, C. A. Yoria, and R. H. Crymes, eds., *Teaching and Learning: Trends in Research and Practice*, (selected papers from the 1977 TESOL Convention). Washington, D.C.: TESOL Georgetown University, 1977.

Stengal, E. "On Learning a New Language," *International Journal of Psychoanalysis*, 1937, *20*, 471-479.

Swain, M. "Future Directions in Second Language Research," in C. A. Henning, ed., *Proceedings of the Los Angeles Second Language Research Forum*. Los Angeles: UCLA Department of English (TESL), 1977.

Tucker, G. R. "Can a Second Language be Taught?" paper presented at the Eleventh Annual TESOL Convention, Miami Beach, Fla., April 26-May 1, 1977.

Tucker, G. R., E. Hamayan, and F. H. Genesee. "Affective, Cognitive, and Social Factors in Second Language Acquisition," *Canadian Modern Language Review*, 1976, *32*, 214-226.

STUDY AND DISCUSSION QUESTIONS

(1) Pick a language contact situation that you are familiar with and discuss the social factors that either promote or inhibit contact between the two groups.

(2) Discuss language shock and culture shock experiences you have had and relate them to your success (or lack of it) in learning the languages involved.

(3) Think about what is involved in learning a second language and then try to speculate about what personality and cognitive style characteristics, other than the ones mentioned in this chapter, might be important in becoming bilingual.

(4) Recall your experience in pursuing a second language and try to think of aspects of the language you *learned* consciously (i.e., through monitoring) and those aspects you *acquired* unconsciously (i.e., without monitoring).

(5) Discuss which factors you think are more important in second language acquisition: trait variables (i.e., personality and cognitive style factors) or state variables (i.e., personal or situational factors).

(6) Examine the taxonomy of factors involved in second language acquisition presented in Table 8-1 and discuss what field you think would provide the best training for a researcher in second language acquisition: sociology, psychology, biology, linguistics, or education.

(7) Write a language learning autobiography which relates your language learning experiences to the social and psychological factors discussed in this chapter.

(8) Those students who are currently studying a foreign language might keep diaries of their reactions to the language, the people who speak it, the teacher, and the method of instruction. The diaries could then be analyzed for personal or situational factors such as those discussed in this chapter.

(9) Through the psychology department at your college or university, obtain personality and cognitive style tests, administer them to your class, and then have the class attempt to determine whether the students who find second language learning easy have different personality and cognitive style profiles than those who find it difficult.

9

THE NATURE OF LANGUAGE TEACHING

Peter Strevens

INTRODUCTION

Acquisition: learning/teaching

This paper is concerned with the nature of institutionalized foreign language learning—the process which takes place when a learner sets out to learn a language other than his primary language (mother tongue or native language), given the mediation of a teacher and within a deliberately organized framework of instruction. The rather cumbersome definition used above is necessary in order to distinguish the language learning/teaching process (LL/LT) from "picking up a language" without formal instruction, whether during the acquisition of the primary language or while subsequently achieving some command of a foreign language by informal and unorganized means.[1]

Is language teaching simply applied psycholinguistics?

Discussion of the effectiveness of language teaching and of ways to improve the achievement of learners has been inhibited in recent years by two hidden assumptions about the applicability to foreign language learning and teaching of psycholinguistic research into first language acquisition and the unstructured picking up of a foreign language. These assumptions are, first, that psycholinguistic research *is* directly relevant to language teaching, and second, that this research is not only relevant but uniquely so: that it is the *most* relevant research and by implication that no other area of knowledge or understanding—certainly not the rather low-valued craft of teaching—is of significance for language teaching. It is no part of the intention of this paper to criticize or to diminish the importance, in their own field, of the principal findings of language acquisition research. A great deal of valuable understanding has been gained through this research, much of which is reflected elsewhere in the chapters of this book. What this chapter will attempt to do, however, is to suggest that the language learning/teaching process is a highly complex set of events in which many elements coexist and interact which have no counterpart in psycholinguistic models of first language acquisition, and that current psycholinguistic theory applies to only a small area of the total field of foreign language learning/teaching. The conclusion will be drawn that perhaps the most relevant and helpful intellectual contribution that can be made to language teaching is the development of models of LL/LT considered *in its own terms*. To rephrase the distinction, first language acquisition and LL/LT belong in different universes of discourse which overlap in only limited ways. To see language teaching as simply applied psycholinguistics is to misunderstand the relationships between a predominantly intellectual activity and a predominantly practical one, and to ignore the immense and subtle complexity of education, methodology, and teaching. Language teaching, too, needs an intellectual basis, but the simple importation of a theory developed in a quite different area does not meet this need.

Can teaching affect learning?

Having stated the stance of this paper to be that the study of the LL/LT process is *sui generis* and not subject to any single external discipline, it is further necessary to state that the basic philosophy of the paper is interventionist, accepting as rational and realistic the proposition that teaching *can* affect learning. There are those who deny this, and who regard the effects of teaching as being either negligible, counterproductive, or uncontrollable; and who in consequence conceive the function of a teacher as being limited to a combination of language informant, attention-getter and pupil-minder. There is indeed a great deal of low-grade language teaching throughout the world, to which these limitations may apply to varying degrees. Many institutionalized programs produce average levels of achievement so low as to invite the criticism that simple contact with speakers of the language might at least do no worse. But the undoubted existence of *inferior* language teaching in no way obscures the existence—equally real, but often overlooked—of *superior* language teaching, in which learners achieve high levels of command of languages in direct response to deliberate schemes of learning and teaching.[2]

The temptation to oversimplify

If it is the case that psycholinguistic research fosters the belief that certain universal human characteristics of first language acquisition are the sole or principal determinants of success in LL/LT, it is also true that the language-teaching profession has similarly regarded its own practices and activities (usually labeled "method" or "methodology") as the principal determinant. From either standpoint, the argument has seemed to lie between a preference for the one or the other, for the intellectual rigor of psycholinguistics, or the humane art of teaching; and this polarization of views has virtually ignored the possibility not only that *both* these features may be important, but that others too may be crucial. Yet close study shows that the process as a whole is complex, not simple, that a number of elements, of very different kinds, have to be taken into account, and that in some cases a shortcoming in one or more of these elements can be largely compensated by unusual excellence in others.

The value of identifying fundamentals

The purpose of identifying elements of the language learning/teaching process is to provide organizing principles for simplifying our thinking about a highly complex event. The test of whether the elements are well chosen is a pragmatic one: do they account for everything that happens in language teaching? Can we allocate to some place in the total scheme of elements all those features of learning and teaching languages that have a bearing on the effectiveness of the process? Does the analysis into elements help us to understand why levels of achievement may be higher in one set of circumstances and lower in another? Will it enable us to identify the major impediments to success and to specify what has to be altered in order to bring about major improvements in language learning/teaching achievements? The main section of this paper attempts to offer a contribution toward these aims.

PRINCIPAL ELEMENTS

Four fundamental divisions

At a high level of generality, the principal components of this analysis[3] are:

The Learner
The Teacher
The Community
The Language Teaching Profession

Having reduced the complexity of LL/LT in this apparently arbitrary way to a mere four main headings, much of the remainder of the paper will be devoted to "recomplexifying" them, so to speak. But before embarking upon a detailed discussion of the contribution which each makes to the whole process, it is necessary to insist that the reduction to four principal components is not just an arbitrary change of scale. On the contrary, the various considerations that are lumped together under the heading of "The Learner," to take an example, are all more closely related to each other than to considerations under other headings, for example those under the heading of "The Community," and so forth. Of course there are marginal cases and interconnections. But the division into four groups of elements does reflect real affinities, as well as reducing the total complexity to a manageably small group of bases.

The ordering of the separate components

Once one expresses these four basic divisions, the question arises whether they are all of equal importance, or whether some are prior to others or in some way more important. In other words, are there any principles for determining a most appropriate ordering of these components?

The superficial answer to such a question depends on one's focus of attention. Thus, a teacher-centered outlook might lead one to begin with "The Teacher"; a sociolinguistic outlook would give priority to "The Community"; a narrowly applied linguistic outlook might concentrate first upon "The Language Teaching Profession." But in this chapter we are considering a *process* (the language learning/teaching process), i.e., a sequence of events during which something gets changed. And in order to account for all the many variable factors which affect the course and effectiveness and nature of the process, a particular sequence of these components seems to impose itself.

If it is the learner who gets changed—if the learner is the focus of the entire process—then it is reasonable to conceive of the total process as concentrating eventually upon that combination of features which characterize The Learner, so that a flow-diagram of the process would lead eventually to The Learner as the final component.

At the other end of the process we can identify the origins of institutionalized language teaching as being sociolinguistic in nature. It is thus The Community which supplies the general social conditions of tolerance, encouragement, and facilitation for learners to be taught. The flow-diagram thus has its terminal conditions established, as seen in Fig. 9-1.

If we are proposing no more than four components in all, and if the first and the fourth are now located, the remaining problem of sequence is to decide which of the two remaining components precedes the other (or whether they should be treated simultaneously rather than in

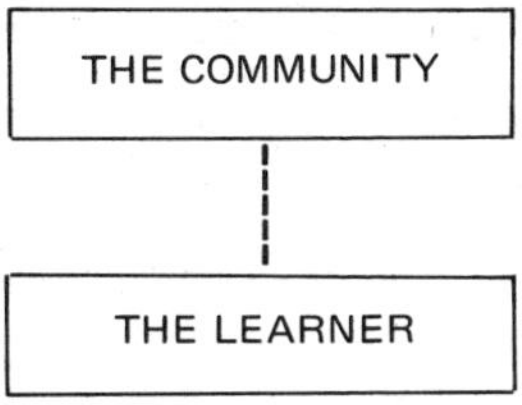

```
┌─────────────────────────┐
│   THE COMMUNITY         │
└─────────────────────────┘
            ┊
┌─────────────────────────┐
│   THE LEARNER           │
└─────────────────────────┘
```

Figure 9-1

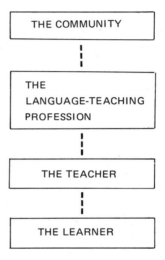

Figure 9-2

sequence). Viewed in this light there appear to be sound reasons for treating The Language Teaching Profession as depending closely upon The Community, and The Teacher as being linked intimately with The Learner. The flow-diagram then becomes as in Fig. 9-2.

This is the sequence of components that will be adopted here, and while it is certainly true that many back-connections exist from later components to earlier ones (for example, the influence which a language learner's degree of success or failure has upon his family and therefore upon the community, by way of creating a climate of higher or lower expectancies of achievement), nevertheless the principal sequence of operations appears to flow in the direction as we have indicated.

The four components of the model
The Community

The organized learning and teaching of languages is essentially social in character. The great majority of teachers are public servants, engaged in the implementation of the public will that tuition in such and such languages shall be made available; they are typically paid by the community, trained at the expense of the community, administered and supported and brigaded by the mediation of a branch of central or local government. Language teaching, in short, is an integral part of a community's total educational provision.

This much is obvious: is it not also banal and trivial? It is a major contention of this paper that beneath the surface banality of the way in which a community organizes its education, including (among many other subjects) foreign language teaching, lie a number of hidden but critical choices, influences, exclusions, preferences, or prejudices.

In order to understand the underlying importance of The Community for language learning it is necessary to distinguish two separate elements within this component:

    (a) the public will

    (b) administration and organization

The first of these, the public will, consists of the current consensus at any time that particular languages should be learned within the community; the second, administration and organization, senses the public will and interprets it by allocating funds, training teachers, providing buildings, and so forth. Looked at in different terms, one aspect of the community's contribution to the overall language learning/ teaching process is the expression of an intention that particular languages should be learned (and therefore taught); the other is to sanction the entire *system* of learning and teaching which brings the learner and the teacher together and encourages or constrains the learner's achievement.

The public will, then, determines in large part which foreign languages are available to learners. Its influence is usually quiescent: it is noticed principally at times of change. When Malaysia, as an act of policy, deliberately adopts Bahasa Malaysia as its national language, the consequences for the learning and teaching of languages in that country are profound and far-reaching. When the people of Quebec elect a pro-French government and understandably seek to redress the anti-French balance in legislation and administration, the consequences for the learning and teaching of languages in the Province turn out to go far beyond the simple promotion of French and to arouse the hostility not only of the English-speaking minority but also the indigenous Indian and Eskimo population, as well as the large communities of European immigrants, for all of whom future prosperity has been equated with learning English, not French. When the European community considers the principal barriers to easy communication and circulation among its members, the consequences for language teaching go beyond the simple favoring of neighboring European languages in existing schools and extend to deliberate, large-scale schemes of systems development in language learning and teaching (Trim, 1973, 1974; Van Ek, 1977).

But equally important as a consequence of the public will is the creation of general levels of expectation, within a community, for the achievement in language learning of its citizens. It is possible to argue that the generally high level of achievement in learning English in Sweden results more from the fulfillment of high public expectations than from a general level of outstandingly good language teaching. (There *are* outstanding teachers, but even in Sweden they are the exception rather than the rule.) People learn English rather well because above all, it can be argued, they take it for granted that they will do so.

Here can be seen at work an interconnection between The Community and The Learner. As we shall see in a later section, the learner's expectations about his own possibilities of achievement form part of the profile of his individuality as a learner, which in turn influences his performance. This feature is frequently lumped together under the catchall heading of *motivation*: the learner's willingness to learn a language, his reasons for giving time and effort to the learning task, his perception of the benefit he will gain from doing so—all these are affected in a fundamental way by the attitudes, prejudices, fashions, and intentions which make up the sociolinguistic situation in the community to which he belongs: i.e., the public will.

The existence of the second subcategory, administration and organization, is a recognition of the fact that language teaching, like the provision for tuition in any other subject, is totally dependent upon a "ministry of education" or its equivalent. Yet this is a double-edged blessing. On the one hand the bureaucratic structure for employing teachers and organizing schools and classes puts education onto a footing of large-scale organization, while the provision of training facilities and the development of a career-long progression of events and stages attracts suitable people to teaching and retains them once they have been inducted. To that extent this element of administration provides the almost indispensable framework of organization within which learners and teachers come into contact with each other. Yet on the other hand some aspects of the very system which creates opportunities for learning and teaching may make it difficult or impossible for either learning, teaching, or both, to take place at all—or at least to do so effectively.

Examples of this paradoxical situation are easy to find. They include overcrowded classes, low standards of teacher recruitment, lack of provision of books and materials, the creation of "examination neurosis" under the guise of achievement testing, and many more.

Earlier in this paper we mentioned the existence of inferior as well as superior language learning and teaching. It is unfortunately the case that the differences between the two extremes very often rest on features of administration and organization: in the inferior case, adequate teaching and learning are frustrated by faults in the system; in the superior case, merely adequate teaching and learning are enhanced by a high-quality system.

It seems to be the situation in many parts of the world that the great progress in language-teaching professionalism which has taken place in recent years has not been assimilated into the administrative and organizational framework of general education within which language teaching exists as one "subject" among many.[4] Thus language teaching is offered as if all that the teachers know about carrying it out with maximum effectiveness is what their predecessors knew, 70 or 100 years ago, when the subject was first incorporated into organized education. In other words, there is frequently insufficient interaction between the administrative element of The Community and the next component to which we shall turn, The Language Teaching Profession.

The Language Teaching Profession

The term "profession" is here used in two distinct but complementary ways. First, it relates to those disciplines, in the academic or quasi-academic sense, which contribute to our understanding of the nature of language learning and teaching—i.e., linguistics, psychology, educational theory, social theory, scientific method, principles of educational technology, etc.—and which are "available," so to speak, in broadly similar ways throughout the world by way of universities, research institutes, and similar centers of intellectual activity. But second, the term profession also relates to those principles by which teachers of language organize themselves, select the succeeding generations of their fellows, set entry standards (e.g., of age, personal education, character, etc.), insist upon special training for entrants to the profession, support their colleagues throughout their careers, study continually to raise the level of effectiveness of that which they do, and above all, maintain the ethic of social responsibility and devotion to the interests of their pupils (Strevens, 1978).

It is essential to realize that we are discussing a profession—an *industry* might almost be a more appropriate term—of truly immense size. Millions of language teachers teach scores of millions of language learners, distributed the world over. Within this occupational community of some millions of teachers there exists a large subset comprising those who are responsible for standards of teacher training, for awareness of relevant developments in other disciplines and other places, for the promotion of research, for the continued drive toward greater effectiveness—in short, for the intellectual basis and the evolutionary drive of the profession.

Of course, all members of this subset are not located in one place or one country. They are found spread among the staff of many training colleges, university departments, research centers and specialized institutes, in many countries. They have their own networks of information, cross-fertilization, visits, exchanges, publications, etc. Their function, essentially, is to mediate between the contributory disciplines on the one hand, and the practical tasks and problems of the language teaching classroom on the other.

Two observations are required here: in the first place, the contributory disciplines, necessary though they are for the profession in its broadest sense, do not in themselves provide a sufficient basis for ensuring the effective learning and teaching of languages. It is perfectly possible for an individual teacher to be exceptionally successful in encouraging optimum learning in his or her pupils without ever having heard of linguistics or even psychology, let alone having studied these subjects. For the learner, an awareness of the disciplines is even less directly relevant to his progress in learning a foreign language. What *is* essential, however, is that the profession as a whole should possess, distributed in an appropriate way through its various levels, a sufficient number of members with interest in and understanding of the *why* of their profession, not just the *what* and *how*.

The second observation is that there is a distinction to be made between *professionalism* and *instructional techniques*. Of course techniques are a part of being professional, but they are not the whole of it. It is possible to discern three different stages of language teaching activity (Strevens, 1978). The first is that of the *instructor*, who is able to manipulate the techniques of language instruction, who knows the course-books and materials in use for his particular pupils, and who presents the foreign language material with adequate competence to his or her students. The second is that of the *teacher*, who is a good instructor and more. The good teacher cherishes his pupils, knows them, understands their individuality as learners, recognizes their learning preferences and their difficulties, and sees their language learning progress on a time-scale greater than simply that of the class, the week, the semester, or the year. The third is that of the *educator*, who is a good teacher, but whose perspective is wider, who thinks of the students in relation to the whole of their needs for tuition and training, and who is aware of the interrelations between the techniques of language teaching, the contributory disciplines, and the needs of society.

It is a feature of the tremendous rise in professionalism in the past 15 years that language teaching now provides suitable training and encouragement for all its members to become competent as instructors, for the majority to become competent and caring as teachers, and for a sufficient proportion to become language educators, capable of maintaining and extending the intellectual basis and the practical effectiveness of language teaching, and of meeting new needs for language learning with innovative, appropriate, principled, acceptable, and successful responses.

The Teacher

Each of the two main components already touched upon, The Community and The Profession, are reductions from great complexity to a single mnemonic label. So it is, too, with The Teacher. It is here that nearly all aspects of teaching, as a deliberate activity, will be included, so that under the heading "The Teacher" it becomes necessary to consider at least the following elements:

(a)   the teacher

minimum qualities of a teacher

teacher training (see also (b))

upkeep of command of the foreign language and upgrading of professionalism

(b)   teacher training

criteria for selection

components of *skills, information, theory*

initial training, further training, "higher echelon" training (including applied linguistics)

(c)   teaching

approach: particular philosophies or ideologies or myths of language-learning/teaching

methodology: the full range of techniques for promoting effective learning

syllabus design: principles for deciding what to teach, in which sequence, and how organized

materials production: principles for creating suitable ancillaries

testing

selection of teaching type

(d)   constraints on teaching/learning effectiveness

physical impediments: fatigue, extremes of temperature, overcrowding, distraction

organizational impediments: insufficient total time for instruction, too much time, insufficient intensity, lack of premises, materials, and staff, absenteeism

psychological impediments: negative social attitudes, examination neuroses, intimidating teacher-pupil relationships

It will be obvious that this component of our analysis is extremely complex, and each of the four elements within it merits a chapter—indeed, a book—to itself.[5] Here we shall confine ourselves to a brief explanatory comment on each element of the component labeled The Teacher, which incorporates not only the characteristics of the teacher but also the training and preparation for the task, the whole gamut of instructional procedures, and those features which diminish the effectiveness of learning and teaching.

(a)   The Teacher: Again we must notice an ambiguity. In the widest sense, the teacher is the human agency responsible for presenting foreign language material to a learner. He or she may be either physically present (as in the conventional case of a teacher working with a class or group), or, in the case of self-study courses, embodied within the handbook and possibly in accompanying recordings, or, in computer-assisted instruction, known to the learner only through instructions he receives as to his optimum learning procedures. Many other manifestations of the teacher are possible in this metaphorical use of the term, referring to the progenitor and/or presenter of learning material. The other sense of the word "teacher" is the technical and professional one which distinguishes between individuals whose capabilities merit the label and those who do not. In this sense, a teacher is identified by the possession of certain characteristics which affect his ability to perform as a language teacher.

Cutting through the great range of possible specialized abilities, an absolute minimum statement of the requirements of an adequate language teacher might be the following (see also Perren, 1968, and Strevens, 1974, 1977b):

a nondiscouraging personality

adequate classroom command of the language being taught

adequate presentational skills as a teacher

In addition to these minimum requirements for any given individual teacher, the sound continuation of the profession requires that the majority of teachers should also possess and display dedication to learning in general and to language learning in particular. This entails two parallel and continuous lines of concern: first, a high degree of awareness of the learners as individuals, of their progress and difficulties, and of the best means at any time of promoting their continued learning; and second, a high degree of self-awareness as a teacher, including conscious efforts to improve his or her command of the foreign language (or at the very least, taking steps to counter the gradual attrition in one's foreign language ability that normally occurs with the passage of time), and seeking always to extend and improve the grasp and understanding of the profession by keeping in touch with changing ideas and techniques.

(b)   Teacher Training: Teachers being, by definition, among the educated rather than the uneducated members of society, the selection and training of language teachers necessarily includes attention to the individual teacher's personal education, as well as his or her professional training, and ideally should include a measure of temperamental suitability and of a sense of vocation, difficult though these criteria are to identify.

The vocational and professional aspects of teacher training must depend for the detail of their design upon who the trainees are and in what circumstances they will be employed. But a few general principles can be adduced. First, there is a difference in kind between *initial training*, in which the aspirant is first introduced to the nature of the profession, and all *further training*.

Second, within initial training there are two main streams of content: (1) general training as a teacher, irrespective of any particular subject specialty, and (2) special training as a teacher of a specified foreign language. These are usually combined in a single multifaceted course, but both are normally present.

Third, initial training will deal with an appropriate mixture— appropriate, that is, to the prior education of the trainee, the level and type of educational establishment the trainee expects to be employed in, the duration and intensity of the training course, and the available competencies within the training staff—of the three basic components of vocational training: a component of *practical skills*, a component of relevant *information*, and a component of *principle and theory*. Achieving the best mixture in a given training institution is a difficult task. But the difficulty generally centers around the ratio of *skills* to *theory*. Too little theory, and a teaching force is created which can perform well in the classroom but lacks the understanding to change with the times and to cope with new conditions. Too much theory, and the teaching force may become separated from the practical demands of the learners, or prove to follow pseudointellectual fashions.

A fourth general principle of teacher training provides a possible solution to the difficulty of getting the mixture right: ideally, all teachers should receive the chance of *further* training, either in the form of "in-service" training, or by being withdrawn from teaching in order to be given additional full-time training, not just once but at suitable intervals throughout their careers. If such opportunities are available, additional training in principle and theory can be provided for those whose professional work especially requires it, and for those whose personal abilities can best assimilate and utilize it, while at the same time *all* teachers can keep up with new ideas, share their experience, consider the future, and in general give a professional dynamism to language teaching.

It is interesting to observe that in recent years the teaching of English as a foreign language has gone further than the teaching of French, German, or most other languages, both in the nature of its provision of further training and in the numbers of teachers who are enabled and encouraged to take advantage of this provision. In Britain, for example, each year since about 1970 roughly 150 qualified, graduate teachers, each with about five years of teaching experience, have taken one-year higher-degree courses of further training, described as "M.A. in Applied Linguistics," "M.A. in English and Linguistics," "M.A. in TEFL," or some equivalent label. These are the individuals who become language advisers, inspectors, syllabus designers, team leaders—they constitute a high and growing proportion of the upper echelon of the profession.

But more than numbers is involved. The crucial feature of these courses has been their content, and above all the high intellectual level at which much of the content is offered. Typically, these courses of further training assume the prior possession of sound initial training together with solid practical experience of teaching. They then offer a range of subjects, including advanced work in methodology and practical aspects of language learning and teaching, but also including the opportunity of becoming familiar with relevant work in linguistics, psycholinguistics, sociolinguistics, educational theory, experimental design, test construction—in short, the contributory disciplines referred to during our discussion of The Profession. It is this amalgam of relevant work in all the contributory disciplines that is usually referred to, in Britain, as *applied linguistics* (Allen and Corder, 1973; Strevens, 1977b; Corder and Roulet, 1973; Wilkins, 1972).[6]

The point at issue here concerns the importance within teacher training of further training, and especially of provision for sufficient language teachers to receive training for the higher echelons of the profession. In the teaching of English as a foreign language such provision has existed for over a decade: the teaching of other foreign languages tends to suffer by comparison, and will continue to do so until additional advanced further training can be provided for teachers of those languages, too.

(c)   Teaching: This is the element which has received the greatest amount of attention in the past. As was noted earlier, teachers have been inclined to assume that it was exclusively, or at least principally, those variables which they controlled that had the greatest influence upon learners' achievement. It is not the intention of this paper to suggest that teaching is unimportant, but rather to point out that its importance is not unique, and that teachers need to be aware of many other factors in the total language learning/teaching process.

Since so much attention has been paid to this area, we shall confine ourselves here to a brief justification of the subdivisions it seems necessary to make.

(1)   Approach: Beginning with the most general consideration, language teaching from time to time throws up sets of integrated, interrelated ideas, philosophies, techniques, and possibly also materials. Examples are: direct method, audiolingual method, cognitive code teaching. An ideological set of concepts of this kind can be called an "approach." (It must be stressed that the effective learning and teaching of languages is not dependent upon adherence to any approach, still less to one particular approach rather than any other.) The principal effect of an approach is to concentrate enthusiasm and energy: it is concerned with polemics, propaganda, and politics, rather than with pedagogy *tout pur*.

The next two elements within this component of The Teacher require a word of prior explanation. Until recently the single term "method" (e.g., Mackey, 1965) has been used to refer simultaneously to criteria for organizing the content of teaching courses and the teaching techniques for presenting them. However, so much intellectual effort has been applied to the first of these in recent years, with such far-reaching results, that it has become essential to recognize "syllabus" as an essential category in its own right, distinct from "methodology."

(2)   Syllabus. One stage closer to the learner than approach, then, is the syllabus. More accurately, it is *principles of syllabus design* that we are concerned with. Ever since it became the accepted doctrine among language teachers that the effectiveness of learning can be significantly improved by manipulating the *content* and the *sequence* of what is taught, there have been devised a series of refinements and of additional sets of criteria. From *linguistic* to *situational* to *notional/functional* to *communicative* syllabuses, the sophistication has lately increased dramatically (Wilkins, 1976). This is an area in which the relevant disciplines, especially through the synthesis of applied linguistics, have recently made and continue to make important contributions. It is also the area in which the general trend in education toward learner-centered instruction has the greatest impact, particularly in the form of "special-purpose" language teaching (Strevens, 1977c) and various types of individualization.

(3)   Methodology. Within this main component of the total process, methodology or method has usually seemed to be the most obviously central element, embracing as it does the whole range of presentational techniques, learning/teaching tactics and instructional procedures. It is worth noting, however, that two distinct though related types of activity are included under the heading of methodology. One of these consists of the techniques, procedures, tactics, etc., for deliberately promoting learning; the other concerns relationships between learner and teacher, and especially those activities on the part of the teacher which are calculated to influence and improve the learner's attitudes toward learning and toward the teacher. It is a feature of recent developments in language teaching that the importance of the learner's attitudes toward his task and toward his teacher has been given greater recognition, and that teaching methods have been devised which concentrate upon the establishment of helpful learning attitudes. This aspect of methodology is the principal feature of The Silent Way, Community Language Learning, and even Suggestopedia.

(4)   Materials. The function of this subdivision of The Teacher is difficult to assess, not only because of the sheer diversity of course books, readers, workbooks, reference works, flashcards, wallcharts, recordings, films, filmstrips, videotapes, etc., but also because in any given teaching/learning situation it is the relation and interaction between the materials actually used, the syllabus being followed, and the professional ability of the teachers which is important. In some circumstances, materials can have a teacher-training function in addition to their contribution to the teaching task; in other situations they may enable highly trained teachers to present courses of great sophistication; or they may simply be pedagogical extras chosen almost casually from the great range of the publishers' lists. Whatever their function in a particular case, there is no doubt that "materials" constitutes an important element of The Teacher.

(5)   Testing. Any process that is being deliberately carried out requires a continual supply of information about how far the process has gone, how effectively it is being achieved, what deficiencies it may contain. In the case of language learning and teaching, this information is supplied through testing, both formal and informal. At the extreme of informality, testing is barely distinguishable as a separate element of teaching, since a great many exercises and techniques of instruction incorporate ways for the teacher (and the learner) to check whether that which was taught has been learned, or that which was learned has been accurately and adequately assimilated. At the extreme of formality, as a device for measuring achievement or progress, testing becomes in addition—or instead—a piece of social administration, identifying the learner as having "passed" or "failed," as meriting (or not meriting) promotion or acceptance for some purpose quite distinct from that of language learning. Between these extremes there exists a growing array of techniques for testing the whole range of language activities. Against the convenience and advantage of the new availability of tests of various kinds must be set the very real danger that teachers may confuse testing with teaching, may use simple testing techniques as if they were equally effective in teaching, and may spend so much time on testing that teaching (and, more important, learning) flies out the window.

(6)   Selection of Teaching Type. Teachers of languages often fail to recognize that different teaching takes place according to certain dimensions or variables. The kind of difference that occurs is

sometimes methodological, sometimes out of pace and intensity, sometimes a question of entire pedagogical outlook. These variables are:

Pupil age: different teaching is appropriate to *young children, adolescents,* and *adults*

Level of proficiency: different teaching is appropriate for *beginners, intermediate* level, and *advanced* level learners

Educational framework: different teaching is required in a context of *general education,* or *acquiring a practical command,* "culture-free," and of *special-purpose* learning, e.g., vocational or educational ends

Learner volition: different teaching may sometimes be appropriate, depending on whether the learner is a *volunteer* or a *nonvolunteer*

Language of instruction: different teaching is required if the foreign language instruction is carried out—the *mother tongue,* or in the *target language* itself, or in some *other foreign language.*

Target language status: different teaching is indicated depending on whether the language being learned has the status, in the situation where it is being learned, of a *second language* or a *foreign language*

The expression "teaching type" is used here in order to suggest that these six variables each have different values in particular situations, and that therefore the most appropriate teaching for any given situation is indicated by a profile along these six variables (Strevens, 1977b).

(7) Constraints on Teaching/Learning Effectiveness. Accompanying all organized language learning is the potentiality for the effectiveness of the process to be constrained or restricted by impediments, which may be of three kinds: *physical, organizational* or *psychological.* Physical impediments include the obvious ones of fatigue and extremes of heat or cold; it is necessary also to guard against the constant distractions that sometimes occur in schools and against overcrowding, which not only reduces the available share of teacher-attention per pupil, but also frequently produces real physical discomforts and distractions.

Organizational impediments—frequently imposed by educational administrators many years ago and subsequently accepted as if they were unchallengeable facts of life—relate above all to the quantity and intensity of tuition. There is a good deal of shared experience in the language teaching profession to suggest that within broad limits the rate of learning per hour of instruction improves with greater intensity; and also that while it is obviously true that enough total time of instruction has to be provided in order for the learner to reach any particular goal, it may well be the case that some school language courses spend too many years on too little content, thereby virtually ensuring low standards of achievement. Other organizational impediments include the lack of premises, books or equipment, or suitable staff; absenteeism of students or staff is yet another way in which faults in organization can reduce the effectiveness of teaching.

This concludes the summary of the four elements which make up this major component, The Teacher. We now come to the last, yet in some ways the most important component, The Learner. In it we shall consider what contribution the learner brings to the learning/teaching process. We shall also deal with the psychological makeup of the learner and the fact that sometimes there are impediments of a psychological nature that reflect negative social attitudes (for example, learners do not find it easy to learn, and teachers find it difficult to teach a language which is unpopular in the community). Or a teacher and a learner may develop strong likes or dislikes for each other that get in the way of learning. Or anxieties about examinations may have a similar effect.

The Learner
The essence of this component is the fact that every learner of a foreign language is an individual, with his own profile of characteristics that mark him as different from all other learners, even though he obviously also shares the universal characteristics of all humans. Research in psycholinguistics has tended to concentrate (though with notable exceptions: see especially Tucker, 1976 and Schumann, 1978) upon the universals. What the teacher notices and, indeed, what the teacher has to work with when teaching is the individuality.

Learners differ in a large number of ways (Strevens, 1977b) which can be loosely divided into two groups.

> *Group 1:* age; *willingness* to give time and effort to learning; *special language abilities* (a "good ear," superior talent at mimicry, a good verbal memory, etc.); *learning stamina* over a long period; *previous linguistic experience,* (a) in the mother tongue (e.g., whether literate or not, what command of different varieties, etc.), (b) in other foreign languages including the extent to which these are cognate with the language currently being learned; *general educational experience.*

> *Group 2: personal optimum learning rate; preferred learning styles* or strategies; *minimum success-need; self-view as a language learner,* including level of expectations of success; *relations with teachers.*

Group 1 contains, on the whole, "givens" with which the teacher must come to terms; Group 2, on the other hand, contains qualities within which the management of learning (another name for teaching) can be manipulated by a skilled teacher to produce the best possible result. Indeed, it is a partial definition of a good teacher that he or she is capable of identifying the profile of qualities of each learner, and of so conducting the management of learning that each individual achieves as nearly as possible his own optimum rate of language learning.

We have now completed a brief outline of the four fundamental components of the language learning/teaching process. In the remaining section of the paper we shall consider commonly occurring reasons for failure in learning languages, as well as common conditions for success, and we shall relate them to the four-component model already described.

FAILURE AND SUCCESS IN LEARNING AND TEACHING LANGUAGES

Variability of achievement

The terms "failure" and "success" are relative: they make sense only in relation to the degree of achievement of particular aims and goals. The important point, however, is that teachers and learners alike observe the existence of variability in achievement, while the teachers' experience goes a stage further and recognizes a number of factors to be commonly associated with greater or less achievement respectively.[7]

(a)   Factors commonly associated with below-average achievement:

(1)   unwilling learners

(2)   low expectations of success

(3)   unattainable aims and objectives

(4)   unsuitable syllabus (or no syllabus)

(5)   confusion between language learning and the study of literature (or, more recently, linguistics)

(6)   physical organizational and psychological shortcomings

(7)   insufficient or excessive time or intensity of tuition

(8)   poor materials not compensated by good teachers

(9)   inadequate teacher training

(10)   incompetent class teaching and lack of interest in learners

(b) Factors commonly associated with above-average achievement:

(1) willing learners

(2) high expectations of success

(3) realistic and attainable aims

(4) suitable syllabus

(5) competent organization of teaching/learning situation

(6) sufficient time, not excessive, at reasonably high rate of intensity

(7) helpful materials

(8) teachers adequately trained

(9) teachers display professionalism and devotion to learners

Analysis of failure and success

We should now recall the four basic components of our theoretical model of the process and consider the origins of below-average achievement.

C   The Community

P   The Profession

T   The Teacher

L   The Learner

Origins of "failure"

(1) Unwilling learners. Poor learning (or even no learning at all) takes place when the learner is unwilling to give time, effort, and attention to the task. In the first instance, then, the responsibility for low achievement lies with the learner. Sometimes the reasons for unwillingness are trivial, and can be partly or wholly countered by tactful cajoling on the part of the teacher. Sometimes the unwillingness stems from social attitudes which defy the teacher's best efforts.

L

(2) Low expectations of success. This obstacle to learning is very often personal to the learner, who may have persuaded himself or been persuaded by family or friends that he will not do well. But sometimes there is a national myth, shared by the community that, for example, "The English can't learn foreign languages." The skillful teacher can do a good deal to overcome these low expectations, for instance by simple demonstrations of personal success in learning.

L

(3) Unattainable aims and objectives. In some countries, the officially promulgated syllabus or program supposes the imparting

C of skill in the spoken language, to a high standard by the end of 10 or 12 years, whereas in fact the majority of teachers lack the command of the spoken language necessary for the achievement of these aims, and everyone accepts a very low terminal standard of achievement. Responsibility for this rests principally with the community, in that the public will is being incompetently put into practice. But as the sophistication of the profession and of individual teachers increases, so it becomes more and more a part of their duty to recognize where the defect lies and to press for the necessary changes to be brought in.

P (4) Confusion of aims. Where learners are taught what is basically a course in literary texts or in linguistic theory, in the expectation that they will thereby acquire adequate command of the foreign language, it is basically the profession that is at fault, for having misled the community's administration of education, though the same reservation about the growing responsibility of the teachers also applies here.

C (5) Physical, organization, and psychological shortcomings. In the majority of cases, these obstacles are squarely the responsibility of the community—that is to say, of the administration and organization of education.

C (6) Insufficient or excessive time or intensity. Again, it is almost always the community's administrators of education who lay down procedures for allocating tuition time to particular subjects. Yet even here, as more teachers are trained for the higher echelons, their responsibility grows for pointing out ways of improving the situation.

T (7) Poor materials not compensated by good teachers. This stems chiefly from inadequate standards of teacher training, though the profession can play a part in encouraging the community's administrators to initiate action on both fronts: the preparation of better materials and the improvement of teacher training.

C (8) Inadequate teacher training. Usually this is due to the community's servants not being able to obtain enough money to improve matters. Taking a worldwide view, enough understanding and experience now exist, within the profession and among individual teachers at the advanced level, to be able to specify immediate action that would produce drastic improvements.

T
(9) Incompetent class teaching and lack of interest in the learners. Here the teachers are squarely at fault; the community and the profession between them need to organize for change.

Conditions for "success"

We are now in a position to use the four-component model of the nature of the learning process to suggest how possibilities of high achievement can be maximized.

But success cannot be absolutely *predicted*, any more than failure can, by the simple presence of one factor or group of factors. Almost the only absolute statements that one can make are, first, that unwilling learners are unlikely to learn while, conversely, willing learners are likely to learn well; and second, that enough learning time must be provided. In most other respects excellence in one area can compensate for inadequacy in another, while major hindrances in one area can largely nullify excellence elsewhere.

Where then can we confidently expect to find success? Each of our components need to be included, since the overall process involves them all, in suitable interaction.

> The Community: the community needs to have positive attitudes toward a particular language (or the society and culture of those who use it); in addition, it needs to be served by an administration which encourages, in a professionally understanding way, the creation of a helpful learning/teaching system, free from gross impediments.

> The Profession: the language teaching profession needs to provide its teachers with support of all kinds: information, access to the contributory disciplines, a network of centers of excellence, etc.

> The Teacher: the teacher needs adequate training (including a sufficiently large higher echelon), suitable syllabuses and materials, helpful testing arrangements, and above all to display devotion toward his or her pupils.

> The Learner: the learner needs to be a *willing* learner, and to give the necessary time, effort, and social collaboration to the task.

Willing learners, devoted and well-prepared teachers, support from the profession and from the community. These would seem to be the fundamental ingredients to success. Many teachers will comment that there is nothing surprising in that. But the intention of this paper has been to show, first, that behind and beyond the obvious truths lies a set of interrelationships of great complexity, and second, that teachers and the profession now understand a great deal about the total process, and therefore we now bear a new responsibility for ensuring that changes are made, improvements are sought, and failure (where it habitually occurs) is no longer tolerated but is replaced by success.

NOTES

1. In an important paper, Lamendella (1977) points out the need for distinguishing between "... *primary language acquisition* and two distinct types of *nonprimary language acquisition: secondary language acquisition* and *foreign language learning.*" Lamendella's arguments are adduced from general principles of neurofunctional organization.

2. Lamendella's 1977 article cited in Note 1 equates *Foreign Language Learning* with "... a tedious process ..." whose end-product is the possession of "... only rudimentary communicative abilities in real-world situations." The existence of high-grade learning/teaching is nowhere mentioned.

3. In a previous paper (Strevens 1977a) I have referred to only three elements: learner, teacher, system. But using the label "system" obscures a crucial distinction between that part of the total circumstances which depends upon society and that part which depends upon the worldwide profession of language teaching. Hence my preference here for a four-part analysis.

4. It is one of the great achievements of the Culture Learning Institute of the East-West Center, in Hawaii, that they have offered for several years courses designed specifically for educational administrators responsible for English-language education in South-East Asia, Japan, and the South Pacific. See also Beeby (1966).

5. Mackey (1965) is a pioneer work in analyzing the great range and complexity of language teaching in its modern forms. See also the important contributions of Rivers (1964 and 1968) and of Tucker (1976).

6. It is interesting to observe that when theoretical concerns become central, direct relevance to language teaching diminishes. The possession of a Ph.D. in *theoretical* linguistics, for example, important though it may be for linguistics, is but rarely capable of making a useful contribution to advanced work in the learning and teaching of languages. Too much linguistics is too much, in this context; and linguistics alone is not enough. Hence the observable value of "applied linguistics," which brings together selected (relevant) portions of *all* the disciplines concerned.

7. These considerations are discussed in greater detail in Strevens (1977a); they also form a central theme in this author's forthcoming book, *Conditions for Success in Language Teaching*, Oxford University Press, 1979.

REFERENCES

Allen, J. P. B., and S. P. Corder, eds. *The Edinburg Course in Applied Linguistics*, 4 Vols. London: Oxford University Press, 1973-1977.

Beeby, C. E. *The Quality of Education in Developing Countries.* Harvard, 1966.

Corder, S. P. *Introducing Applied Linguistics.* London: Penguin, 1973.

Corder, S. P., and E. Roulet, eds. *Linguistic Insights in Applied Linguistics.* Brussells, AIMAV, and Paris, Didier, 1973.

Lamendella, John T. "General Principles of Neurofunctional Organization and their Manifestation in Primary and Nonprimary Language Acquisition," *Language Learning,* 1977, *27,* 155-196.

Larsen-Freeman, D., and V. Strom. "The Construction of a Second Language Acquisition Index of Development," *Language Learning,* 1977, *1,* 123-134.

Mackey, William F. *Language Teaching Analysis.* London: Longman, 1965.

Perren, G. E., ed. *Teachers of English as a Second Language: their Training and Preparation.* Cambridge University Press, 1968.

Rivers, W. M. *The Psychologist and the Foreign Language Teacher.* University of Chicago Press, 1964.

———. *Teaching Foreign Language Skills.* University of Chicago Press, 1968.

Schumann, J. "Affective and Social Factors in Second Language Learning," *Foreign Language Annals* (in press).

Strevens, Peter. "Some Basic Principles of Teacher Training," *ELT Journal, XXIX,* No. 1, 1974. London: Oxford University Press, 19-27.

———. "A Theoretical Model of the Language Learning/Teaching Process," *Working Papers in Bilingualism, N. 11.* Toronto: O.I.S.E., 1976, 129-152. (A revised version of this paper appears in Strevens, 1977b.)

———. "Causes of Failure and Conditions for Success in the Learning and Teaching of Languages," in D. Brown, ed., *On TESOL 77.* TESOL, Washington, D.C., 1977a.

———. *New Orientations in the Teaching of English.* London: Oxford University Press, 1977b.

———. "Special-Purpose Language Learning: A Perspective," *Language Teaching and Linguistics: Abstracts. 10,* No. 3, 1977c, 145-163.

———. "From the Classroom to the World; from Student to Citizen, from Teacher to Educator," *Foreign Language Annals,* 1978 (in press).

Trim, J. L. *Draft Outline for a European Unit/Credit System for Modern Language Learning by Adults.* Strasbourg: Council of Europe, 1973.

———. "A Unit/Credit System for Adult Language Learning," in G. Perren, ed., *Teaching Languages to Adults for Special Purposes.* CILT Reports and Papers No. 11, London, 1974.

Tucker, G. R. *Cross Disciplinary Perspectives in Bilingual Education: A Linguistic Review Paper.* Arlington, Va.: Center for Applied Linguistics, 1976.

Van Ek, J. *The Threshold Level.* Strasbourg: Council of Europe, 1975.

Wilkins, D. A. *Notional Syllabuses.* London: Oxford University Press, 1976.

STUDY AND DISCUSSION QUESTIONS

(1) Discuss the similarities and differences between:
    (a) first language acquisition
    (b) "picking up" a foreign language
    (c) learning a foreign language with the aid of a teacher.

(2) What examples are known to you of (a) superior language learning and teaching; (b) inferior language learning and teaching? Consider possible reasons, using the categories employed in this chapter.

(3) List the languages commonly taught in your community. Are any of them higher valued than others? Are any languages taught which are low valued (unpopular)? Discuss the differences (a) for the learner, (b) for the teacher, in the teaching of low valued as compared with high valued languages.

(4) What machinery exists in your community for enabling language teachers to become aware of relevant work in linguistics, psycholinguistics, sociolinguistics, applied linguistics, educational theory, experimental design, testing?

(5) To what extent are educational administrators (including inspectors and educational officials) in your community aware of modern developments in language learning and teaching? Could teachers do more to help administrators to be up-to-date in these areas?

(6) Consider the training of language teachers in your community. In the light of current experience, do you regard *initial* training as being satisfactory? What consequential changes would your proposals entail for the training institutions? Now consider *further* training in the same light.

(7) How far have developments in syllabus design been reflected in the language courses known to you?

(8) Turn to the discussion of constraints on the effectiveness of learning and teaching (pp. 198-199). How many of those mentioned exist in the teaching system within your experience? What action would be needed in order to bring about improvements? Have teachers (or others) attempted to make changes? Can you identify the obstacles to change? What can be done about them?

(9) In the discussion of reasons for failure (p. 197) how many of these listed are familiar to you? How could they be remedied?

(10) Consider the conditions for success (p. 198). Which of these are present in your own experience? Draw up your own list of qualities and abilities for a good teacher, in your own circumstances.

$$======== 10 ========$$

THE IMPLEMENTATION OF
LANGUAGE TEACHING PROGRAMS[1]

G. Richard Tucker

During the past decade there has occurred both at home and abroad a great deal of research, theorizing, and discussion about various facets of language learning and language teaching. The continuing dialogue has involved at various times parents, educators, researchers, and even policy makers at the highest levels. This really should not seem surprising considering the fact that there are many more bilinguals in the world than monolinguals and that there are many more students who by choice or by necessity attend schools where the medium of instruction is their second or later-acquired language than who attend schools taught in their mother tongues.

In recent years, the topic of second language learning and teaching has attracted the attention of an increasing number of researchers drawn from a wide range of academic disciplines. In addition to educators concerned with discovering and applying new and better pedagogical techniques, we now find an active group of anthropologists, linguists, psychologists, and sociologists engaged in the systematic study of the complex interplay among affective, cognitive, social, and other factors in second language acquisition.

A number of scholars have proposed useful models or frameworks within which we can examine questions related to second language learning and teaching (see, for example, Fox, 1975; Paulston, 1974; Schumann, 1976a; Strevens, 1976). I believe that we can usefully

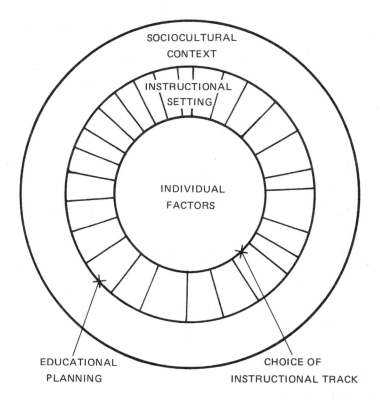

Figure 10-1   Context for Language Learning and Teaching

represent the domain graphically by using three concentric circles (see Fig. 10-1). The outermost represents the *sociocultural* context—the ambiance in which the language is spoken natively, in which it is to be learned as a second or foreign language and is to be used for diverse purposes. It comprises elements such as (1) the official position and allocated role(s) of the target language in the community, nation, or region; (2) the perceived status of the language and its speakers; (3) the existence of structures which encourage or facilitate the use of the target language; (4) the size and cohesiveness of the groups in contact; and

(5) the correspondence between their values, attitudes, and traditions (cf., Schumann, 1976b).

The middle circle represents the *instructional* or pedagogical setting—the context in which the language is to be "formally" transmitted from a teacher or other resource person to the learner. Salient components at this level are factors such as (1) the goals, whether explicit or implicit for second language teaching; (2) the pedagogical techniques to be employed (I am going to restrict my remarks for the most part to second language learning which goes on within the confines of a classroom since one of the other papers in this collection alludes to issues posed by informal learning); (3) the design of the syllabus including the choice or development and sequencing of materials and the allocation of time; (4) the training and language proficiency of the teacher as well as the attitudes of teachers and administrators; and (5) the procedures for evaluation. The interface between these two circles is effected by educational planning within the context of national or regional priorities.

The innermost circle represents *individual* factors. The second language learner brings with him to the learning environment a variety of attitudes, biological predispositions, learned behaviors, and societal experiences that affect the course, the duration, and the speed of second language learning. Important factors at this level may be elements such as (1) age; (2) intelligence and language aptitude; (3) learning style or the general cognitive processes drawn upon; (4) personality characteristics; and (5) motivation and attitude. The interface between the innermost and the middle circle is effected when the learner by choice or by necessity begins to follow one of a large variety of instructional tracks. (The components or elements that I have identified at each level are, of course, only illustrative; they are by no means exclusive.)

We will now briefly consider the contributions or relationships among some of the factors or elements of the three concentric circles which I used to define the context for second language learning and teaching.

NATIONAL POLICY, EDUCATIONAL PLANNING, AND LANGUAGE TEACHING

I want to begin at the outermost or sociocultural level by suggesting that it is necessary to examine various aspects of second language learning and teaching within the broad framework of educational planning. The selection of a language to be taught or to be used as a medium of instruction clearly constitutes an important aspect of educational and of national planning (see, for example, Fishman, 1974). I have come to believe over the last ten years on the basis of extensive experiences in

North America, the Middle-East and southeast Asia that despite research, experimentation, or innovation, second language teaching programs or bilingual education programs will *not* succeed or thrive unless they are consistent with government policy, whether explicit or implicit, or with the carefully and clearly expressed goals of local educational authorities (see, for example, Harrison, Prator, and Tucker, 1974; Tucker, 1977). Educational or national policy serves to define explicitly the parameters within which language teaching programs can be developed.

Let me present a few examples. Consider first the Sudan—a linguistically diverse, geographically immense country with the potential, as yet unrealized, to become a major agricultural resource for the Arab World. During the time of the Anglo-Egyptian Sudan, English was the medium of instruction in many of the schools throughout the country. More recently, a number of small but incrementally rather dramatic changes have occurred which have eroded the official position of English within the country but have not diminished its importance. In the northern provinces of the country, Arabic is now the exclusive medium of instruction in the government school system. The introduction of English as a subject for study was changed from grade 5 to grade 7; the number of periods per week devoted to English instruction was reduced by two; the length of individual periods for all subjects was reduced; English was declared to be no longer a required "pass" subject for the secondary school leaving examination; *but* English remains the medium of instruction at the University of Khartoum—a distinguished institution with a mixture of Sudanese and expatriate professors and a continuing British tradition of utilizing the services of external examiners for degree candidates. It has long been rumored that the university will eventually arabicize but that probably will not happen for some years yet.

The situation in the north of the Sudan contrasts sharply with that in the six southern provinces. In the south, English continues to be the major link language and, in fact, is used in many different situations to link the north and the south. In the south, it has been decided to use one of at least nine local vernaculars as the initial medium of primary education, with English and Arabic to be taught as second languages and English to be used as the medium of instruction at the senior secondary level. This radical difference in policy between north and south represents a major concession by the north—a concession articulated in the Addis Ababa agreement of 1972 which concluded a 17-year civil war in which language was one of the precipitating factors. If the country is to survive politically, linguistic diversity must not only be tolerated, but encouraged.

In the Sudan, then, a series of major educational and national policy decisions have affected the course of English-language teaching, leading on the one hand to desperation on the part of some northern teachers who must now train students under circumstances relatively less hospitable than those a decade ago and on the other hand to optimism on the part of southern teachers who see once again official sanction and concern for their efforts.

Consider now the situation of Canada—in particular, the Province of Quebec. With the passage in 1974 of the Official Language Act, French became the sole official language of the province; but not, it must be remembered, of the country where the policy of the Federal government through the Official Languages Act explicitly advocates the encouragement of multiculturalism through bilingualism. A number of associated regulations were promulgated to ensure that French in Quebec will become the *de facto* as well as the *de jure* language. For example, demonstrable proficiency in French is now a requisite for membership in professional groups such as the corporation of dentists or psychologists or physicians. In addition, companies are required to obtain "francization" certificates to be eligible to compete for government contracts, subsidies, etc. To qualify, French must not only be the actual working language of the organization, but Francophones must also be represented at various levels of the company hierarchy including upper management positions.

Perhaps the single most important and controversial provision of the Act, however, was that which limited access to English-medium schools to Anglophones or to other pupils who *already* possessed a "sufficient knowledge" of English to profit from instruction in the language. (At the time of writing, fall 1977, even more stringent legislation—Bill 101—was being debated in the Quebec National Assembly.) The government's decision to implement this section of the Act by utilizing examinations of dubious validity and reliability for screening purposes has resulted in the launching of legal action by groups representing both immigrant parents and, more interestingly, French-Canadian parents. The passage and implementation of the Act has meant that a majority of the Quebec population has been abruptly denied access to two popular and successful sources of English-language training: (1) following some portion of their education in English-medium schools, or (2) working at jobs where English was the *de facto* language of wider communication. Note, in particular, that even French-English bilingual education is specifically prohibited for non-Anglophones or non-English dominant immigrants. Despite this government action, the need for English by

Quebec residents—Anglophone, Francophone, or other immigrant—who wish to pursue business or trading opportunities with representatives from an increasingly large array of industrialized or developing countries has *not* diminished. The onus of responsibility for meeting this need thus falls on the ESL program within the French educational sector. There is no reason to believe that the program as presently designed and staffed can meet the challenge.

Acheson, d'Anglejan, de Bagheera, and Tucker (1977), recently conducted a survey of 112 provincial ESL teachers participating in a government-sponsored in-service training program. Despite the fact that the Anglophone population of Quebec is at least 400,000, fewer than 2% of the teachers were English mother tongue. Only 21% had previously completed an ESL training program; a majority reported that they were teaching English because it was essentially the only job opening available to them; and as a group the teachers' English-language proficiency scores on the Michigan Test of English Language Proficiency were such that they would *not* have qualified for admission to the majority of North American English-medium universities. Furthermore, and perhaps most discouraging, there was no indication that the teachers represented in this sample would be able to contribute to the promotion among their students of a sensitivity to and appreciation for the cultural values of the Anglo-Canadian group.

How different the situations in the Province of Quebec and in the south of the Sudan and how different are likely to be the outcomes of the English-language teaching programs in these two disparate settings!

The point that I wanted to make through these two examples is that educational or national policy does define the parameters within which language-teaching programs can be developed. Furthermore, it is obvious that social pressures motivated by a diverse array of contributory factors can lead to policy change. The results *per se* of empirical research—even when widely publicized—however, rarely do. I would like to conclude this section by calling attention to the usefulness of various language-planning activities such as sociolinguistic surveys as tools which may provide baseline information to assist in the national development of language-teaching programs. I will return to this topic in a later section.

Let me turn next to the innermost or *individual* level. A plethora of studies has been conducted which seek to examine, to measure, or to manipulate a diverse array of individual characteristics. For example, researchers have investigated in various permutations the relationship among age (cf. Krashen, 1973; Ramsey and Wright, 1974), affective factors (cf. Brown, 1973; Chastain, 1975; Gardner and Lambert, 1972;

Gardner, Symthe, Clément and Gliksman, 1976; Jacobson and Imhoof, 1974; Schumann, 1975; Taylor, 1974; Teitlebaum, Edwards, Hudson, and Hudson, 1975), ability factors (cf. Carroll, 1974; Gardner and Lambert, 1972), learning stages or style (cf. Naiman, Fröelich and Stern, 1975; Rosansky, 1974), and second language learning. Two general conclusions can be drawn from these studies: (1) aptitude and attitude/motivation comprise statistically independent and significant predictors of language-learning success; and (2) youthful versus adult learners *may* approach the language-learning task differently and hence profit from different teaching approaches. The influences of personality variables and differences in cognitive or learning style are as yet little understood and research should be continued in these areas. The major application of these studies derives from the fact that teachers can affect or manipulate attitude and motivation and can design programs of instruction appropriate to the age, experience, ability, and interest of their students. The apparent popularity and success of "English for Special Purposes" programs lends credence to this claim (see, for example, ESPMENA).

During the past two years, a few researchers working at this level have begun to phrase their questions and shape their data-gathering techniques slightly differently. They are attempting to define the constellation of individual factors associated with successful second language learning and furthermore to determine whether the effects of these factors can be modulated by the language teaching program which a student is following (cf. Cohen, 1977; Naiman, Fröelich and Stern, 1975; Rubin, 1975; Tucker, Hamayan and Genesee, 1976). The results of the few studies conducted to date indicate that the study of individual differences in second language learning and factors associated with them can be usefully pursued using multivariate statistical procedures. This area, I believe, constitutes an important future research direction.

Let me turn finally to the remaining level—the *instructional* setting and its associated factors. On the basis of my experience in various settings around the world during the last ten years, I have come to conclude that much more serious attention needs to be given to the task of defining, publicizing, and implementing locally appropriate language-teaching goals. For example, is it realistic to expect all pupils to develop native-speaker control in each of the four skills of the target language? Should the objective, rather, be for the individual to develop native-like receptive skills together with the communicative ability necessary to express his ideas? How do prospective teachers, employers, or other target-language speakers react to spoken or written messages that, although comprehensible, are marked by various lexical, phonological, or syntactic deviations (see, for example, research by Johannson, 1973;

Quirk and Svartvik, 1966; Schachter, Tyson and Diffley, 1976)? It may, for example, be perfectly acceptable for an English-Canadian member of the Ontario Provincial Parliament who lives in Toronto to comprehend spoken and written French with ease while producing utterances which are markedly deviant. It would, however, be totally unacceptable for an English-Canadian member of the Quebec National Assembly to perform similarly. The task of defining a set of locally appropriate goals undoubtedly necessitates an understanding of the sociolinguistic context in which the graduates of the language program will live and work (see Cohen, 1975a; Harrison, Prator and Tucker, 1975).

As mentioned in a preceding section, within the past decade sociolinguistic or language policy surveys have been conducted in a number of countries. They have been designed to provide information about the patterns of language use within a particular region or country, the aims for language teaching, the dimensions of the language-teaching effort, the various resources available to implement the programs—all within the context of the actual demonstrated needs which people have for the target language(s) in diverse daily activities (see, for example, Bender, Bowen, Cooper, and Ferguson, 1976; Harrison, Prator, and Tucker, 1975; Ladefoged, Criper, and Glick, 1972; Royal Commission on Bilingualism and Biculturalism, 1963; Whiteley, 1974). Such surveys are based on the assumption that people's needs for a particular target language should be allowed to influence the scope and design of the language-teaching program—an assumption which has certainly not characterized the development of programs in many countries. I have suggested elsewhere (Tucker and d'Anglejan, 1971) that the first step in establishing an innovative language-teaching program "should involve a small-scale sociolinguistic survey of the local community where the program will be situated." In practice, this is rarely done.

But how are language-teaching objectives to be developed? Consider the directive in the "Official Language Act" of the Province of Quebec:

> The curricula must ensure that pupils receiving their instruction in English acquire a knowledge of spoken and written French, and the Ministry of Education shall adopt the necessary measures to that effect.

> The Ministry of Education must also take the necessary measures to ensure instruction in English as a second language to pupils whose language of instruction is French.
> —Bill No. 22, Title III, Chapter V, Article 44

I realize you may argue that the task of the legislature is simply to provide the mandate under which appropriate experts will articulate more explicitly the goals or objectives of the language-teaching program.

But consider the set of specific objectives for Jordanian students who by the end of the Compulsory Cycle (i.e., after studying English as a foreign language for five years from grades 5-9), are expected to be able to:

(1) Understand simple English spoken at a normal speed

(2) Communicate sensibly with an English-speaking person, within certain reasonable areas

(3) Read simple English with ease, fluency and understanding

(4) Write a basic paragraph in English, using the basic structure of the language (*English Curriculum: Compulsory Stage*, 1969)

I have previously claimed (see Harrison, Prator, and Tucker, 1975) that "these 'specific' aims typify the conventional goals so often cited for language study. They lack precision, and fail to make clear precisely what degree of English proficiency students are expected to achieve." I went on to suggest that operationally defined behavioral objectives appeared to be a necessary prerequisite to effective program development and that ultimately the success of an English-language program must be measured by the ability of school graduates to obtain suitable employment which would permit them to grow individually and to contribute directly to the social and economic development of their country. In retrospect, my suggestion seems naive and likewise without precision, and for the present I shall simply identify this as an area which requires additional thought and development.

We will now consider another major factor which shapes the actual language-teaching program—the examination system. In many countries, regions, states, or provinces the final English-language attainment of each school graduate is evaluated by his success or failure on the English paper of a secondary certificate examination (this is true, for example, in Egypt, Jordan, Quebec). It has been my repeated observation that the form and content of this examination affects the manner and substance of English-language teaching: and furthermore that even where there exist relatively explicit objectives for ELT there is often a lack of correspondence between the objectives and the examination (see Bending, 1976). In such cases, despite their professional preparation and despite the resources at their disposal, teachers often elect to concentrate their attention on "preparing" their students for the required examination. It is not inconceivable that students who pass the English paper of the Egyptian Thannawiyya amma or of the Quebec matriculation exam can also communicate accurately and confidently, but this remains for the most part untested. Educators are now beginning to turn their attention to this domain, and I predict that it will become an increasingly important research area.

In addition to the ideas described above, theoretical insights and research results of the past decade have profoundly affected work at the instructional level. One of the important pedagogical notions which derives from insights about native-language learning is that the major focus of second language classroom activity should be on communication—not just of simulated dialogues—but on genuine communication where the validity of students' utterances will be judged on the basis of their content rather than on the appropriateness of their grammatical form (Diller, 1975; Tucker and d'Anglejan, 1975). The apparent acceptance of this notion manifests itself in diverse ways: (1) by the adoption of seemingly radical objectives and techniques on the part of some teachers (e.g., the development of communicative competence at the possible expense of grammatical perfection, Savignon, 1972); (2) by the switch from structurally graded to notionally based syllabi (O'Neill, 1976); (3) by a widespread move toward the implementation of apparently successful bilingual education programs in many parts of North America (see Alatis and Twadell, 1976; Troike and Modiano, 1975); and (4) by the development of English-for-special-purposes texts and courses throughout much of the third world where English occupies the role of an important foreign or second language. Such innovations attempt to capitalize on the observation that a student can effectively acquire a second language when the task of learning the language becomes incidental to the task of communicating with someone about something which is inherently interesting.

This shift in focus calls, of course, for a reassessment of the role and training of the second language teacher—a reassessment which at least one major professional organization has recently conducted (TESOL, 1976). The second language teacher will often be called upon to work in close partnership with teachers of content subjects (see, for example, Cohen, 1975b). The language specialist not only must be a fluent speaker of the target language, but also during the course of professional preparation should have acquired an understanding of current theories of language acquisition and should be familiar with and attuned to the sociocultural traditions of the students. It should be emphasized that there remain enormous variations and healthy controversy about the optimal manner of implementing programs of formal instruction for children or for adults (cf. Diller, 1975; Krashen and Seliger, 1975) today as there were 50 years ago (Jesperson, 1904; Palmer, 1921).

In summary, I know of no "scientific" data or empirical evidence which demonstrate conclusively that we have yet designed the ideal program or programs by which a second language can be *taught*; but we do know that almost any student (and we see ample evidence) placed in the appropriate milieu, given ample opportunity, and the support of his parents, peers, and teachers can successfully *acquire* a second language— the paradox may be semantic or illusory but clearly the challenge to provide effective second language training to an increasingly large and heterogeneous group of students remains.

NOTE

1. I have drawn extensively in this paper on material presented at the 1977 TESOL conference at Miami Beach under the title "Can a Second Language Be Taught?"

REFERENCES

d'Anglejan, A., P. Acheson, I. de Bagheera, and G. R. Tucker. "English as the second language of Quebec: A teacher profile," paper presented at TESOL convention, Miami Beach, Fla., 1977.

Alatis, J. E., and K. Twadell, eds. *English as a Second Language in Bilingual Education.* Washington: TESOL, 1976.

Bender, M. L., J. D. Bowen, R. L. Cooper, and C. A. Ferguson, eds. *Language in Ethiopia.* London: Oxford University Press, 1976.

Bending, H. B. "Motivation in an examination-geared school," *ELT*, 1976, *30*, 315-320.

Brown, H. D. "Affective variables in second language acquisition," *Language Learning*, 1973, *23*, 231-244.

Carroll, J. B. "Aptitude in Second language learning," *Proceedings of the Fifth Symposium of the Canadian Association of Applied Linguistics*, 1974.

Chastain, K. "Affective and ability factors in second-language acquisition," *Language Learning*, 1975, *25*, 153-161.

Cohen, A. D. *A Sociolinguistic Approach to Bilingual Education.* Rowley, Mass.: Newbury House, 1975a.

———. "Error correction and the training of language teachers," *Modern Language Journal*, 1975b, *59*, 414-422.

———. "Successful second language speakers: a review of the research literature," *Israeli Journal of Applied Linguistics*, 1977, 3-22.

Diller, K. C. "Some new trends for applied linguistics and foreign language teaching in the United States," *TESOL Quarterly*, 1975, *9*, 65-73.

ESPMENA, English for special purposes in the Middle East and North Africa, English Language Servicing Unit, University of Khartoum, Sudan.

Fishman, J. A. "Language modernization and planning in comparison with other types of national modernization and planning," in J. A. Fishman, ed., *Advances in Language Planning.* The Hague: Mouton, 1974, 79-102.

Fox, M. J. *Language in Education: Problems and Prospects in Research and Training.* New York: The Ford Foundation, 1975.

Gardner, R. C., and W. E. Lambert. *Attitudes and Motivation in Second Language Learning.* Rowley, Mass.: Newbury House, 1972.

Gardner, R. C., P. C. Smythe, R. Clément, and L. Gliksman. "Second language learning: a social psychological perspective," *Canadian Modern Language Review*, 1976, *32*, 198-213.

Harrison, W., C. Prator, and G. R. Tucker. *English-Language Policy Survey of Jordan*. Arlington, Va.: Center for applied Linguistics, 1975.

Jacobsen, M., and M. Imhoof. "Predicting success in learning a second language," *Modern Language Journal*, 1974, *55*, 329-336.

Jespersen, O. *How to Teach a Foreign Language*. London: George Allen & Unwin Ltd., 1904.

Johansson, S. "The identification and evaluation of errors in foreign languages: a functional approach," in J. Svartvik, ed., *Errata: Papers in ERROR Analysis*. Lund, Sweden, CWK Gleerup, 1973, 102-114.

Jordan, Ministry of Education, Curricula and Textbooks Division. *English Curriculum: Compulsory Stage*. Amman: Cooperative Printing Presses Workers Society, 2nd ed., 1969.

Krashen, S. "Lateralization, language learning and the critical period: Some new evidence," *Language Learning*, 1973, *23*, 63-74.

Krashen, S. D., and H. W. Seliger. "The essential contributions of formal instruction in adult second language learning," *TESOL Quarterly*, 1975, *9*, 173-183.

Ladefoged, P., R. Glick, and C. Criper. *Language in Uganda*. Nairobi: Oxford University Press, 1972.

Naiman, N., M. Fröelich, and H. H. Stern. "The good language learner," Modern Language Centre, Ontario Institute for Studies in Education, Multilith, 1975.

O'Neill, T. "The teaching of notions," in *English Language Teaching for the Arab World*. London: Oxford University Press, 1976, 10-15.

Palmer, H. E. *The Oral Method of Teaching Languages*. Cambridge: W. Heffer & Sons Ltd., 1921.

Paulston, C. B. "Implications of language learning theory for language planning: concerns in bilingual education," papers in Applied Linguistics, Bilingual Education Series: 1. Arlington, Va.: Center for Applied Linguistics, 1974.

Quirk, R., and J. Svartvik. *Investigating Linguistics Acceptability*. The Hague: Mouton, 1966.

Ramsey, C. A., and E. N. Wright. "Age and second language learning," *The Journal of Social Psychology*, 1974, *94*, 115-121.

Rosansky, E. "The critical period for the development of language: some cognitive developmental considerations," *Working Papers on Bilingualism*, 1975, *6*, 92-102.

Royal Commission on Bilingualism and Biculturalism. Ottawa: Queen's Printer, 1963.

Rubin, J. "What the Good language learner can teach us," *TESOL Quarterly*, 1975, *9*, 41-51.

Savignon, S. *Communicative Competence: An Experiment in Foreign-Language Teaching*. Philadelphia: Center for Curriculum Development, 1972.

Schachter, J., A. F. Tyson, and F. J. Diffley. "Learner intuitions about grammaticality," *Language Learning*, 1976, *26*, 67-76.

Schumann, J. H. "Second language acquisition research: Getting a more global look at the learner," *Language Learning*, 1976a, special issue no. 4 (papers in second-language acquisition), 15-28.

———. "Social distance as a factor in second language acquisition," *Language Learning*, 1976b, *26*, 135-143.

Schumann, J. H. "Affective factors and the problem of age in second language acquisition," *Language Learning,* 1975, *25,* 209-235.

Strevens, P. "A theoretical model of the language learning/language teaching process. *Working Papers in Bilingualism,* 1976, *11,* 129-152.

Taylor, B. P. "Toward a theory of language acquisition," *Language Learning,* 1974, *24,* 23-35.

Teitelbaum, H., A. Edwards, and A. Hudson, and A. Hudson. "Ethnic attitudes and the acquisition of Spanish as a second language," *Language Learning,* 1975, *25,* 255-266.

TESOL. Position paper on the role of English as a second language in bilingual education, March, 1976.

Troike, R. C., and N. Modiano, eds. *Proceedings of the First Inter-American Conference on Bilingual Education.* Arlington, Va.: Center for Applied Linguistics, 1975.

Tucker, G. R. "Some observations concerning bilingualism and second-language teaching in developing countries and in North America," in P. A. Hornby, ed., *Bilingualism: Psychological Social and Educational Implications.* New York: Academic Press, 1977, 141-146.

Tucker, G. R., and A. d'Anglejan. "Some thoughts concerning bilingual education programs," *The Modern Language Journal,* 1971, *55,* 491-493.

———. "New directions in second language teaching," in R. C. Troike and N. Modiano, eds., *Proceedings of the First Inter-American Conference on Bilingual Education.* Arlington, Va.: Center for Applied Linguistics, 1975, 63-72.

Tucker, G. R., E. Hamayan, and F. H. Genesee. "Affective, cognitive and social factors in second language acquisition," *The Canadian Modern Language Review,* 1976, *32,* 214-226.

Whiteley, W. H., ed. *Language in Kenya.* Nairobi: Oxford University Press, 1974.

STUDY AND DISCUSSION QUESTIONS

(1) In this paper it is argued that language-teaching programs occur within a sociocultural context and are shaped by and contribute to national and educational planning. Compare and contrast language-teaching policy in two countries that you are familiar with to provide examples to illustrate this statement.

(2) Tucker states that serious attention needs to be given to the task of defining, publicizing, and implementing locally appropriate language-teaching goals. To what degree are foreign language teaching goals in your school, institution, or community locally appropriate, and how if necessary could they be made more so?

(3) Discuss the relationship between teaching practices, the form and content of the national examination system, and the objectives of English language-teaching programs.

(4) Examine the objectives for foreign or second language teaching programs in your country and the curriculum or syllabuses for such programs that exist. To what degree do such syllabuses reflect realistic and appropriate language-teaching objectives?

(5) Several contributors to this book, including Tucker, suggest that the major focus of activity in the classroom should be on meaningful communication. To what degree can this be taken as a general organizing principle of language-teaching activities? What other factors are relevant to a discussion of organizing principles for classroom language-teaching activities?

(6) In what ways can teachers affect the attitudes and motivation of their students and contribute to the design of programs of instruction appropriate to the age, ability, experience, and interest of their students?

(7) Tucker suggests that an examination of the constellation of factors associated with language learning using multivariate techniques is a useful research direction to pursue, as is a closer examination of the dynamics of classroom language usage and patterns of interaction. Prepare an observation matrix or similar research tool that could be used to study the dynamics of classroom language usage and interaction, and test its usefulness in a foreign or second language classroom.

(8) Do you agree with the suggestion that the theoretical validity of a particular approach and considerations of methodological sophistication may be relatively minor ingredients in the development of a successful and total second language education program when compared with sociocultural or attitudinal considerations?

LANGUAGE LEARNING
IN AND OUT OF CLASSROOMS

Alison d'Anglejan

Quebec is an industrialized society which is now experiencing the direct impact of recent and abrupt language policy changes (Tucker, this volume). It is difficult to accept with any measure of confidence or composure traditional academic solutions to the urgent problems of second language learning and teaching. Generations of Quebec children have spent ten or twelve years in second language classes only to emerge functionally unilingual at the end of their schooling. On the other hand, we can cite countless examples of bilingual citizens who move, with no apparent effort, from one language to the other and who have acquired this skill in the street or in the workplace. As language policy changes put increasing pressure on both the population and the educational establishment, it is hoped that this paper will provide a reminder to all that classrooms are only one, and not necessarily the best, of many contexts in which a second language can be learned.

The paper will focus on language learning in and out of classrooms. By examining some of the general principles underlying formal classroom learning and informal or incidental learning, I shall attempt to clarify the difference between the two and to determine the scope of each. Finally, drawing on examples from various parts of the world, I shall discuss the use of innovation both in the classroom and out as a means of exploiting the potential for informal second language acquisition within a community.

THE NATURE OF INFORMAL AND
FORMAL LEARNING

In their attempts to gain a better understanding of the process by which individuals acquire knowledge or skills, educators are showing increased interest in the nature of informal and formal learning, and in the relationship between the two. Impetus for this broadening of focus has come in part from the failure of schools to provide an adequate learning environment for certain minority groups—the poor, the culturally different, and even the unusually gifted. Further impetus has been derived from the work of cognitive anthropologists and psychologists in cross-cultural settings and by the need to develop educational programs in third world countries where local traditions are often at variance with Western educational practices.

It is clear to even the casual observer of societies in which little, if any, formal schooling is available that a great deal of complex learning does take place. Sophisticated hunting, fishing, and agricultural practices are passed on from generation to generation. Children learn to build boats and to weave baskets, rugs, or cloth in intricate geometric patterns; additional languages or dialects necessary for religious rites, trade, or wider social contacts are added to the mother tongue. Typically in such settings, the structure of social processes and institutions permits the child to acquire through observation and direct participation the values, attitudes, customs, and skills which define adult behavior in his culture (Scribner and Cole, 1973).

Mead (1964) points out that in informal learning, the adult, or model, rarely articulates the set of rules underlying a particular practice but instead provides a demonstration of it. Since learning takes place in real situations where the meaning is evident from the context, much of it can occur without the need for its principles to be articulated by either the learner or the teacher. However, opportunities are provided for the learner to gain feedback about the appropriateness of his or her performance.

Even in nonliterate societies, anthropologists have found some evidence of formal education, that is, the organization and transmission of knowledge for didactic purposes in a specific setting. Gladwin's (1970) analysis of the procedures used by navigators in a Polynesian culture to teach the complex skills of navigation provides one of the most complete descriptions of a formal learning situation in a nonliterate society. However, it is not clear from this study or from other anthropological works whether such formal learning settings are simply extensions of the ways of learning that operate in everyday life or whether they engender new learning processes.

According to Scribner and Cole (1973) one common characteristic of both formal and informal learning contexts is that in both, individuals transmit knowledge and skills with a high positive social value. Learning is not depersonalized but is closely linked to the social status of persons acting as teachers. Thus, empathy and identification with persons and their social roles rather than the appeal of the subject matter per se appear to be critical correlates of informal learning and of noninstitutional formal learning.

Whereas studies of learning in nonliterate societies are still few and fragmentary, the same cannot be said of investigations of formal education. Unfortunately, the majority of these focus on teaching methods or the evaluation of achievement at the group level and actually provide very little information about the relationship between that which is taught by the teacher and that which is learned by the student.

In spite of the deficiencies of much current educational research, some general statements about the nature of formal learning can certainly be made. In contrast with informal settings, schools emphasize what is being taught rather than the person who is doing the teaching. Students are expected to learn by relating themselves to the subject matter and by relegating to a much lower level of consciousness and importance their identification and empathy with the teacher. Bruner (1966) notes that school learning is removed from the context of socially relevant action and is embedded within a context of language and symbolic activity. As a consequence, sources of information upon which the learner may draw in the classroom are sharply reduced, observation is of limited value, and learning is highly dependent on the medium of language. In addition, the learning process is frequently initiated through the formal verbalization of rules or principles underlying the tasks to be mastered. This is in striking contrast with informal learning of the type described earlier in which typically neither the teacher nor the learner is expected to articulate the rules which underlie social values, cultural practices, or specific tasks. Learning grows through experience with reality and it may well be that the capacity to learn informally is enhanced by repeated opportunities to do so. It is equally likely that the ability to benefit from formal teaching grows through school experiences.

Lave (1977) recently explored the effects of schooling on "everyday" cognition in an experimental situation. She studied the ability of Liberian tailors with varying amounts of schooling to perform certain arithmetic and measurement operations of some complexity by administering two kinds of tasks. One involved new arithmetic and measurement problems within the familiar context of tailoring. The other involved equivalent tasks presented in an academic form. The general finding was that each kind of experience (tailoring and schooling) promoted transfer *within* that specific context but did not generalize across contexts. Bullock (1974) has remarked that "all genuine learning involves discovery, and it is as ridiculous to suppose that teaching begins and ends with 'instruction' as it is to suppose that 'learning by discovery' means leaving children to their own resources." However, it is not at all clear how formal and informal learning interact, nor what the implications for learning are of the incongruities evident in the two processes.

NATIVE LANGUAGE LEARNING

Let us now focus more specifically on the area of language learning and see what it can tell us about the relationship between formal instruction and incidental acquisition.

Given a minimal set of necessary and sufficient conditions, all children learn to talk. They are thought to construct for themselves the complex system of rules which underlie the language spoken by those around them, acquiring as they grow increasingly sophisticated linguistic mechanisms for conveying subtleties of meaning. Brown (1973) has described child language acquisition as a process of creative construction whereby the child formulates hypotheses regarding the grammar of his native language which he revises systematically until the discrepancies between his own structures and those of adults in his environment are resolved. Clearly, the human being's propensity for language acquisition has its roots in his biological makeup and he approaches the task with an innate capacity for linguistic analysis and intuitions about the nature of grammar. Consequently, learning to speak, like learning to walk, involves a number of identifiable and predictable stages and reveals strong patterns of similarity across languages and cultures (Brown, 1973). Native language acquisition provides a remarkable example of informal learning. The incredibly complex set of rules which prescribe the grammar of any language are beyond the conscious awareness of the child and the adult. Some researchers believe them to be innate (Chomsky, 1965; McNeill, 1970). Others (Skinner, 1957; Hebb, Lambert, and Tucker, 1973) consider that their acquisition can be accounted for by principles involved in perceptual and cognitive learning.

Studies focusing on the interactions between mothers and their very young children (Condon and Sanders, 1974; Bullowa, 1973) reveal the powerful interpersonal bond which appears to lay the foundation for the development of language. Research by Snow and others (Snow and

Ferguson, 1977) examining the characteristics of language addressed to children by their mothers and other adults in their environment suggests that such persons play an important role in enhancing language learning by directing to the child speech which is more simple, more redundant, and generally more tractable than that addressed to adults. Baby talk thus provides a transparent sample of speech in which linguistic rules are salient and easily perceived. Studies (Brown, 1973) also show that mothers play a formal role in the language-learning process by providing feedback to children regarding the appropriateness of their utterances. However, this feedback generally concerns the content and not the form of the utterance. It is interesting to note in these studies of adult-child interactions that certain characteristic formalized behaviors on the part of adults which are present in the context of native language acquisition are consonant with the principles of informal learning. They facilitate the natural process of language acquisition by making it easier for the child to perceive for himself not only grammatical rules but also the relationship between meaning and form. Instances of behavior incongruent with informal learning principles have been noted—e.g., attempts to teach "correct" grammatical forms to very young children—but Cazden's (1965) research shows that teaching behavior of this sort, focusing on the form rather than the function of language, does not seem to facilitate language acquisition. Thus, the language-learning process is an unconscious one embedded in the context of everyday activities and not dependent on explicit teaching provided by an adult. Furthermore, empathy, imitation, and identification, which Mead (1964) has described as the cornerstone of informal learning, are clearly evident in the process of native language acquisition.

By the time the child goes to school he has mastered most of the basic grammatical features of his language. Others are acquired progressively between the ages of five and ten (Palermo and Molfese, 1972; C. Chomsky, 1969). As for the learning of vocabulary, it is one of the aspects of language development which continues throughout life.

It is generally in the schoolroom that children first encounter formal language teaching which is the introduction to literacy. They learn to read and write, and certain rules of grammar are made explicit. Thus, a French child is taught how to make appropriate gender agreements and, often laboriously, to conjugate verbs, something he does with relative ease when left to his own devices. Certain rules underlying unconscious language usage are raised to a level of consciousness and are learned as a body of knowledge. For many children, the necessity of acquiring a new dialect, or school register, represents a break in the continuity with the language of the home. It is interesting that these new language skills, introduced in the classroom and generally in a manner which contravenes the principles of informal learning, are not mastered with equal facility by all children. The child's ability to acquire the tools of literacy may well depend upon his understanding and acceptance of the purpose that they are eventually to serve, and the extent to which literacy is valued by those in his community. Hoggart (1957) points out the cultural bias favoring middle class values and interests which runs through literature. While attitudes toward literacy which shape the language curriculum in most schools may be isomorphic with those of middle class families throughout the world, they conflict with the value systems of many cultural subgroups in both literate and nonliterate societies. The challenge of literacy is that of helping the child see beyond the constraints of the printed word to the exciting world on the other side. He must come to accept the printed word as a means of participating vicariously in experiences to which he does not have immediate access, in other words as a means to a worthwhile end.

Within most literate societies a broad range of individual differences can be noted with respect to levels of literacy. Many adults possess only the marginal reading and writing skills which may be necessary for survival in their community. Others, typically from middle class homes, or ones in which literacy is cherished, develop high level skills, but it is difficult to determine whether this competence should be attributed exclusively to the effects of formal education or in part to informal learning nurtured by a particular type of home environment. It is probable that both are involved and that they interact harmoniously.

SECOND LANGUAGE LEARNING

The area of second language acquisition is a challenging one in which to examine the implications of formal and informal learning. Contemporary theoretical views tend to support the position that first and second language learning are essentially analogous processes (Macnamara, 1975; Ervin-Tripp, 1974; Tucker and d'Anglejan, 1972). The second language learner, like the young child, constructs for himself the rule system of the target language and progresses in a systematic manner toward increased mastery of the second code (Corder, 1967; Dulay and Burt, 1974; Hatch, this volume). However, the analogy must be examined in depth if we are to even begin to understand the paradox posed by the commonly noted failure of many, if not most, second language learners to achieve verbal fluency as a result of classroom instruction, in contrast with the universal success of young children in acquiring their native tongue.

Krashen (1976, 1977) has proposed a "monitor-model" for second language performance which accounts for puzzling phenomena such as discrepancies in oral and written second language performance and differences between learners' careful classroom speech and their performance in unstructured situations.

According to the model, adult second language learners concurrently develop two possibly independent linguistic systems for second language performance, one *acquired*, incidentally and unconsciously through a creative construction process, the other consciously *learned* as the result of formal instruction. Linguistic production in the second language is made possible by the acquired system, with the learned system acting as a monitor. Under certain conditions—when speakers have sufficient processing time or when they are focused on grammatical form—the monitor inspects and appropriately alters the output of the acquired system. However, in rapid spontaneous speech, or when the speaker is tired or distracted, monitoring cannot take place and he must rely entirely on the output of the acquired system. Krashen provides evidence that there are wide individual differences with respect to the use of the monitor. Overusers may be quite handicapped in spontaneous communication by an excessive reliance on their conscious knowledge of linguistic rules and an unwillingness to trust their acquired system. Conversely, underusers appear to be uninfluenced by most error correction and do not appear to utilize conscious linguistic knowledge in their second language performance. The model, with its ability to account for individual differences, provides a powerful explanatory mechanism for the variability evident in second language performance resulting from both formal and informal learning. While Krashen's model purports to explain adult second language performance, I believe it can be usefully extended to classroom language learning by children.

The traditional approach to second language teaching

The traditional approach familiar to most language teachers involves the explicit teaching of the language per se. Students are introduced to the target language as a school subject by a teacher who, ideally, has native or near native fluency. Students listen to, repeat, practice, and then expand the specific structures presented by the teacher. Basic vocabulary is taught, and students must practice grammatical structures until their control of the sequences becomes automatic. Generally, the introduction of reading and writing follows the development of listening and speaking skills. Some approaches avoid the explicit teaching of grammatical rules on the assumption that the learner will be able to generalize from target sentences to the production of novel forms. Others include the formal learning of syntactic and morphological rules as a means of short-cutting the process of rule induction. The prime focus of most language programs is the development of oral communication skills through the use of dialogues and manipulative exercises. However, it should be noted that what is commonly regarded as "communication" in the second language classroom rarely corresponds to any acceptable definition of what might be termed communication outside the classroom. As Macnamara (1973) has observed, rarely do the language teacher and the student have any genuinely important or exciting things to say to each other, and the teacher's preoccupation with the form of the student's utterances rather than with their content is hardly conducive to the stimulation of spontaneous verbal interchange. Long (1977) has shown that feedback supplied by teachers in traditional second language classrooms focuses primarily on linguistic form, that it is at the best ambiguous and at the worst misleading.

Both from a qualitative and a quantitative standpoint, the sample of the target language to which the classroom learner is exposed tends to be sharply reduced and affords limited potential for the formation and testing of hypotheses regarding syntactic and morphological rules. Whereas the young child's communicative intentions are, at least in the early stages, relatively limited, predictable, and closely related to the experiences which he shares with his mother or caretaker, the same cannot be said of the older child or adult approaching a second language. Cognitively mature learners will want to understand and express ideas which call for a wide range of syntactic structures, verb tenses, or vocabulary. Their communicative needs will quite likely not concur with the programmed presentation prescribed by the instructional materials or syllabus. Furthermore, the limited exposure to spontaneous speech of native speakers in the classroom setting provides little opportunity for the formation and testing of hypotheses necessary for the induction of syntactic and morphological rules.

The importance of appropriate "intake" for the second language learner has been pointed out by many authors (Krashen, 1976; Wagner-Gough and Hatch, 1975). In addition to being exposed to a spontaneous and authentic input of the target language, the learner also requires an input of speech addressed directly to himself. The role of this input can be likened to that of the input or baby talk which the mother provides for her young child. It makes rules more salient and helps the learner to perceive more easily the relationship between meaning and form. Ferguson (1975) has shown that native speakers intuitively direct a simplified form of the language to nonnative speakers. However little information is available regarding the characteristics of teachers' speech in the formal second language classroom.

The shortcomings inherent in the traditional classroom approach to language learning may be exacerbated by the fact that the amount of curriculum time devoted to second language instruction is typically small. Nonetheless, many studies (Upshur, 1968; Mason, 1971; Saegert, Scott, Perkins, and Tucker, 1975) appear to indicate that the number of hours, or years of formal second language study is not in itself a strong predictor of second language achievement as measured by proficiency tests, particularly ones measuring oral fluency.

The explicit teaching of grammar, while useful in the carrying out of classroom activities such as transformation exercises or skills, or written work, does not appear to transfer readily to situations out of the classroom, where the learner must draw upon his knowledge of the target language in face-to-face interchange with native speakers. (Krashen's hypothesis is helpful in understanding this phenomenon.) Furthermore, the lack of experience with the rules of discourse, and with some of the nonverbal, kinesic, or ethnolinguistic idiosyncracies of native speakers may well contribute to the problems which the classroom learner encounters when he moves out into the community of native speakers (Richards, 1977). Words and structures learned in the classroom may be virtually unrecognizable when they occur in the normal discourse of native speakers.

This lack of transferability of classroom learning to unstructured situations is one of the prime criticisms of second language instruction. In Quebec, after twelve years of formal instruction in French, many high school graduates are able to pass written examinations in French language and literature, but show a limited level of oral fluency in interactions with native speakers and a tendency to retreat from situations in which they might be called upon to speak French. Ironically, there seems to be an assumption on the part of educators that if students persevere through college level courses, the elusive communicative skills will eventually emerge. There is little evidence that this is so. However, we still know virtually nothing about how near or how far such students are from functional fluency in the target language. Could they cope with university studies in French? Could they hold down a job in a French-speaking environment? Is their production acceptable to native speakers? Few attempts have been made to determine in any systematic way what additional experiences would be required to produce verbal fluency.

Innovative approaches to
second language learning within the classroom

The second general approach to language learning within a formal setting is based on the rationale that the student can most effectively acquire fluency in a second language when the task of language learning becomes incidental to that of gaining knowledge about a specific topic (geography, math, or basketball) via the target language through communication with a native speaker. Students enrolled in such programs are taught regular school subjects through the medium of the target language. There is considerable research evidence to support the fact that they are able to learn subject matter effectively while at the same time acquiring high level functional fluency in the second language (Swain, this volume). However, there are indications that in immersion situations where the teacher is the sole native speaker of the language and where the native language of the learners is homogeneous, the prolonged absence of contact with a target language peer group, or significant intercultural contact, leads to the development of a somewhat pidginized form of the language. Learners do become able to express themselves—some with greater ease than others—but their syntax shows evidence of simplification and frequent reliance on the rule system of the mother tongue (Spilka, 1976; Selinker, Swain, and Dumas, 1975). The fact that pidginization does not appear to occur when individual children are immersed in classrooms with many native speakers (Macnamara, 1976) suggests that social psychological factors such as identification with a peer group may play a critical role in enhancing or impeding effective acquisition of the target language.

Let us return briefly to our discussion of the principles underlying informal and formal learning and see if they can be useful in explaining success or failure in achieving fluency in a second language classroom. As we noted earlier in our discussion, native language acquisition appears to conform remarkably closely to the principles of informal learning. It is embedded in a context of social interaction. It does not involve the formal articulation of a set of rules. It results from the opportunity for sustained verbal exchange with a model with whom the learner identifies closely who provides a tractable input of the target language and feedback about the appropriateness of the learners' utterances. In the typical second language program, most, if not all, of these principles are violated. Students who follow these programs do in many instances successfully acquire reasonably good literacy skills, such as those which the child in his mother tongue learns at school. However, it is in the area of verbal fluency that the results tend to be disappointing. Immersion-type programs conform more closely to the principles of informal learning; however, the absence of an influential peer group of native speakers apparently cannot be compensated for by the presence of a sole adult model in the classroom. The result is the development of a classroom dialect which is functionally adequate for communication, yet deviates phonologically, syntactically, and morphologically from the native model.

Second language learning in informal contexts

It is not difficult in a multilingual community to find numerous examples of thoroughly successful informal second language acquisition. Few of the millions of immigrants from central and western Europe who have come to Canada during the past three decades would attribute their present skills in English or French to formal classroom instruction. Those who entered public schools, universities, or occupational settings which allowed them to interact socially or professionally with native speakers by whom they were accepted, acquired the language quickly and effectively. Those who remained encapsulated in ethnic communities—older persons, married women, or workers in factories with high concentrations of immigrants—and had little occasion or need for contact outside their group failed to do so. I do not believe that there is any reason to suspect that formal second language classes would have had a noticeable impact on this latter group so long as it remained cut off from the host community. There have been several studies carried out which suggest that this is so.

Schumann (1976) studied the impact of extensive formal English language instruction on the performance of a culturally isolated Spanish-speaking immigrant. He showed that whereas instruction radically improved performance in an artificial, highly monitored, elicitation task, it had virtually no effect on the learner's spontaneous speech used in communication with native speakers of English. Schumann concluded that formal language instruction is not powerful enough to overcome the pidginization engendered by social and psychological isolation.

In a recent study of the informal acquisition of German syntax by Italian and Spanish migrant workers, Dittmar and Klein (1977) looked at the relationship among a variety of extralinguistic variables (e.g., contact with Germans during leisure time; age at the time of immigration; contact with Germans at work; duration of stay) and second language learning. The degree of contact with Germans during leisure time was the most important factor governing the level of second language performance.

A study conducted in Nigeria (Obanya, 1976) examined the manner in which immigrants to Ibadan had managed to learn Yoruba, the language of that community, and their motivation for doing so. Among the 500 respondents, the most important reason for learning Yoruba appeared to be the need for survival in a Yoruba-speaking environment, the need to mix and to interact with the host community, socially or occupationally. Furthermore, the largest number of respondents appeared to have learned the language informally through a process of immersion, mixing freely with native speakers. Language acquisition was thus the outcome, rather than the cause, of finding a job or making friends.

The findings of the Nigerian research are in marked contrast with those reported by Bibeau (1976) in an evaluation of the impact of a program established by the Canadian government to improve the second language proficiency of Canadian civil servants in accordance with the requirements of Federal language policy. Employees were freed from their jobs, at full pay, for periods of as long as one year to attend intensive second language classes. While many progressed, as evidenced by their ability to move to a higher grade level in the continous training program, the majority remained disfluent in the second language and became resentful at being taken away from their jobs as economists, custom officers, or clerks, and placed in the alien environment of the second language classroom. Few reported any genuine opportunities either in their jobs or social life to interact with members of the target language group. While their motivation in instrumental terms was high—many required second language proficiency certification to retain or move into jobs designated as bilingual—the absence of an authentic "language barrier" or practical need for the second language, and the absence of contact with native speakers could not be overcome by systematic language training.

In contrast, a highly successful innovative program to train Vietnamese immigrants to the United States is being carried out in California by the San Diego County Welfare Department. The program rests on the assumption that an immigrant finding a job in an English-speaking environment in which he is accepted by the host group will acquire English. Thus students are given a short ten-week classroom training program in English and are then individually placed in occupational settings appropriate to their training and interests. The Welfare Department continues to pay them a subsistence allowance and maintains contact during a trial period. Employers provide work, tools and an emotionally supportive environment. This project is reported to be the most successful model for the adaptation of Vietnamese immigrants to the United States. In Montreal, we are currently experimenting with a similar model for adult immigrants who appear to make virtually no progress in government-sponsored intensive 30-week courses in French as a second language. Since such students seem unable to benefit from formal instruction, we have proposed that after a short trial period of classroom instruction they be placed in carefully chosen occupational slots in French-speaking environments for a period equal to that for which they would receive financial support to attend language classes. Thus an Arabic-speaking female immigrant might be placed in a day care center and a Greek draftsman might be taken in by an architect's office. In all cases care must be taken to avoid the placement of a learner in an environment in which there are concentrations of members of his own ethnic group. Contact with the language school is to be maintained through a weekly three-hour visit during which two or three immigrants will meet with a member of the research team and a language teacher to discuss their experiences and receive, if so desired, help with language or social adaptation difficulties.

At this point, we can only speculate as to the likely outcome of this project; however, evidence from the San Diego program, and from reports of successful informal language learning in second language occupational settings suggest that it will provide a fertile environment for the informal acquisition of second language fluency. It is our belief that the level of fluency which the learner will achieve will depend on a variety of factors such as the distance between his own and the target culture, and the degree to which he is verbal and articulate in his native language. The learner's occupational status and level of literacy in his first language will also be important variables. In work settings where reading and writing play virtually no role and are not regarded as salient achievements, there is little reason to expect these skills to develop as a spin-off from the second-language immersion situation. In settings where reading and writing are of greater importance and are valued skills in the native culture of the learner, functional efficiency in reading and writing the second language will be acquired. Ferguson (1977) notes that the use of a similar writing system in two languages tends to promote positive transfer, and basic literacy skills can often be transferred from one language to the other. The fact that complex writing systems, such as Chinese, Japanese, and Korean may not transfer so readily to another language may contribute to the burden of acquiring literacy. It is likely that some systematic training would accelerate the acquisition of literacy. Lagarde and Vigier (1974) describe a successful project for the training of literacy skills for Portuguese migrant workers in France who have acquired French informally. Interestingly the workers, who have no demonstrated need for second language literacy skills in their work, requested such training in preference to a program focusing on oral skills.

There appears to be a growing, although somewhat reluctant willingness among educators to accept the fact that no second language program can be expected to provide all things to all people. If students have not attained functional oral fluency after many years of formal study, then there is reason to look elsewhere for opportunities to develop this skill. On the other hand, many would argue (Savignon, 1972) that the potential for the development of communicative ability within the classroom has scarcely been tapped and that carry-overs from the audiolingual tenets of the 1960s disguised as communicative activities cannot be viewed as a serious test of the constraints inevitably inherent in the classroom environment.

In order to enhance the potential of the classroom as a favorable environment for the acquisition of verbal fluency, Corder (1977) calls for a redefinition of the role of the teacher and the learner to one in which both are equal partners in a cooperative enterprise. The learner must seek out the linguistic data and process it when he needs it and can assimilate it. It must be the learner and not the teacher who sets the pace. The role of the teacher is that of responding to the developing communicative needs of the learner by making the appropriate linguistic data available "on request." If the focus of the second language classroom is to be on developing the learner's ability to get the message across, then the teacher's feedback must be related to the communicative appropriateness and not the linguistic form of the student's utterances. It is not easy for teachers to adjust to this new role, particularly if they have been trained to encourage their students to avoid error and to produce only well-formed sentences. Anxiety is often brought on by awareness that students will be tested on their grammatical skills rather than on their communicative competence at the end of their program of study. At the present time, the notion of communicative competence is beginning to be understood by the language-teaching establishment. However, the means to measure objectively oral fluency are as yet tentative and exploratory.

We have recently gained additional insight into the problems inherent in changing the focus of classroom activities through our ongoing research with immigrants to Quebec. Exploring the potential of the classroom as an environment for the development of communicative skills for adult immigrants, we have devised an experimental program modeled along the lines of those described by Savignon (1972) and Allwright (1976). Systematic second language training involving the explicit teaching of syntax and morphology is limited to approximately one hour a day. The remaining five hours are devoted to problem-solving or information-seeking activities conducted exclusively in the target language, such as learning how to use the city's transit service, how supermarkets function, how to cash a check, obtain a driver's license, rent an apartment, or enroll a child in school. Authentic documents and videotape recordings are used to bring actual verbal interchanges into the classroom. Students go out in pairs to buy shoes, cash checks, and perform the activities which will give them feedback about their ability to communicate in the real world. A pilot class of slow learners has just completed this 20-week innovative course. Data from the evaluation are not yet available. However, many insights have been gained from discussions with the three participating teachers. For all, the project has called for a radical reversal of the principles of language teaching which they had been taught. Although they were enthusiastic about the program and understood through preparatory reading and in-service workshops the orientation of the program, all admitted to experiencing moments of doubt and uncertainty with respect to the outcome of the project. These doubts resulted partly from feelings of alienation from the other teachers in the language school who continued to use a highly structured audiolingual method in their classes. Administrators of the school, while in principle favorable to the new approach, tended to reveal ambivalent views as to its probable success. Interestingly, students themselves often expressed the feeling that they were in some way being shortchanged. They pointed out that the other groups had completed "the red book" or "the green book" while they had been studying city maps and learning about the educational system.

Our weekly videotapes of the classroom sessions corroborate the participating teachers' observations regarding the wide range of individual differences among the students in terms of their willingness to seek out information and generate input from the teacher. We hope, by examining students' scores on tests of nonverbal I.Q. and cognitive style and data from a sociolinguistic questionnaire, to understand better the constellation of personal characteristics which are associated with what Seliger (1977) has termed high or low input generators.

The impressionistic view of the teachers is that the project, designed primarily for students who seem to make no measurable progress in regular classes, was relatively successful. The students gained a greater degree of self-confidence in their ability to function in a French environment. Our prediction is that while these learners are still far from fluent in French they are more self-confident and less likely to shy away from contacts with native speakers of the target language than are those who have spent an equivalent length of time doing pattern practice, imitation exercises, or simulated dialogues. We believe that ultimately it is the possibility of contacts with native speakers that will bring about the development of verbal fluency and linguistic accuracy in our learners.

CONCLUSION

Our review of the literature relating to the nature of formal and informal learning has provided convincing evidence that complex skills can be acquired in the absence of formal instruction. Since language or communication is in fact behavior, and not a body of knowledge, it seems normal that it should essentially be acquired as the result of communicative interaction between the learner and a well-disposed native speaker. This is clearly the case in native language acquisition, which is universally successful. If there is sufficient reason for a society to officially promote second language teaching on a widespread basis, there should be equally sound reasons for promoting and sustaining intercultural contacts at the individual level. There is something alarming in the growth of the second language educational establishment in contemporary North American society. It suggests we are placing on the shoulders of educators a responsibility which should be shared to a much greater extent by society in general.

There is sound theoretical, empirical, and anecdotal support for the position that verbal fluency in a second language is most effectively acquired when the learning context corresponds to that described for informal learning and where it is possible for the language to be acquired rather than learned. Direct participation in communication with native speakers as well as social or professional contact with the target-language group provides the authentic linguistic input data, feedback on performance, and psychological support which are the prerequisites for second language acquisition. Interestingly, in many societies prevailing social structures perpetuate cultural and linguistic isolation. It is often and, I believe, inappropriately assumed that individuals or groups who remain culturally isolated do so because of their inadequate second language skills. It is my contention that the converse is more often true: cultural isolation is the cause of the failure to acquire the second language. This philosophy underlies our current experimental program to restructure the environment in which immigrants to Quebec learn French, so that contact with supportive native speakers in an occupational setting replaces contact with other immigrants in a language classroom. It should be noted that this calls for a certain amount of conscious social engineering. Left to his own devices to pick up the language, the typical learner might gravitate toward his own cultural group and not seek out native speakers of the target language with whom to interact. There is reason to believe that simply rubbing shoulders with native speakers is not sufficient—the learner must receive an input of the second language directed to him by a concerned native speaker. This input must be embedded in a context of social interaction.

In spite of my firm belief in the human being's ability to acquire a second language informally, I am convinced that classrooms will continue to provide an important setting for second language learning. They will certainly have a vital role to play in assuring literacy in a second language. In communities which offer no possibilities for contact with speakers of the target language, communicative competency training will complement formal language teaching. Furthermore, as an increasingly fine-grained picture of the second language acquisition process emerges from the research literature, we can look forward to changes in the structure of classroom activities and innovative attempt to encourage language *acquisition* by adults in formal instructional settings. This new orientation will call for a radical reshaping of teacher training programs, instructional materials, and evaluation criteria. Most of all, it will call for a better understanding of the learner and increased respect for the natural capacity for language acquisition which he brings with him into the classroom.

REFERENCES

Allwright, R. "Language Learning Through Communication Practice," *ELT. Documents, British Council*, 1976, *3*, 2-15.

Bibeau, G. *Report of the Independent Study on the Language Training Programmes of the Public Service of Canada (General Report).* Ottawa: Public Service of Canada, 1976.

Brown, R. *A First Language: The Early Stages.* Cambridge, Mass.: Harvard University Press, 1973.

Bruner, J. S., in J. S. Bruner, R. R. Oliver, P. M. Greenfield, *Studies in Cognitive Growth.* New York: Wiley, 1966.

Bullock, A. *A Language for Life.* London: H.M.S.O., 1974.

Bullowa, M. "When Infant and Adult Communicate How Do they Synchronize their Behaviors?" Paper presented at the Biennial Meeting of the International Society for the Study of Behavioral Development. Ann Arbor, Mich., 1973.

Cazden, C. B. "Environmental Assistance to the Child's Acquisition of Grammar," Ph.D. dissertation, Harvard University, 1965.

Chomsky, C. *The Acquisition of Syntax in Children from 5-10.* Cambridge, Mass.: M.I.T. Press, 1969.

Chomsky, N. *Aspects of the Theory of Syntax.* Cambridge, Mass.: M.I.T. Press, 1965.

Condon, W. S., and L. W. Sander. "Synchrony Demonstrated Between Movements of Neonate and Adult Speech." *Child Development,* 1974, *45,* 456-462.

Corder, S. P. "The Significance of Learners' Errors," *IRAL,* 1967, *5,* 161-169.

———. *Language Teaching and Learning: A Social Encounter.* Paper presented at TESOL Convention, Miami, Fla., 1977.

Dittmar, N., and W. Klein. "The Acquisition of German Syntax by Foreign Migrant Workers," *The Heidelberg Project on Pidgin-Deutsch.* Unpublished mimeograph, 1977.

Dulay, H. C., and M. K. Burt. "Natural Sequences in Child Second Language Acquisition," *Working Papers on Bilingualism,* 1974, *3,* 44-67.

Ervin-Tripp, S. M. "Is Second Language Learning Like the First?" *TESOL Quarterly,* 1974, *8,* 111-127.

Ferguson, C. A. "Towards a Characterization of English Foreigner Talk," *Anthropological Linguistics,* 1975, *17,* 1-14.

———. "Linguistic Theory," in *Bilingual Education: Current Perspectives.* Washington, D.C.: Center for Applied Linguistics, 1977.

Gladwin, T. *East is a Big Bird.* Cambridge: Harvard University Press, 1970.

Hebb, D. O., W. E. Lambert, and G. R. Tucker. "Language, Thought, and Experience," *Modern Language Journal,* 1971, *55,* 212-222.

Hoggart, R. *The Uses of Literacy.* Harmondsworth, Middlesex: Penguin Books, 1957.

Kennedy, G. "Conditions for Language Learning," in J. W. Oller and J. C. Richards, eds., *Focus on the Learner.* Rowley, Mass.: Newbury House, 1973.

Krashen, S. D. "The Monitor Model for Second Language Performance," in *Viewpoints on English as a Second Language.* M. Burt, H. Dulay, and M. Finnochiaro, eds. New York: Regents Publishing Company, 1975.

———. "Formal and Informal Linguistic Environments in Language Acquisition and Language Learning," *TESOL Quarterly,* 1976, *10,* 157-168.

———. "Some Issues Relating to the Monitor Model," paper presented at the 1977 TESOL Conference, Miami, Fla.

Lagarde, J. P., and C. Vigier. "L'alphabétisation et insertion linguistique des travailleurs étrangers. *Mélanges Pedagogiques.* Centre de Recherches et d'Applications Pédagogiques en Langues. Université de Nancy II, France, 1974.

Lave, J. "Tailor-Made Experiments and Evaluating the Intellectual Consequences of Apprenticeship Training," *Quarterly Newsletter of the Institute for Comparative Human Development,* 1977, *1* (2), 1-3.

Long, M. H. "Teacher Feedback on Learner Error—Mapping Cognitions," paper presented at the Eleventh Annual TESOL Convention, Miami, Fla., 1977.

Macnamara, J. "Nurseries, Streets, and Classrooms: Some Comparisons and Deductions," *Modern Language Journal, 57,* 1973, 250-254.

———. "Comparison Between First and Second Language Learning," *Working Papers on Bilingualism,* 1975, *7,* 71-95.

Macnamara, J., J. Svarc, and S. Horner. "Attending a Primary School of the Other Language in Montreal," in *The Bilingual Child.* New York: The Academic Press, 1976.

Mason, C. "The Relevance of Intensive Training in English as a Foreign Language for University Students," *Language Learning, 21,* 197-204.

McNeill, D. *The Acquisition of Language: The Study of Developmental Psycholinguistics.* New York: Harper & Row, 1970.

Mead, M. *Continuities in Cultural Evolution.* New Haven: Yale University Press, 1964.

Obanya, Pai. "Second Language Learning Out of School." *I.T.L. Review of Applied Linguistics,* 1976, *31,* 15-26.

Palermo, D. S., and D. L. Molfese. "Language Acquisition from Age Five Onward," *Psychological Bulletin,* 1972, *78,* 409-428.

Richards, J. C. "The Ethnography of Second Language Communication," working paper prepared for discussion at the Nordic Summer Institute on Interlanguage Studies, Copenhagen, 1977.

Saegert, J., S. Scott, J. Perkins, and G. R. Tucker. "A Note on the Relationship Between English Proficiency, Years of Study, and Medium of Instruction," *Language Learning,* 1974, *24,* 99-104.

Savignon, S. J. *Communicative Competence: An Experiment in Foreign Language Teaching.* Philadelphia: The Center for Curriculum Development, 1972.

Schumann, J. H. "Second Language Acquisition: The Pidginization Hypothesis," *Language Learning, 26,* 391-408.

Scribner, S., and M. Cole. "Cognitive Consequences of Formal and Informal Learning," *Science,* 1973, *182,* 553-559.

Seliger, H. W. "Does Practice Make Perfect?: A Study of Interaction Patterns and L2 Competence," paper presented at the First Annual Second Language Research Forum, Los Angeles, Feb., 1977.

Selinker, L., M. Swain, and G. Dumas. "The Interlanguage Hypothesis Extended to Children," *Language Learning,* 1975, *25,* 139-152.

Skinner, B. F. *Verbal Behavior.* New York: Appleton-Century Crofts, 1957.

Snow, C. E., and C. A. Ferguson. *Talking to Children.* Cambridge: Cambridge University Press, 1977.

Spilka, I. "Assessment of Second Language Performance," *The Canadian Modern Language Review,* 1976, *5,* 543-562.

Tucker, G. R., and A. d'Anglejan. "Language Learning Processes," in D. Lange, ed., *The Britannica Review of Foreign Language Education,* 1970, *3,* 163-182.

Upshur, J. "Four Experiments on the Relation Between Foreign Language Teaching and Learning," *Language Learning,* 1968, *18,* 111-124.

Wagner-Gough, J., and E. Hatch. "The Importance of Input Data in Second Language Acquisition Studies," *Language Learning, 25,* 297-308.

STUDY AND DISCUSSION QUESTIONS

(1) The belief that all learning comes from books and, by extension, takes place in schools seems prevalent in today's society. In what way might this philosophy undermine attempts to promote informal language acquisition?

(2) D'Anglejan does not appear to make a distinction between second language learning by children and adults. Consider the contexts in which both are typically exposed to formal second language teaching. Is her position justified?

(3) According to Krashen's "monitor-model," second language learners may have to trade off accuracy for verbal fluency in spontaneous conversation with native speakers. How important is grammatical accuracy in oral communication? Can you note examples of deviant or poorly formed sentences in the speech of native speakers with whom you interact?

(4) Examine some widely used second language textbooks. Does the speech used in dialogues conform to that which the learner is likely to hear outside the classroom? Are the suggested communication activities really drills or are they designed to encourage the learner to express his own thoughts and ideas?

(5) D'Anglejan suggests that successful second language acquisition is the *result* rather than the *cause* of opportunities for interaction with speakers of the target language. Examine this hypothesis in the light of observations of typical patterns of social interaction in your own community.

(6) Discuss the pros and cons of emphasizing communicative competency training in areas where second language learners have no opportunity to encounter speakers of the target language.

(7) D'Anglejan stresses the importance of cross-cultural contacts at the individual level in promoting effective second language acquisition. What types of social intervention would you propose for child and adult immigrants, respectively?

(8) The observation that a second language is more successfully learned when it is used as a medium of instruction rather than taught as a subject *per se* is somewhat puzzling. What explanations can you offer for this phenomenon?

(9) How might formal classroom time be used to help students become more efficient at acquiring a second language in informal contexts?

(10) Are the difficulties which many minority group students encounter in mastering literacy skills in English necessarily related to their lack of familiarity with the target language? In what way would ESL training for such students need to differ from the basic literacy training offered to English-speaking students from a similar socioeconomic background?

HOME-SCHOOL LANGUAGE SWITCHING

Merrill Swain

The term "home-school language switch" has been used to refer to contexts in which the language of communication at home is different from the language of instruction in school[1]—a situation not uncommon for students in many parts of the world. Under these circumstances, second language learning necessarily becomes an integral part of the students' lives. In this chapter, three types of programs involving a home-school language switch are described and compared in order to account for contradictory research findings which have emerged not only in relation to second language learning, but academic achievement as well.

SECOND LANGUAGE IMMERSION

Immersion refers to a situation in which children from the same linguistic and cultural background who have had no prior contact with the school language are put together in a classroom setting in which the second language is used as the medium of instruction.

One example of an immersion program is that of French immersion in Canada. The initiative for such a program in the public school system began with a small group of parents in St. Lambert, a suburb of Montreal, whose primary concern was that the level of French attained by their children in a traditional French-as-a-second-language (FSL) program would not be sufficient to meet their needs in a community and country that was increasingly emphasizing the importance of French as a *langue de travail*. As one parent put it, "many of us had learned French in high school, but had graduated with very little proficiency in it, in addition to having a big inferiority complex about second language learning" (Parkes, 1972). They did not want the same for their children—they wanted their children to be able to function in an environment in which the language of work was French. Nothing was said about attaining a native-like command of the language. They were, however, convinced that if French was used as a medium of communication—as a means to an end rather than as an end in itself—second language learning would be enhanced.

Today, French immersion programs exist in every province and in every major city of Canada. The students in a French immersion program are for the most part English-speaking children who have had little or no exposure to French before entering school. English is the language of their home and immediate community environment.

The typical format of a French immersion program at the primary grade levels is that all instruction is given in French until grade 2 or grade 3, when English Language Arts is introduced and taught in English for approximately an hour a day. With each successive year thereafter a larger proportion of the curriculum is taught in English until an approximately equal balance is reached between the time devoted to instruction in each language.

The term *immersion* has led to many a misconception of what actually occurs in a French immersion class. Although it *is* the case that French is the only language used by the teacher, it is *not* the case that it is the only language used by the children. During much of the first year in a primary-level French immersion program, the children continue to speak English among themselves and to their teacher, who, although a native speaker of French, is bilingual, and therefore can understand the children when they use their native language. It is not until the second year of the program that the teacher begins to insist that the children attempt to express their ideas in French and, through a gradual transition, French comes to be established as the language of the classroom.

Many of the French immersion programs in Canada have been evaluated, and the results have been remarkably consistent across programs and geographical areas (see Swain, 1974 for a review, and Swain, 1976a for a bibliography of research on immersion education).

Generally speaking, in the evaluations of French immersion programs, four basic questions have been examined:

(1) Are the children enrolled in the French immersion program more proficient in French than they would be if they took an FSL program (20-40 minutes a day of formal French instruction)?

(2) Does prolonged exposure to a second language result in some loss of facility in the students' native language?

(3) Does instruction in a second language about a specific subject (for example, mathematics) affect the students' achievement in that subject?

(4) Does the learning of a second language affect the child's I.Q. and general cognitive development?

Answers to these questions have been sought by administering tests of French language skills, English language skills, subject-area knowledge, and I.Q. to the students in the French immersion program and comparing their results with those of students with similar background characteristics enrolled in a regular English program and studying FSL.

Generally speaking, the results show:

(1) French immersion programs lead to the development of French skills far superior to those of students following an FSL program. How the French immersion children perform in relation to native speakers of French will be discussed below.

(2) Prior to the introduction of formal training in English Language Arts, students in the primary French immersion program do not perform as well as their English-taught peers in English skills. However, they quickly catch up to their peers if they are introduced to formal instruction in English Language Arts at the grade 2, 3, or 4 level. In fact, the data suggest that in some aspects of English language skills, the immersion students outperform their English-instructed peers by grade 5 or 6.

(3) Where achievement in subject areas taught in French has been tested in English, French immersion students perform as well as their English-taught peers.

(4) Students who have attended several years of a primary French immersion program do not appear to be disadvantaged in terms of cognitive development. They continue to perform as well on standardized I.Q. tests as their English-taught peers. Additionally, there is some evidence which suggests that by the later grades, certain aspects of cognitive functioning may have been enhanced (see Cummins, in press, 1978b, for a review).

Thus the overall picture which emerges from the studies related to primary-level French immersion programs is a positive one. Many educators have referred to the documented success of the French immersion programs in Canada as evidence that it is in fact possible to learn both a second language *and* subject matter at the same time. Indeed the success of the immersion programs has led to a tenuous extension of this line of reasoning. The success of the immersion program has been used to argue against the necessity of education in the mother tongue in cases where the mother tongue is not the same as that used in the schools. In other words the French immersion program has, for some educators, legitimized home-school language switching, and has provided an argument against vernacular education for minority language groups. It is, therefore, important to examine closely the validity of this generalization. To do so, we will examine another type of program which has often been referred to as immersion but which has been relabeled as *submersion* to draw attention to essential differences (Cohen and Swain, 1976).

SECOND LANGUAGE SUBMERSION

Second language submersion refers to the situation encountered by some children wherein they must make a home-school language switch, while others can already function in the school language. Within the same classroom, then, one might find children who have no knowledge of the school language, varying degrees of facility in the school language through contact with the wider community, and native speakers of the school language.

Typical of this situation are the children of migrant workers, first and second generation immigrants, as well as the children of our indigenous populations for whom low academic achievement, low target-language proficiency, low self-esteem, and first language loss have been reported in submersion programs (see, for example, Yarborough, 1967; Skutnabb-Kangas and Toukomaa, 1976).

The contradictory results for children experiencing a home-school language switch in an immersion program and in a submersion program indicate clearly the need to look beyond the home-school language switch as a causal variable. Some of the factors which contribute to an explanation of the differences in linguistic and academic outcomes between the two programs have been discussed by Cohen and Swain (1976), Burnaby (1976), and Paulston (in press).

First, it is the case that most of the children enrolled in the French immersion programs are from middle to upper-middle class homes; whereas many children involved in the submersion type of home-school language switch programs are from lower-working class homes. It is a recognized fact that socioeconomic class correlates with school achievement. Thus, with children in the French immersion program it is not surprising to find that although working class children do as well academically and linguistically in French immersion programs as their working class counterparts in English programs, it is not the case that they do as well as middle class children in similar programs (Bruck, Jakimik and Tucker, in press). (Similar conclusions hold true for children with learning disabilities and below-average intelligence; see Genesee, 1976 for a review.) Similarly, there is evidence to suggest that children from middle class homes who undergo a submersion experience can come to pass for native speakers of the target language without any noticeable loss in the first language (Macnamara, Svarc, and Horner, 1976). Thus comparisons of results across programs without taking account of socioeconomic differences are obviously inadequate.

The way in which socioeconomic class affects second language learning and academic achievement is not well understood. Cummins (1978a, in press) has suggested that the development of skills in a second language is a function of the level of the child's first language competence at the time when intensive exposure to the language begins (developmental interdependence hypothesis).[2,3] Cummins points out that in the case of most middle class Anglophone children in Canadian immersion programs, the first language is adequately developed and reinforced by the out-of-school environment, while this may not be the case among lower class or "disadvantaged" minority language children. If the developmental interdependence hypothesis is correct, then children whose first language is not adequately developed should not be exposed to a language switch until it is. Developing and maintaining the first language will provide the potential for equivalently high levels to be attained in the second language.

Cummins has also proposed the "threshold" hypothesis—its import being linked intimately with the developmental interdependence hypothesis. Basically the threshold hypothesis claims that one must attain a threshold level of competence in the second language in order to be able to profit by instruction in that language. But because the level of competence in the second language is dependent on the level attained in the first language, it is important to ensure that the threshold level is also attained in the first language. It must not be forgotten, however, that not only might socioeconomic variables be related to first language development, but also so will variables such as language use patterns in the home and perceived prestige value of the home and school languages.

Concerning the perceived status of the languages in question, in the French immersion program the children are members of the dominant linguistic and cultural group. Learning the second language does not portend the gradual replacement of the first language and the loss of cultural identity associated with that language. Furthermore the second language being learned is a socially relevant, nationally, and internationally recognized language, through which individual economic advantages may accrue to the learner. Lambert (1977) has referred to this situation, that is, where the first language is maintained while a second language is being learned, as an "additive" form of bilingualism. This is in contrast to the situation faced by many immigrant groups and indigenous populations who perceive knowledge of the majority school language to be the gateway to social and economic gains, and the home language to be of no consequence except in enabling them to communicate with their friends and relatives. The overwhelming use of the dominant language in school and in the wider community often results in a "subtractive" form of bilingualism (Lambert, 1977), where the learning of the second language may reflect some degree of loss of the first language and culture.

Program variables also have been considered to play an important role. As has been noted, the French immersion program involves a home-school language switch which is the same language switch for all children, and where all children begin the program with essentially the same level of competence in the school language—nil. In the submersion program, the children experiencing the language switch are mixed together with students whose native language is that of the school. In the immersion program, the use of the second language by the children receives praise and reward, leading to feelings of progress and accomplishment. In the submersion program, use of the second language with competence and fluency is *expected*. Limited proficiency is often treated as a sign of limited intellectual and academic ability, resulting in feelings of inferiority and lack of self-esteem. In the immersion program, second language learning is a recognized goal, and attended to by the teachers. In the submersion program, second language learning is presumed to have occurred, and students are instructed as if they were native speakers of the school language. The teachers in the French immersion program can understand the children's home language and respond appropriately. The teachers in the submersion program typically cannot understand the home language or languages being used by their students, who are left frustrated by their inability to make their needs known and their ideas understood. Furthermore the teachers may have little understanding of the complexity of the task facing the second language learners as they grapple with new ideas presented in a form intended for native speakers. In the French immersion program the children's home language is introduced as a subject at some stage in their educational program, providing institutional recognition of the importance of that language. In the submersion program, the home language is neither taught nor used, reinforcing the attitude that it is of little import.

Participation in a French immersion program is *optional*—at the choice of the parents—thereby ensuring the interest and support of the parents. Participation in a submersion program is obligatory. No other options are available to the children. Because of the home-school language difference parents are reluctant or unable to communicate with school personnel about their interests or concerns related to their child's development within the educational setting.

Thus, submersion and immersion programs are clearly different programs which lead to different results. Those who have recognized the failure of submersion home-school language switch programs have argued that what is needed is education in the vernacular, an argument not incompatible with Cummins's hypotheses.

TRANSITIONAL AND MAINTENANCE BILINGUAL EDUCATION PROGRAMS

Transitional and maintenance bilingual education programs both involve a home-school language switch. Both, however, involve beginning the educational process in the home language of the children, shifting at a later stage to the partial use of the language typically used in the school setting (maintenance bilingual education programs) or to the complete use of the language typically used in the school setting (transitional bilingual education programs).

Through this process, educators are hoping to accomplish several things at once: increase the level of academic achievement, strengthen self-image, and develop second language skills. Whereas in the immersion program, the main aim is to develop second language skills without a *decrease* in academic achievement or mother tongue development, in the immersion program, no one is concerned with improving the child's self-image; it is not judged to be low. The fact that different criteria of success have been applied to each program indicates that it is not valid to simply look at the success-rate of the programs in order to determine whether a program of home-school language switch or of vernacular education is better.

In the case of the transitional and maintenance programs, there is evidence to suggest that in many—but by no means in all—programs, measures of first *and* second language skills, of academic achievement, and of self-concept were higher among those participating in the bilingual program than those participating in a unilingual (submersion) program (see, for example, Belkin, Graham, Paulston, and Williams, 1977; Skutnabb-Kangas and Toukomaa, 1976; Claydon, Knight, and Rado, 1977). In the French immersion program all programs have been judged successful because a second language is learned without loss in academic achievement or mother tongue skills relative to children in the regular English program. But what does a comparison of this sort mean? Very little indeed. A comparison of those goals which the programs have in common would be considerably more meaningful. One goal which the programs have in common is second language learning.

SECOND LANGUAGE LEARNING

In considering the studies associated with the programs, it is important to note that many of the comparisons of the second language skills of the French immersion children have been in relation to children who have learned French as a *second* language through more traditional language-teaching programs; whereas comparisons of the children in the other programs have been in relation to children who are *native* speakers of the target language.

Consider for example, the following description of the second language skills of French immersion children as summarized by Tucker and d'Anglejan (1972):

In addition and at no cost they can also read, write, speak and understand French in a way that English pupils who follow a traditional program of French as a second language never do. These children have already acquired a mastery of the basic elements of French phonology, morphology, and syntax; and they have not developed the inhibition which so often characterizes the performance of the foreign or second language student.

More recently, comparisons with the French used by native speakers of the same age have become more frequent. Swain (in press) concluded that:

The results reveal consistently superior performance of the immersion students relative to students following a program of FSL instruction. Furthermore, immersion students perform better than at least 30% of native-French students who served as norming populations for the standardized tests employed. After six or seven years in an immersion program, student performance in the areas of listening and reading approaches native-like levels; whereas in the areas of speaking and writing, many differences between immersion and francophone students still remain. Second language acquisition research, as well as teacher opinion, suggest that additional language "input" through sustained interaction with francophone peers is an essential component of a program if the attainment of native-like speaking abilities is to be a program goal.

What are some of the differences between the speech of the French immersion students and students whose first language is French? To date almost no systematic analyses have been undertaken which have compared in detail the French spoken by the immersion students with that used by their Francophone peers. One exception is a study (Harley and Swain, 1977, in press) which examines the productive control of the verb system in French by grade 5 immersion children in a completely English-speaking community, grade 5 French-English bilingual children, and grade 5 unilingual French children from Quebec. The data analyzed for this study were obtained through individual interviews conducted by a native French-speaking adult.

Questions were directed to in-school and out-of-school topics of relevance and intrinsic interest to children of the age group concerned. The interviewer was free to extend the conversation in any direction that seemed appropriate, and was asked to introduce a minimum set of questions in as natural an order as possible. This set of questions was designed to elicit a variety of discourse types—narrative, descriptive, and expository—which might be expected to contain differences in time, aspect, and modality, with a corresponding variety of verb forms. For example, the students were invited to tell the interviewer about personal experiences from the past, to describe some classroom activities, and to talk about their dreams for the future.

The study was carried out with a view to determining whether or not there are systematic differences in the spoken French of the immersion pupils vis-à-vis the comparison groups. The findings indicate that there are such differences. In general, the immersion children may be said to be operating with simpler and gramatically less redundant verb systems. They tend to lack forms which are of minimal import for the conveyance of ideational meaning, or for which grammatically less complex alternative means of conveying the appropriate meaning exist. The forms and rules that they have mastered appear to be those that are the most generalized in the target verb system (for example, the first conjugation -er verb pattern). In the area of verb syntax, it appears that where French has a more complex system than English (for example, in the form and placement of object pronouns), the immersion children tend to opt for a simpler pattern that approximates the one that they are already familiar with in their mother tongue. It is significant, however, that in the area of vocabulary, of major importance in the realization of meaning, the immersion children seem, in general, to be relatively close to the comparison groups.

One interpretation of the systematic differences between the immersion children's speech and that of the comparison groups is that such differences are clearly connected with the language acquisition setting in which the immersion children find themselves. The French immersion classroom provides a setting for second language acquisition that resembles a natural language acquisition setting in some important respects. Not only do the pupils receive several hours of exposure to French each day, but they have the opportunity to use the second language for real communication about a wide variety of topics. Indeed it may be hypothesized that, as in a natural setting, it is their communicative needs that largely determine what French is acquired. Their communicative needs in the classroom are oriented most strongly toward the conveyance of cognitive meaning, and once the children have reached a point in their language development where they can make themselves understood to their teacher and classmates (as they clearly have), there is no strong social incentive to develop further toward native-speaker norms. Many of the errors noted in the speech of the grade-5 immersion students appear to be *fossilized*; that is, they appear to have been in their speech for several years (see, e.g., Swain, 1974, 1976b; Selinker, Swain, and Dumas, 1975) and show little sign of being eradicated.

What makes the French immersion setting different from the natural setting is that the children are for the most part exposed, in any one year, to only one native French-speaking model—the teacher. Otherwise, the spoken French language input that they receive is largely that of their nonnative French-speaking classmates in interaction with the teacher or with each other. This and the lack of interaction with native French-speaking peers suggests that there may be insufficient input, or social stimulus, for the immersion children to develop completely native-like speech patterns. This isolation, or "social distance" from native speaking peers, experienced by the immersion students may, however, be quite similar in important ways to that experienced by some language learners in natural settings (Schumann, 1976). It is interesting to note that the simplification evident in the immersion children's speech is similar in kind to that found in the speech of many "natural" second language learners, in whose speech certain forms may also become fossilized (see, for example, Schumann, in press).

Although a similarly detailed, comparative study of the product of second language learning in the other home-school language switch settings described has not been undertaken, it is highly probable that the learners attain a more native-like command of the second language, especially if interaction with native speakers of the target language is one of the critical variables: children in the submersion programs have contact with native-speaking children of the target language both within and out of school; children in the bilingual education programs typically have contact with native speakers out of school. Perhaps what the linguistic product of the French immersion program represents is the best that can be accomplished in terms of developing second language skills in a school setting alone.

However, the extent to which native-like command of the second language is accomplished at the expense of the first language, is the extent to which a valuable resource has been lost, both to the individual and to the society. And if the threshold and developmental interdependence hypotheses are substantiated, then the extent to which the first language is not developed must be seen as a limiting factor in second-language development. One of the important educational tasks of the future is to structure school settings so that they convert subtractive forms of bilingualism into additive ones. This structure will necessarily involve a home-school language switch at some stage in the educational process, but when and how much must be determined in relation to the linguistic and socioeconomic characteristics of the learner and of the learning environment.

NOTES

1. Although I refer to *languages* of the home and school throughout this paper, the situations described incorporate as well those in which home and school *dialects* differ.

2. Cummins appears to use "language competence" and "cognitive competence" interchangeably, by which he means "the ability to make effective use of the cognitive functions of the language, i.e., to use language effectively as an instrument of thought and represent cognitive operations by means of language" (in press, 1978b, footnote 21).

3. This description is obviously not applicable to the situation where two languages are learned simultaneously from birth.

REFERENCES

Belkin, J., J. Graham, C. Paulston, and E. Williams. "Appendix B: Excerpts from abstracts of U.S. dissertations on bilingual education," in C. B. Paulston, ed., *Research in Bilingual Education: Current Perspectives,* Arlington, Va.: Center for Applied Linguistics, 1977.

Bruck, M., J. Jakimik, and G. R. Tucker. "Are French programs suitable for working class children?" in W. Engel, ed., *Prospects in Child Language,* Amsterdam: Royal Vangorcum, in press.

Burnaby, B. "Language in native education," in M. Swain, ed., *Bilingualism in Canadian Education: Issues and Research.* Yearbook of the Canadian Society for the Study of Education, 3, Edmonton, Alta.: Western Industrial Research Centre, 1976, 62-85.

Claydon, L., T. Knight, and M. Rado. *Curriculum and Culture: Schooling in a Pluralistic Society,* Sydney, Australia: George Allen and Unwin, 1977.

Cohen, A. D., and M. Swain. "Bilingual education: The immersion model in the North American context," *TESOL Quarterly,* 1976, *10* (1), 45-53. Reprinted in J. E. Alatis and K. Twaddell, eds., *English as a Second Language in Bilingual Education,* Washington, D.C.: TESOL, 1976, 55-63.

Cummins, J. "The influence of bilingualism on cognitive growth: A synthesis of research findings and explanatory hypotheses," *Working Papers on Bilingualism,* 1976, *9,* 1-43.

———. "Educational implications of mother tongue maintenance in minority language groups," *The Canadian Modern Language Review,* February, 1978a, in press.

———. "The cognitive development of children in immersion programs," *The Canadian Modern Language Review,* 1978b, in press.

Genesee, F. "The suitability of immersion programs for all children," *The Canadian Modern Language Review,* 1976, *32* (5), 494-515.

Harley, B., and M. Swain. "An analysis of the spoken French of five French immersion pupils," *Working Papers on Bilingualism,* 1977, *14,* 31-46.

———. "An analysis of the verb system used by young learners of French," *Interlanguage Studies Bulletin,* 1978, *3* (1), in press.

Hébert, R. *Rendement académique et langue d'enseignement chez les élèves franco-manitobains.* Saint-Boniface, Manitoba: Centre de recherches du Collège Universitaire de Saint-Boniface, 1976.

Lambert, W. E. "The effects of bilingualism on the individual: Cognitive and sociocultural consequences," in P. A. Hornby, ed., *Bilingualism: Psychological, Social, and Educational Implications,* New York: Academic Press, 1977, 15-27.

Macnamara, J., J. Svarc, and S. Horner. "Attending a primary school of the other language in Montreal," in A. Simoes, Jr., ed., *The Bilingual Child: Research and Analysis of Existing Educational Themes,* New York: Academic Press, 1976, 113-131.

Parkes, M. "Perspectives on the Montreal programs," in M. Swain, ed., *Bilingual Schooling: Some Experiences in Canada and the United States.* Toronto: The Ontario Institute for Studies in Education, 1972, 22-27.

Paulston, C. B. "Bilingual bicultural education," *Review of Research in Education,* in press.

Schumann, J. H. "Social distance as a factor in second language acquisition," *Language Learning,* 1976, *26* (1), 135-143.

———. *The Pidginization Process: A Model for Second Language Learning.* Rowley, Mass.: Newbury House, in press.

Selinker, L., M. Swain, and G. Dumas. "The interlanguage hypothesis extended to children," *Language Learning,* 1975, *25* (1), 139-152.

Skutnabb-Kangas, T., and P. Toukomaa. *Teaching Migrant Children Mother Tongue and Learning the Language of the Host Country in the Context of the Socio-Cultural Situation of the Migrant Family.* Tampere, Finland: Tutkimuksia Research Reports, 1976.

Swain, M. "French immersion programs across Canada: Research findings," *The Canadian Modern Language Review,* 1974, *31* (2), 117-129.

———. "Bibliography: Research on immersion education for the majority child," *The Canadian Modern Language Review,* 1976a, *32* (5), 592-596.

Swain, M. "Changes in errors: Random or systematic?" in G. Nickel, ed., *Proceedings of the Fourth International Congress of Applied Linguistics,* 2, Stuttgart: Hochschulverlag, 1976b, 345-358.

———. "French immersion: Early, late or partial?" *The Canadian Modern Language Review,* 1978, in press.

Swain, M., and M. Bruck, eds. "Immersion education for the majority child," *The Canadian Modern Language Review,* 1976, *32,* entire no. 5.

Tucker, G. R., and A. d'Anglejan. "An approach to bilingual education: The St. Lambert Experiment," in M. Swain, ed., *Bilingual Schooling: Some Experiences in Canada and the United States.* Toronto: The Ontario Institute for Studies in Ontario, 1972, 15-21.

Yarborough, R. W. *Bilingual Education* Hearings before the Special Subcommittee on Bilingual Education of the Committee on Labor and Public Welfare, United States Senate, Ninetieth Congress, two parts. Washington: U.S. Government Printing Office, 1967.

STUDY AND DISCUSSION QUESTIONS

(1) What characteristics of the learner are important in structuring a program of home-school language switch?

(2) What characteristics of the environment are important in structuring a program of home-school language switch?

(3) Consider the nature of the advantages obtained through an additive form of bilingualism.

(4) Compare two different settings that you are familiar with where a home-school language switch occurs. Discuss the relevant political, social, cultural, individual, teacher, and other variables that you think would be crucial in accounting for the relative success or failure of such programs.

(5) Develop a plan for a program which includes a home-school language switch based on a specified set of learner and environmental characteristics.

(6) Develop hypotheses concerning the way in which a specified set of learner and environmental characteristics may interact with the learning processes in a home-school language switch program.

(7) In what circumstances do you think it would be reasonable to argue *against* the necessity of education in the mother tongue for minority language groups, and in what circumstances do you think it would be unreasonable to advance such an argument?

(8) If you had the choice of placing your child in an immersion program, what questions would you want to be sure about before committing yourself to a decision?

$$=========== 13 ===========$$

STRATEGIES FOR INDIVIDUALIZED
LANGUAGE LEARNING AND TEACHING

Ted Rodgers

There are a number of senses in which the terms *individualized* and *individualization* are used and understood in contemporary educational discussions. Basically all discussions of individualized language instruction assume the following:

(1) Individual language learners have different learning needs, styles, and interests.

(2) Individual language teachers have different skills, styles, and interests.

(3) Individualized learning/teaching strategies and activities are those designed to anticipate and be responsive to these differences.

(4) Observed individual differences are of many kinds: strategies and activities can be designed to accommodate these observed individual differences in many different ways.

INDIVIDUALIZATION AS PERSONALIZATION

A major current thrust in contemporary language learning as exemplified in approaches such as The Silent Way, Community Language Learning, and a variety of other proposals to teach *communicative competence* can be said to represent more individualized, in the sense of more personalized, approaches to language learning and teaching. In this broad sense, individualizing instruction refers to organizing the presentation of new language structures and vocabulary in ways that maximize the learners' capacity to say (or write) something he or she *cares* to say (or write) as early as possible in the language learning process.

These "new" approaches, focusing on a more personalized approach to second language learning, have several features which distinguish them qualitatively from their most recent predecessors. Some of these features, as I see them, are as follows:

(1) More emphasis on message meanings; less on formal structures

(2) More emphasis on communicating; less on correctness

(3) More emphasis on problem solving, intuiting, hunching, context interpreting strategies; less on modeling, mimicry, and memory

(4) More emphasis on creating content as well as utterance in the new language; less on using set content and situation

(5) More emphasis on student-student interaction; less on teacher-student interaction

(6) More emphasis on extra-linguistic devices—pedagogical (manipulatives, games, enactments, etc.) as well as paralinguistic (gesture, tone, expression); less on linguistic content *per se*

(7) More emphasis on physical teaching environments which encourage group observation and participation; less on physical arrangements favoring teacher attending only

(8) More attention to positive first-language transfer; less on first language interference.

Discussion of these contemporary personalized and communicative approaches and methodologies are considered in more detail elsewhere in the present volume. I wish to restrict my discussion here to a related but somewhat narrower view of individualization than that suggested above. I will focus on several particular instructional techniques and activities which have been successfully used as teaching components with a variety of methodologies and in a variety of differing types of language-learning situations. These techniques have been developed and used in settings which most would describe as typical and even traditional language-teaching classrooms. Since many of the readers of this book are assumed to be operating in such classrooms, I have restricted my discussion to those techniques most readily adaptable to such settings.

I would now like to define the basic premises underlying instructional individualization, in the limited sense suggested above, trying to be more specific about the assumed types of learning/teaching differences. This will be followed by discussions of some strategies and activities that are designed to accommodate these learning/teaching differences.

ASSUMED LEARNING/TEACHING DIFFERENCES

(1) Students learn at different rates of speed

(2) Students learn through different media (textbooks, films, programmed texts, games, physical activities, etc.)

(3) Students are interested and competent in different kinds of educational content (language arts, mathematics, science, social studies, physical education, etc.)

(4) Students learn through different styles of content/process organization (deductive, inductive, discovery, learning by doing, memorizational, etc.)

(5) Students have differing abilities and preferences in modes of reporting their learning (paper and pencil tests, written reports, two-person conversations, oral reports, etc.)

(6) Students respond differently to different forms of feedback, reinforcement, and reward (teacher praise, peer recognition, competitive grades, money, written certification, etc.)

(7) Students perform differently in different group arrangements (working alone, peer-tutoring, small group activities, whole class instruction, theater presentation, etc.)

(8) Students' learning efficiency varies differentially according to time of study (longer versus shorter study periods, morning versus afternoon, beginning of class period versus end of class period, first term versus last term, etc.)

(9) Students' learning efficiency varies differentially according to place or study (in-class study, library study, laboratory study, home study, etc.)

(10) Differences in teachers' teaching reflect all of the above factors as well as other factors unique to teachers and teaching.

To individualize instruction, generally, is to employ instructional activities and systems which accommodate any or all of these differences among individuals in learning and teaching. To discuss activities for individualized instruction, then, is to relate proposed instructional activities and instructional systems to these kinds of assumed learning/ teaching differences among individuals. The requirements for individualized teaching/learning are (1) the activities themselves and the materials that support them, (2) a procedure for measuring and matching students and activities, and (3) a management system that makes it all possible in real time in real classes. I refer to these requirements: Materials, Measurement/matching, Management—as the three Ms of individualized instruction.

THE THREE Ms OF INDIVIDUALIZED INSTRUCTION

Materials

If you have a lot of students doing a lot of different things, obviously the need for diverse materials is greater than if you have a lot of students doing the same thing at the same time. If you have a lot of students working on activities of their own, in pairs, or in small groups, then obviously the internal explanatory detail and accessibility of such activities must necessarily be greater than is the case for large-group choral exercises or whole class copy-book activities. To individualize classrooms you must have activities for students to do. Hopefully, interesting, educational, self-directing, self-checking, learning promotional . . . activities, but activities, materials, and lots of them.

This does not mean that these materials need be expensive or commercial or even pretested, evaluated, and "Good-Housekeeping-approved." But materials in variety and quantity there must be. For the present purpose we are assuming unavailability, for a variety of reasons, of the flashier prepackaged individualized materials, of the Hawaii English Project or SRA Reading Kit type. We assume that the materials with which an individual teacher can begin to equip a classroom will be (a) teacher-made, (b) student-made, (c) parent-provided, or (d) found objects. If slick commercial materials are available, so much the better. If not, then these other materials sources must be fully exploited.

Measurement/matching

The measurement/matching system must give answers to questions such as the following: How and under what circumstances should a student be introduced to an individualized program? How do you determine when a student has achieved the objectives of a particular subprogram (or is incapable of achieving the objectives) and can and/or should move on to some other subprogram? How should students be grouped in activities so as to maximize learning for all students? How should students be evaluated in terms of formal requirements (if such evaluation is mandatory)? How are students to be made aware of their own progress? How are parents and other interested parties to be made aware of student progress? All these are concerns of a program's measurement component. The requirement for measurement in individualized instruction does not necessarily imply a complex quantitatively based evaluation system. Measurement/matching concerns are more those of assignment and routing than of making final judgments in quantitative terms.

Management

If there has been one obvious and general shortcoming in the variety of attempts that have been made to individualize classrooms, it has been in the lack of imagination (and hard work) applied to systematically organizing the parts of individualized instruction. Many teachers and students have come unglued after about a week of the booming, buzzing, bumbling chaos which often accompanies introduction of a new set of individualized learning materials. The design of a management system for such materials may, in fact, be more critical than the particular set of materials themselves. How are materials interrelated? How inventoried? How are materials stored, displayed, repaired, replaced, revised? How are pupils routed to materials appropriate to their learning needs and relevant to their interests? How does the rest of the class survive and function while the teacher is directing attention to an individual or small group? How are records kept? How are progress reports designed, completed, and routed to the appropriate audiences? All these (and more) are questions dealing with the management of an individualized learning program. The problem of management is the more severe in that, by and large, such management issues are rarely dealt with in preservice teacher-training courses on individualized instruction. At the other end, materials developers are inevitably more concerned with selling materials than systems. Typically the management suggestions accompanying commercial materials are too few, too untested, too general, and too optimistic about the degree to which the materials themselves will absorb students and free teachers from organizational, disciplinary, and other management problems.

Second language teaching presents some additional and severe management hurdles in individualizing instruction. These hurdles are called *direction-giving* and *feedback*. Direction-giving, in oral or graphic form, is usually done in language. Where language learning is the goal, it is difficult to use the relatively complex language typical of instructional directions as the means. This is particularly true in individualized situations where every student may be simultaneously getting a different set of directions. Feedback is required so that each student knows how s/he is doing and what s/he needs to do next. Often the language teacher, or at least a relatively competent user of the language, is required to monitor and respond to learner responses. This is particularly true in oral work. In individualized learning situations there usually just aren't enough competent monitor respondents to go around. These two problems need to be acknowledged early and often. The success of individualized language-learning programs most often hinges on the degree to which these problems have been solved or in some manner cleverly circumvented.

From this point on, I will be focusing more on activities (i.e., materials in use) and less on management and measurement/matching systems. It cannot be overemphasized, however, that the types of activities suggested are of use only in situations in which well worked out systems for program management and progress measurement accompany the activities.

SOME INDIVIDUALIZED LANGUAGE-LEARNING STRATEGIES AND ACTIVITIES

The remainder of this paper describes several instructional ideas which qualify within the constraints listed above. These ideas have been realized in classroom programs which have had a successful track record. For these, the minimal requirements for materials, measurement/matching, and management systems have been designed and used by somebody somewhere.

For the strategies described I have borrowed or given the names below:

(1) programmed learning
(2) sequential learning kits
(3) factlets
(4) contracts
(5) flow-charting
(6) group work
(7) each one-teach one
(8) games
(9) simulations

Programmed learning

The key notion of programmed learning is the idea that a student can be directed (by a nonhuman agency) through a series of predetermined steps (usually many small steps) toward mastery of a specific learning problem. Each program step is linked to the one before and after it. Each step requires active involvement on the part of a student, such as answering a question by writing a specific answer in a spot provided for that answer. The student is also provided direct and immediate feedback regarding each answer, usually in the next program "frame." Programmed learning activities, as customarily used in classrooms, consist of paper and pencil workbooks or worksheets laid out in a linearly sequenced format. The individualized aspect of such materials is that they allow students to proceed at their own pace and to recycle and review steps if they wish.

Three major practical problems, from the perspective of this paper, are (a) the time and patience needed to design and construct linearly programmed materials, (b) the cost of producing and replacing expendable programmed materials, and (c) the typical programmed learning restriction to "read-write" and often "fill-in-the-blank" formats. At least two of these problems (a + b) can be minimized by using programmed design formats to produce programmed materials. Use of such formats can greatly reduce the time necessary to think out and write the necessary programmed steps. Some shortcomings in this approach will be obvious from the example below. The example is from some programmed language-learning materials constructed using a modified cloze procedure. The drill is designed to provide practice in the use of certain function words.

Program Instructions
(probably given orally)
Reading—D-level

Cover the right-hand column with your answer strip. Scan the whole passage to get the overall idea. Then return to the first line. Read the first line and try to determine the words that belong in the blanks. Write the words on your answer strip.

Slide the strip down the column until the first line of answer(s) appears. Compare the answer(s) with what you have written. If your answers vary from those given, try to determine why, then fold over your answer strip and proceed to write answers for the blanks on this line. Check and fold over as before. Continue until you have finished the passage. Put all your answers alongside the answer column. Note how many of your answers are exactly the same as those given in the answer column. Write this number at the bottom of your answer strip. If you have fewer than 8 matches, choose another D-level reading passage from the reading file and begin again. If you have more than 8 matching answers, put your answer strip in the answer box and choose an E-level reading passage from the reading file and begin again.

When I was _____ small boy back _____	a, in
Hammond, the Sunday school picnic was one	
of _____ major events of _____ year. Every	the, the
summer, tension grew week _____ week until	by
_____ great day arrived, and everyone gath-	the
ered at _____ church early in _____ morning	the, the
in _____ splendid concentrate _____ expect-	a, of
ancy, hunger, impatience, and _____ fellow-	good
ship. People _____ assigned to cars, and	were
_____ mounting excitement _____ began	with, they
_____ long drive to Mandeville, over on Lake	the
Pontchartrain.	

In this program the student receives practice (and confirmation) in the use of reading context to select verb forms, prepositions, articles, and idiomatic constituents. Such passages are easy to build "automatically." (They can be built by deleting every nth word or by deleting all or most function words, nouns, modifiers, etc.)

If we consider the second problem of expendability and cost, one can imagine mounting such passages on heavy paper or cardboard (perhaps with lamination) and having students make expendable answer strips the width of the right margin. As students work through the passage they could write their answers on strips, waiting to compare their answers with the key at the end of every section, or they could check every answer as they go, folding over their paper strips to write the next answer. With easily produced programs and minimal expendable materials, programmed learning materials could become practical activity systems in most language classrooms. (Incidentally, cloze-type exercises have been rated as interesting and challenging reading comprehension and writing exercises by a number of study users.) Other sample programs can be found in a very helpful guide entitled, *Programmed Learning and the Language Teacher* by A. P. R. Howarth (Longmans, 1972).

Sequential learning kits

In recent years considerable enthusiasm has developed for learning kit systems. Typical of such kit systems are the SRA Reading Kits. The major feature of such kit materials is that they are developed (in theory) according to a finely graded continuum to lead students from nonperformance to expert performance in the skill area to be mastered. The placement system attempts to locate students on the continuum of skill development at the level of difficulty at which they may be reasonably successful, using already acquired skills and yet sufficiently challenged so that they strive to acquire the new skill increments offered by the materials at that level. A kit will typically contain a variety of materials or exercises within an assumed level of difficulty. For reading kits, the levels of difficulty are determined by the vocabulary difficulty, sentence structure types, passage lengths and topics of the reading selections and, as well, by the type of response expected of the student (e.g., literal recall versus inference) in the reading checks following each reading passage. A reading kit will typically contain ten to fifteen reading levels and ten to fifteen different selections at each level.

The principal objections to such kits are that (1) commercial versions are very expensive, and (2) finely graded sets of materials and diagnostic tests are difficult and time-consuming for teachers to construct on their own. There are, however, several possible alternatives to the purchase of such kits for individual classroom use. Let me suggest a few of these alternatives in outline form. (The examples are for constructing reading kits.)

(1) Buy a kit which can be shared among several classes.

(2) Set up a workshop of talented teachers to produce graded reading passages which all teachers can reproduce, based on the model of a commercial kit.

(3) Cut out or copy short reading passages from interesting sources (magazines, short stories, newspapers, etc.) and grade them impressionistically or by enlisting your students as graders, using cloze procedures.

(4) Reproduce sections of school texts written for different subject areas and different grade levels. Assume the grade levels represent difficulty levels (more or less) and arrange your reading kit selections accordingly.

(5) Get samples of stories written by children at various grade levels. Edit these, write check questions, and arrange them in kit form, as representatives of various levels of reading difficulty.

The other major problem in making kits is that of designing some sort of diagnostic measure that introduces the student into the kit materials at an appropriate level of difficulty. There are several possibly usable schemes for doing this:

(1) Color-code the reading level sections and, on the basis of best judgment, notify each student (by memorandum, preferably) of the color section in which he is to begin his individualized reading study.

(2) Use an individual vocabulary recognition test composed of sample words taken from readings at various kit levels and ask students to pronounce (or, if necessary, define) the individual words. (Word recognition tests of this type have proved to be reasonably reliable indicators of general reading level.) A student's total score on the word recognition test can be used as a basis for placement in an (approximately) appropriate level in the reading program.

(3) Construct a cloze test from a reading passage in the mid-range of difficulty of the kit readings. It has been estimated that a 50% cloze score is minimally adequate to suggest comprehension of reading materials at the level of difficulty of the cloze passage. Thus a student scoring around 50% might be placed in one of the mid-difficulty levels. Those scoring below 50%, in the appropriately lower levels, and those above 50% in the appropriately higher levels of difficulty.

Another feature of the reading kits is a set of exercises sometimes called speed builders. These are sets of cards with short graded passages on them. The student, in addition to reading and answering questions from the longer reading selections at each level, follows a set of continuing practice exercises in which his reading and response is time-limited (e.g., the student is given one minute to read the card and another minute or two to respond to questions based on the content of the short reading passage.) These speed builders appear to be useful components of the reading kits and probably should be included if possible in homemade versions.

Factlets

Factlet is the somewhat colloquial name by which I know an individualized learning system built around small, self-contained, self-directing, topical study packets. A factlet may be organized around a single theme ("Methods of Growing Sugar") or it may be organized around a conceptual question ("Can Computers Think?"). A factlet will typically contain topical activities of several sorts—an introduction to the topic; a dialogue between two knowledgeable people discussing the topic; readings, questions, games, and puzzles related to the topic; cartoons and illustrations highlighting particular aspects of the topic; quizzes; suggested additional resources; study and reporting assignments; an organizational chart showing how this topic (and factlet) is related to other topics (and factlets).

Factlets are particularly useful for modified ESP (English for special purposes) work in general purpose language classes where students may have differing disciplinary and/or vocational interests.

Factlets are individualized in use in that there are usually fewer copies of any one factlet than there are students in a class. Therefore, students will necessarily be working at different points in different factlets at any one time. Students work on topics of their own choosing (within a larger theme of the teacher's choosing) and students work at their own pace. Factlets usually contain internal options for student choice as well.

The factlet system requires some sort of whole class display which suggests generally the content and style of each of the various factlets. The teacher helps students in their selection of a factlet and counsels them regarding problems that arise while working through the factlet. Otherwise, students work largely on their own, although some factlets may be undertaken by two or more students desiring to work as a group. It will usually take anywhere from a day to two weeks to complete a factlet, depending on the topic and student. A factlet, in length, customarily contains ten to twenty pages of written material. Factlets may include tapes and other media sources, although typically they consist principally of reading/writing activities. Factlet responses can be self-checking or can be submitted, upon completion, to the teacher for checking.

It does take some time to prepare factlets. Some of the suggestions offered for the preparation of kit materials might be of use here. Some teachers have had success in having students prepare factlets as one kind of research report. The teacher edits and then uses these as teaching resources (factlets) in subsequent classes. A good deal of direction and modeling is necessary to make this system of factlet construction work, but past experience suggests success is possible.

Contracts

A contract is a formal agreement between two or more persons to do something, stating that the parties to the contract have certain well-defined responsibilities to one another. In an educational contract, a student commits himself to complete certain tasks as his part of the agreement. The teacher commits himself/herself to recognize the student's successful completion of the contract by giving him educational credits for the course or subcourse in which he is enrolled. The student can contract for an A, B, or C grade based on the work he agrees to complete. The contract system is an individualized one in that each contract between student and teacher can be of a different nature, based on what the student and teacher see to be that student's needs and abilities. The student can work on his contract commitment when he wants to, where he wants to, and in whatever order of events he wants to. He can also choose not to work on his contract commitments at all, in which case the contract may state what the result of nonperformance will be.

Contracts are used in a variety of ways—sometimes to decentralize the educational system, sometimes to encourage students to examine more closely educational options open to them, sometimes to try to enforce responsibility on students who display little responsibility, sometimes to designate formally which are the more important and which the less important elements of a study topic.

A typical contract for a study project might look like the following:

Student Contract

Project Name: _____

I will attend _____ class sessions.

I will read resource material from at least _____ sources.

I will talk with at least _____ relevant persons regarding my project.

I will keep a list of new vocabulary words relevant to my project to contain at least _____ words/day for the number of days needed to finish my project.

I will keep a daily journal regarding progress on my project.

I will submit my journal at the end of the contract period.
I will submit a written/oral report of at least _____ words regarding my project finding.
I intend to work for a grade of _____ in this project.
I agree to fulfill all terms of this contract by (date)_____
Any changes in this contract must be initialed by both parties to the contract.

Signed _____ (student)
Witnessed _____ (teacher)
Date_____

The unit/credit system proposed by John Trim and his associates on the Council of Europe project suggests a contract system of a sort. The unit-credit system assumes a number of language learners with different language-learning needs—"components of ability required." Graphically this might look like the following:

Learners	Components of Ability Required							
V	a		c	d	e		g	
W	a	b	c		e			
X	a		c			f	g	h
Y	a	b	c	d				h	i
Z	a		c	d		f	g	

It is assumed that in addition to analyzing the needs of each learner (*measurement* in our terms) and providing learning facilities for each component (*materials* in our terms), the learner would have to be advised on the order in which the components could be taken most profitably (one aspect of *management*). This might well be systematized for each learner in terms of *contract* specifying units to be taken, standards to be met, time and sequence for completion and outcomes anticipated.

In systems like the Hawaii English Program, contracts may be less formal. A child in the planning circle contracts to work in a particular language subprogram. His contract is to continue in that program or until the teacher releases him to work on something else or until the class period ends. The child agrees (contracts) to keep track of the activities he begins and those he completes. This is, essentially, a contract system. Although no written agreements are involved, the child acknowledges his responsibility to do what he has said he will do.

The contract system is attractive in that the teacher can use it with almost any already existing program or content. One can use a contract system with a single textbook in which the students contract to do certain problems or answer certain questions (five easy, three average, one difficult item; all the odd-numbered problems; only the three hardest problems in each problem set, etc.). The contract system is obviously enriched by the quality and quantity of different activities from which the student can choose.

Flow-charting

A flow-chart is a step-by-step diagram of all operations involved in the solution of a particular problem. In classroom use the flow-chart is used as a picture of the activities to be done (in sequence) during a particular period or topic of study. The flow-chart describes all program alternatives and indicates what to do in case of wrong, inadequate, or negative responses to activities. The flow-chart concept is borrowed from the design of computer programs and perhaps thus sounds a bit forbidding to some teachers. The system is basically simple enough and the computer affiliation need not be threatening.

The use of flow-charting allows for individualization in that, although each student begins at the same place, he thereafter proceeds at his own pace and perhaps through a unique set of recommended activities as directed by the flow-chart. The flow-chart is typically posted or otherwise displayed by the teacher in a manner and in a place where it can easily be consulted by students. Shown on pages 264-265 is a flow-chart from a unit within the Hawaii English Program. Note that the flow-chart indicates the theme of a flow-chart sequence, the activities required for all students, optional activities, and the approximate time estimates for each of the required and individual student choice items. Students can follow the flow-chart on their own until they have completed the activities cycle.

Group work

Given large classes and minimal facilities, teachers have been inclined to rely heavily on class-in-chairs-teacher-in-front lecture, demonstration, chalk-talk, and/or dictation modes of instruction. In fact, teachers often assume that no other model is possible given these physical conditions in their classes. Perhaps the first step toward individualization is to examine new group arrangements which can operate within the constraints of large class sizes and inadequate materials. The use of group work activities has proved to be a popular method for giving students some degree of individual attention, according to their needs as perceived by the teacher. Usually the teacher divides the class into three, four, or five groups, assigns students to these groups, works directly with one of the groups and gives the others group work which is largely self-directive.

FLOW CHART — GESTURES
WEEK 1: VISUAL AND VOCAL GESTURES

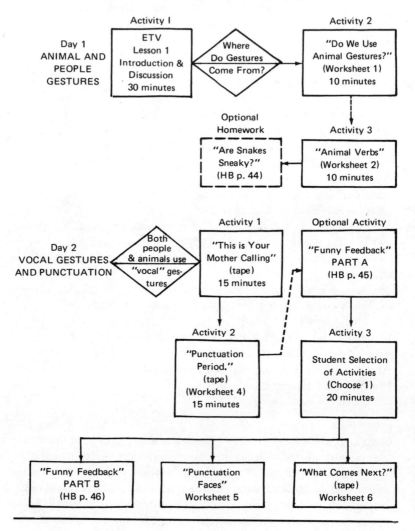

Many of the activities suggested throughout this paper are appropriate for assignment as group work activities.

The major problems in group work concern:

(1) The determination of group composition

(2) The design of group activities which are reasonably self-directing and have relevant content

The flow-chart is a system for organizing individual activities, but it is not the activities per se. I have suggested that the flow-chart might be set up so that students can "play" the flow-chart much as they would play a board game of the Monopoly-type. The flow-chart then becomes an activity itself as well as a chart of activities.

As well as suggesting day-by-day activities, the flow-chart can be used as a shorthand way of directing students within a particular activity. For example, here is a flow-chart for a simple spelling activity:

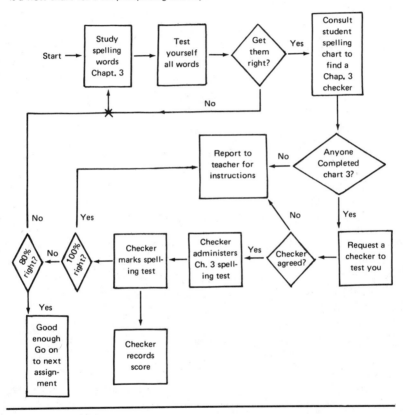

(3) The timing of group activities so that groups come to concluding or stopping points more or less simultaneously

(4) The efficient organization of group activities relative to physical space, movement, monitoring, and reporting

Let us consider the setting up of a group of activities for perhaps an elementary language class. The teacher decides to schedule group work for three groups in three 15-20-minute sections spread over two class periods. Organizational charts might be constructed and posted, for example:

Group Activities	Group A	Group B	Group C
Reading/writing	1	111	11
Oral work	11	1	111
Writing	111	11	1

Group A	Group B	Group C
1. Fazilah	1. Rama	1. Lee
2. etc.	2. etc.	2. etc.
3.	3.	3.
4.	4.	4.
5.	5.	5.
6.	6.	6.

The charts are explained by the teacher.

Groups: Group A, Group B, Group C (children named to be in each group)

Activities: Reading/writing, Oral Work, Writing (description and demonstration of these activities), etc.

Times: Times 1, 11, 111. Who is doing what during what time periods.

Activities description   *Reading/writing.* Students in the Reading/writing group read (on their own) a selection from the reader, passage written on board, worksheet, etc. They are to read as far as they can. Each student is to write in his/her exercise book any word he/she does not fully understand (for later discussion in Oral Work).

Oral Work. Students in the Oral Work Group work with teacher, who conducts oral drills and asks students briefly to read aloud and discuss their reading. Students present unknown words from the activities above for discussion and explanation.

Writing. Students in the Writing Group will copy a writing passage from the board or text into copy books. This may be straight copying, filling-in-blanks, editing each other's writing, etc.

The teacher makes sure students understand the Groups, Times, and Activities. A monitor/reporter is assigned for each group. The groups are then physically organized in their work areas and told to begin. The teacher alerts the groups when a few minutes are left in each time period so that they can bring their group work to a conclusion. The teacher announces the end of each time period and then reviews which groups are to move where and do what. Groups move simultaneously on signal to the new location and activity. The teacher gets the groups settled in and returns to oral work group, and so forth. A number of group activities will encourage cooperative discussion or production by members of the group. The Games section suggests several interactive ideas for group work.

Working in pairs or small groups may be a new experience for many students. Productive group activity does not happen by accident. Students need to know exactly what their goal is, ways they might proceed to reach the goal, and how much time they have. There should be a group leader or secretary when one is needed. Groups for certain activities can be set up by using one of the following methods:

(1) Teacher Grouped

(a) The teacher determines beforehand the number and constitution of the small groups. One teacher listed the groups and group leaders on a large piece of construction paper and tacked it, rolled closed, above the blackboard. When it was time for forming into small groups, the "roster" was unrolled and tacked open. Students arranged themselves as shown on the roster.

(b) Groups are formed on a rotational sequence defined at the beginning of the unit by the teacher. Group membership is always clearly defined but changes for each new small group activity.

(2) Chance Grouped

(a) Students draw cards from a deck or pile of slips which names the subject of the group, or a group number, or a group location in the class. Students join the group defined by the slip they draw.

(b) Students count off. If five groups are to be formed, students count off by fives. All the ones go together, the twos go together, etc.

(c) Groups are alphabetically determined. Students with first (or last) names beginning with letters A, B, C, D go in one group, those beginning with E, F, G, H, I in another, etc.

(d) Groups are determined by the section of the room in which they are seated. This leads to the least reshuffling of students and seats.

(3) Ability Grouped

Following some task, students report to a group as they finish a task or as they get their answers checked "correct." This puts the fastest (most accurate) students in group one, the next fastest students in group two, and so on. Sometimes this is desirable since the groups can work on projects which are most nearly within the capabilities of all members of the group.

Each one—teach one

If one imagined an ideally individualized teaching situation, one might envision a utopia where for every child there was a teacher. Teachers and children, either on a permanent or rotating basis, would be paired off and assigned an office or teaching/learning area. The instructional program and pace would be unique to each pairing of teacher and student. If one means by "teacher" a professionally trained and credentialed educator, then this ideal seems unattainable in any practical situation we can presently imagine. If we take a more humble view of teacher, to mean someone with sufficient knowledge, stature, experience, and maturity to help guide a student through some learning experience, to respond to questions he may have, and to merit his respect, then some more realistic options emerge. Several candidate teachers might qualify in this latter sense—among them parents, teaching aides, older pupils, and peers.

There has been a good deal of discussion regarding the possibilities for engaging these various groups of individuals more immediately and imaginatively in teaching functions. Some proposals have been submitted as to ways in which parents might be more directly involved in the so-called formal education of their own (and other parents') children. Leads could be taken from Scouting and other youth organization programs which often require much fuller engagement of parents as sponsors, tutors, and checkers than do school programs. Some cooperative school programs require the active participation of parents, in some way or other, as one of the contributions toward their children's tuition. One Hawaii school project experimented with the dissemination of Game Packs to the homes of students. These Language Game Packs consisted of a variety of school-program-supportive game ideas and games themselves which could be played by students, siblings, and parents. The Game Pack appeared to be quite popular with students and parents.

Peer-tutoring has also been the subject of considerable experimentation and, in fact, represents a central commitment of a number of educational programs. A notion related to the above is that of using older students as tutors for younger students. In situations where I have observed this in action it appears to work extremely well (the one-room country school could not have functioned without the use of older students as teacher/tutors). Younger students look up to older students, perhaps, more than to anyone else they know. In one-to-one situations, the older students feel responsible for their younger charges. The older students take pride in their roles as teachers and often react with pleasant surprise to the idea that they know how to do something that someone else would like to learn. The usual objections to suggested pairings of younger and older children concern (a) the management and space problems presented by such programs, (b) the idea that older children are being educationally cheated and occupationally exploited by using learning time for teaching time, and (c) the fear that most older students are not responsible, careful, or concerned enough to be good tutors.

A number of in-school big brother/sister experiments have suggested that the management problems are not all that difficult (particularly if both younger and older students come from within the same school). Similarly, studies have suggested that the older students take their roles as teachers seriously and profit from the responsibility and discipline required to be a tutor-teacher. Where classrooms are overcrowded and teachers in short supply, it would seem to make undesirably good sense to use all available teaching resources imaginatively and intensively. I anticipate more attempts to experiment with students as teacher/tutors.

One project which we pilot-tested in Malaysia might be of interest. Older primary students (Standards 5 and 6) were given an English writing assignment as part of their normal class work to produce a reader (story) for a younger (Standard 2 and 3) child. Each student was provided with a student's name for whom they would become an author, samples of the reading level materials the child was working with, and some models, ideas, and warm-up exercises for story writing. The older students then wrote and illustrated a story book (8-16 pages), using the younger child as the central character in the story. The teacher helped students initiate, edit, and complete these writing assignments. Presentation dates were set up, at which time the older students met with the younger students, presented them with the story books, read the stories to them and helped the younger students to learn to read the stories by themselves. Additional meetings both before, during, or after the writing of the stories were also found to be useful. The younger children, many of whom had never had a book of their own before, treasured these books which were (a) books about them, (b) books written by an older student in the school, (c) books that they were able to read to themselves and others.

Games

Game playing, a popular form of home entertainment for centuries, has recently received more serious consideration as a mode of teaching. Interestingly enough, chess, one of the oldest games of which we have record, was originally designed as an instructional game to teach young warriors the strategies of the battlefield. Game playing, having apparently originated as a form of instruction, now appears again to be coming into its own as an instructional activity.

Game use, by its very nature, creates individualized learning situations. As Clark Abt, author of *Serious Games*, observes:

Games are self-teaching. The players learn from their own experience and that of other players within the game. It is most important that the game experience be related by the teacher or instructor to a wider framework, but to the extent that the game itself is self-contained, it requires less teacher effort per time expended than expository methods.

Instructional uses of games may include three basic kinds of tasks: game playing, game critiquing, and game building. I will limit my comments on games largely to game playing. This is not to minimize the usefulness of the game critiquing and game building, however. Having students critique the playing of a particular game represents in many ways an ideal writing task. It engages the students in a topic both highly visible and interesting, with a well-defined chronological, logical, and dramatic structure, with rich opportunities for characterization, presenting data for descriptive, narrative, analytical, or critical exposition, and so on. Similarly, game building involves the student in concentrated application of language- and problem-solving skills. Creative thinking, structural analysis, directed discussion, preparation of outlines, writing of clear and concise directions, construction of game cards or tokens, etc., are all skill applications required of the game maker. One learns a great deal about the subject structure within which a game is set by actually designing such a game. (In this regard, game making has proven to be an excellent teacher-training activity.) The teacher can elicit help from the students in building class games, particularly in the physical construction of game-playing materials. This minimizes the time the teacher must spend in constructing game items, gives students an immediate understanding of what the game materials are and how they are to be used, and increases the students' interest in the game because of their participation in its preparation.

Simulations

Simulations are often listed as game activities. I prefer to separate them from games, in that simulations involve a rather different form of individualization than do games. Simulations customarily ask individuals to "try on" new roles (which they choose or which are chosen for them) and examine what happens to their perspectives and their understanding when they do so. Simulations often require students to open up some aspect of their own personalities and knowledge which, perhaps, they are unaware existed or which they have rarely examined. Specifically, in a simulation:

(1) Players take on roles which are representative of the real world, and then make decisions in response to their assessment of the setting in which they find themselves.

(2) They experience simulated consequences which relate to their decisions and their general performance.

(3) They monitor the results of their actions, and are brought to reflect upon the relationship between their own decisions and the resultant consequences. [1]

Simulations are individualized activities in the very special sense that they allow students to experiment with and examine some of the role attributes and potentials which collectively define their own individuality. Since students take different roles in the simulations, they have opportunities to see other options for "playing the roles" and to compare these with their own. Simulations, in the social studies, especially, have become widely available commercially and represent a sizable share of publication sales in some areas. Classroom simulation kits, like other classroom kits, are often glossily made and expensive. Available simulations kits and/or descriptions cover a wide range of topics:

Business simulation games suggest some of the issues involved when business firms confront problems of pollution ("Blue Wodjet Co."), product distribution ("Decisions"), union-management relations ("Collective Bargaining"), world marketing ("Export Drive"), plant location ("Location of the Metfab Company"), etc.

Social science simulations suggest how professional social scientists go about their jobs. These include archeologists ("Dig"), ecologists ("Dirty Water"), city planners ("Clug"), anthropologists ("Bushmen Hunting"), political scientists ("World Democracy"), sociologists ("Sunshine"), geographers ("Point Roberts"), etc.

Political simulations suggest how governmental organizations make (or fail to make) decisions: city governments ("Metropolitics"), national governments ("Democracy" and "Panatima"), and international organizations ("Mythia"), etc.

Few of the presently available simulations were designed with language learning in mind. However, all of these focus on communication skills, in one form or another, and many provide specific structural practice in all of the language skill areas. Many of these games are also useful in ESP-type classes.

One simulation of perhaps particular interest to language teachers is called "Front Page." "Front Page" simulates some of the operations of a daily newspaper, especially those having to do with editorial, headlining, and layout decisions. The "editorial board" examines incoming news stories submitted by "reporters" and decides which stories should be edited. The description of "Front Page" (Taylor and Walford, 1972) gives complete rules, describes how to construct all simulation components and gives suggestions for introductory and follow-up activities. Other teacher-constructable simulations are also described in this valuable source book.

SUMMARY

I have suggested a number of different activity systems which can be (and have been) successfully used to help individualize classroom language learning. I have tried to limit my suggestions to those which I have evidence to believe are successful in typical contemporary language classrooms. Space has restricted consideration of a number of other activity possibilities and, as well, has restricted the detail accompanying any particular suggestion. I hope that readers are stimulated to modify and amplify the ideas presented and to create new activities and activity systems specifically appropriate to their own situations.

NOTE

1. J. L. Taylor and R. Walford, *Simulation in the Classroom.* (Harmondsworth, England: Penguin, 1972), p. 17.

REFERENCES

Altman, H. B., and R. L. Politzer, eds. *Individualizing Foreign Language Instruction.* Rowley, Mass.: Newbury House, 1971.

Disick, R. S. *Individualization of Instruction: Strategies and Methods.* New York, 1975.

Gougher, R. L., ed. *Individualization of Instruction in Foreign Languages: A Practical Guide.* Center for Curriculum Development, Philadelphia, 1971.

Howatt, A. P. R. *Programmed Learning and the Language Teacher.* London: Longman, 1972.

Logan, G. E. *Individualized Foreign Language Learning: An Organic Process: A Guide to Initiating, Maintaining and Expanding the Process.* Rowley, Mass.: Newbury House, 1973.

Majam, E. E., ed. *Language Learning: The Individual and the Process.* Bloomington, 1966.

STUDY AND DISCUSSION QUESTIONS

(1) The author makes a distinction between "personalized" and "individualized" language instruction. Restate this distinction as you understand it or take exception to it.

(2) Review the descriptions of some contemporary language-teaching methodology such as Silent Way or Community Language Learning, and then revise the author's list of characteristics of contemporary language-teaching methodologies to suit the unique characteristics of the methodology you examine. Add at least two new characteristics you think appropriate.

(3) Critique the list of ten kinds of individual learning/teaching differences the author presents. Make a personal profile of factors which affect your own ability to learn a language (or some other subject of your choice). Rank order the ten points as you think they concern your own learning and state for each point what you feel to be the kind of media, mode, time, etc. which most facilitates your own learning.

(4) Why are direction-giving and feedback necessary components of an individualized learning/teaching system and why do they represent particular problems for language learning/teaching? Suggest five tactics for dealing with or circumventing these problems in some individualized language-learning/teaching situation.

(5) Outline a factlet on a topic of your choice giving a table of components and a sample exercise, activity, or a description for each component.

(6) Describe the content and goals of a two- to four-week section of a second language class. Then design a learning/teaching contract form for the students in, and teacher of, this class.

(7) Review anything else you have read on individualizing language instruction and compare the point of view or emphasis with the author's point of view and emphasis in this paper.